INSIDE QATAR

HIDDEN STORIES FROM ONE OF THE RICHEST NATIONS ON EARTH

JOHN McMANUS

ICON

Published in the UK in 2022
by Icon Books Ltd, Omnibus Business Centre,
39–41 North Road, London N7 9DP
email: info@iconbooks.com
www.iconbooks.com

Sold in the UK, Europe and Asia
by Faber & Faber Ltd, Bloomsbury House,
74–77 Great Russell Street,
London WC1B 3DA or their agents

Distributed in the UK, Europe and Asia
by Grantham Book Services, Trent Road, Grantham NG31 7XQ

Distributed in the USA by Publishers Group West
1700 Fourth Street, Berkeley, CA 94710

Distributed in Australia and New Zealand
by Allen & Unwin Pty Ltd,
PO Box 8500, 83 Alexander Street, Crows Nest, NSW 2065

Distributed in South Africa
by Jonathan Ball, Office B4, The District,
41 Sir Lowry Road, Woodstock 7925

Distributed in India by Penguin Books India
7th Floor, Infinity Tower – C, DLF Cyber City,
Gurgaon 122002, Haryana

Distributed in Canada by Publishers Group Canada
76 Stafford Street, Unit 300, Toronto, Ontario M6J 2S1

ISBN: 978-178578-821-5

Typeset in EB Garamond by Marie Doherty

Printed and bound in Great Britain
by Clays Ltd, Elcograf S.p.A.

To Robin, Sinop and Margot

Contents

A note on particulars

I wanted the book to be accessible for a general reader and so the transliteration of Arabic has been done with an emphasis on making it easy to read rather than strict accuracy. For the sake of consistency, I have used a capital and a hyphen for the widespread 'Al-' prefix (meaning 'the') in all names, places and companies. All dollar figures are US dollars.

I spoke English with everyone I met in Qatar, but very few of them were native English speakers. As far as possible I have left their own words, including idiosyncrasies, intact – not to poke fun or mock, but to convey what it is like to interact with others in English in Doha.

Not everyone I spoke to was happy having their name mentioned. When an asterisk follows the first use of a name, it indicates a pseudonym.

During the course of my research, I was a visiting fellow at Qatar University – an unpaid position. Aside from a one-off honorarium for taking part in a media conference at Northwestern University in Qatar, I did not receive payment from any Qatari institution.

Maps

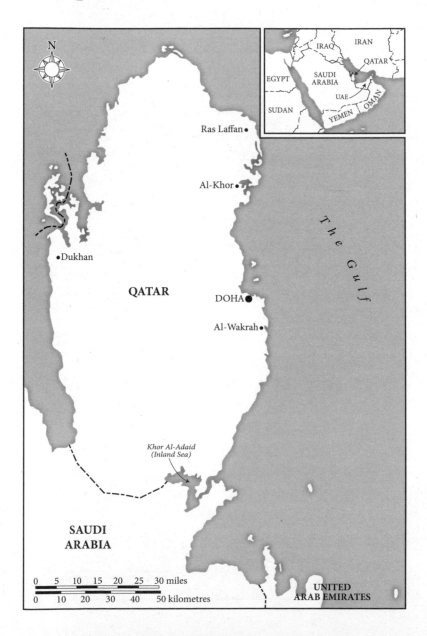

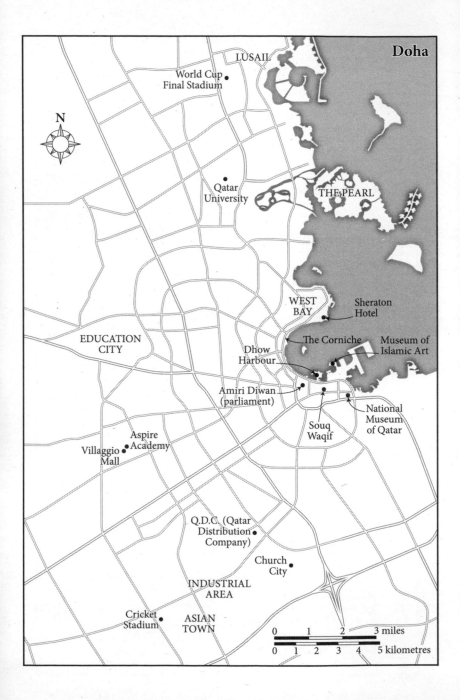

1 'Excuse me, kind sir. I am very ill'

I have gone in the opposite direction.

Away from the coast, the skyscrapers, the world-class museums, the traditional Souq renovated to within an inch of its life. Past the building sites of $600-million stadiums, heading south-west, in search of the answer to a question: what is Qatar like for most people who live here?

As I turn off the expressway, proportions seem to stretch and grow. Roads become longer and straighter. Kilometres of highway unfold without a kink, flanked on the right by a strip mall and then on the left, across scrubby desert, by the squat forms of labour camps.

It is Friday, the one day a week that most people (but not all) have off in Qatar. I now start to see some of them – male workers coming and going. Some are in T-shirts and jeans, others *shalwar kameez*, a few in blazers.

I pull off the main road and into a large car park full of people and vehicles. I open the door and I'm hit by the dusty, humid air. There are car horns and chatter and a restless, tense energy.

What is this place? Who are these people?

In a sense I can answer these questions easily: this is the Industrial Area, the district of Doha reserved for its most numerous residents – the men working low-income jobs. More specifically, this is 'Asian Town', the newly built complex of malls, an amphitheatre and a cricket stadium that is designed to keep them amused and away from the rest of the population.

But in another way I can't answer these questions at all. Having arrived in Doha only days previously, I know nothing of years living apart from your partner and children; of being drawn by the lure of salaries many times what you could earn at home; of feeling disappointed, or worse – exploited, broken – by the ceaseless rotation of camp, bus and building site.

I leave the car and go into the small, covered arcade closest to me. I pass mobile phone vendors, jewellers, shops selling shoes, bags, consumer electronics – even oil-filled radiators, a puzzling sight on a hot spring day but one I would later come to understand after experiencing a Qatari winter. The noise is cacophonous, with passers-by chatting to each other as they promenade and shop assistants shouting at them as they go past.

'Hello my friend!'

The use of English signifies this comment is aimed at me. I spin to see a young man, five-foot-five, beckoning to me from the entrance of his shop.

'You want watch? Hublot. 240 rials [$65].' With nothing better to do, I follow him inside. The shop seems to have a lot of everything. Overflowing shelves rise up to the low ceiling. There is a waist-high glass cabinet, and the man is gesturing manically at items laid out on its top. 'You want scent? Or mobile? Or—this is Kuwaiti scent. Very special.'

I shake my head. 'I don't use cologne.'

'No, me neither,' says the man in agreement. 'You want sex ring?'

'Sorry, what?'

'Sex ring. You can go for two hours.'

My mind cycles through the few things I know about Qatar. The population is overwhelmingly comprised of men, most of whom work six- or seven-day weeks and live in labour camps. Their contact with the opposite sex comes mainly in the form of the occasional interaction with a shop assistant or administrator. Workers have more opportunity for intimacy with each other, of course. But living four to eight people in a dormitory room does not exactly offer a lot of privacy.

'I don't want to go for two hours! Ten minutes is enough,' I say, attempting to defuse the awkwardness with a joke.

The guy looks at me and shrugs.

'OK, so you go for 30 minutes then you pull it off.'

I leave the shop and continue walking. There is a row of currency shops, their posters imploring me to send cash to loved ones in Africa and India. There are cafés selling Pakistani, Sri Lankan, Indian, Nepali and Filipino fare. One shop has a scrum unfolding inside. I watch as people tussle and shout to purchase various bulky, fluorescent suitcases. And everywhere there are men. They sit in clusters on the faded grass and stand in the arcades. They wander in twos and threes, arms round each other's shoulders. They survey posters advertising music concerts and line up in huge queues at cash machines.

These are the men who have built Qatar. It is their tales that fill reports by human rights organisations and draw outrage in the West. It is on their backs that this peninsula the size of Devon and Cornwall, a place that even 30 years ago was a backwater, has become a country of villas, skyscrapers and football stadiums.

I'm finally where I want to be: in Doha to find out for myself what it's really like. And yet I'm struggling. Now that I'm here in person, it feels less like reality and more an immersive video game. I can move around, challenge my senses, but only within a pre-calculated range of interactions, all of which are superficial and slight. I grab a tea from a shop and sit at the benches inside. Looking at the people, I try to find a way in, but the man my age sitting opposite is absorbed by his phone. The greying men in skullcaps to my left are already deep in conversation.

During the rest of the week I occupy a different Qatar to the one these people inhabit. We are separated by walls – walls circling construction sites and walls around camps. Now those walls are removed, I'm beginning to understand that the physical separation is only half of it. It suddenly feels foolhardy to think that I will find a way to understand the lives of those on the other side. I shrink back out, aware of the scale of the challenge I've set for myself.

The car park has become busier. As the sun begins to set, queues are forming alongside big, white buses. Day trip over, workers line up ready to be whisked back to their accommodation.

As I turn to leave, I am stopped by a man.

'Excuse me, kind sir. I am very ill.'

He is wan-faced, the exhaustion round the eyes alerting me to the fact that he is telling the truth.

'I had work accident and went to hospital. Tomorrow I go home to India but need to collect money for flight.'

He is holding his left arm slightly oddly. On cue, he pulls back the long sleeve and reveals a nasty-looking gash of around nine inches tracing up his inside arm. It has been partially stitched, but towards the top a small white bandage has worked free of its moorings, revealing raw and exposed skin.

I get out my wallet and give him 50 rials, around $14. He takes it without thanks and launches into another spiel.

'My family. And I'm 200 short—'

He pulls out a large wad of notes and folds my money in.

'Fifty is good, but if you could give 50 more then I will only be 100 short ...'

I can feel the pricks of irritation. I expected him to be grateful. Fawning, even. The empathy that he should evoke is missing, and I'm not sure why.

I tell him I don't have any more cash.

In my pocket the money laughs, aware of the lie.

'OK sir, thank you.'

He wanders off. My shame lingers.

I had yet to learn an important principle of Qatar, at least for people from my background: if you want to live here guilt-free, then you'd better cultivate steely detachment.

I remember precisely where I was when Qatar was awarded the right to host the 2022 FIFA Men's World Cup.

It was a December morning in 2010. I was sat with my brother in my parents' living room in Leicester, watching the TV with incredulity and amusement. I had heard of Qatar before, but I'm not sure I could have told you much about the place. Small, its wealth derived from petrochemicals, I probably could have guessed. But that would have been it.

It was eight years later that I first visited. Like most football fans, I had spent the intervening time following the news stories that accompanied FIFA's surprising decision to award the contest to Qatar: the accusations of corruption in the bid; the exploitation of workers building the stadiums, unpaid wages, unexplained deaths. That period had also seen me move to Turkey, write a book about football in that country and try – with mixed success – to carve out a niche as a social anthropologist writing about sport in the Middle East. Given all this, I felt almost obliged to get to know the place that would host the Arab world's first football World Cup.

Coming in to land, I asked the air hostess who had sat down opposite me what Doha was like. She laughed nervously.

'Well ... haha.'

My first trip unfolded in a haze of the surreal and mundane. I swam in a November sea the temperature of bath water, drank coffee with consultants in the atriums of world-class museums and attended a top-division football match where I counted a grand total of 116 spectators. All the while, I couldn't shake the feeling that a certain experience was being curated for me. From my interactions, it would have been impossible to know that Qatar's population was 72 per cent male or that, in one of the world's richest countries, many get by on earnings of around 1000 rials ($275) a month. From my air-conditioned taxis, I would look out on the men in overalls sweating and at the walls of enormous villas and I could sense that I was only getting part of the story.

Early mornings were spent on a computer in a coffee shop where I befriended the Nepali barista, Bishnu*, who was little more than a boy, thin as a rake, with a fluff moustache. Bishnu hated the food provided by his company, liked American customers ('If they knock something over, they clean it up. Not asking you to do it') and when he first arrived in Doha it wasn't the heat or the dust that disconcerted him so much as the lack of animals. 'It was four or five months before I saw a dog!' he told me disbelievingly.

Bishnu explained the hierarchy by which the potpourri of Qatar is organised.

'So who's at the top?'

'Of course, the Qatari. Second, European countries and the US. Third, other Arab countries and nationalities.'

I had already grasped that categorising individuals like this was not only encouraged but expected in Doha. Racial logic is visible everywhere. All security guards are black Africans. 'All Asians cook smelly food,' I was told by my estate agent, herself Asian. In a 2020 report, the UN special rapporteur on racism described Qatar as operating 'a quasi-caste system based on national origin'. It made me intensely uncomfortable, but resisting it was a bit like trying to hold back the sea.

'Fourth is like Philippines.'

'Why are they next? Because they speak good English?'

'No! Because their government is strong. The embassy is strong. The fifth, always Nepal, India, Sri Lanka.'

I waited for him to continue but he added, 'That's it.'

'You're at the bottom?'

Bishnu let out a cathartic laugh.

'Yeah.'

I let Bishnu in on my plan. That I wanted to learn what Qatar was really like. To prise apart the different layers of experience, uncover how life truly unfolds for people living and working here. 'Does that sound crazy?'

'Yes!' he replied with a laugh.

'Why?' I asked, a little hurt at his reaction.

'Well,' said Bishnu, gearing up to be tactful.

'Some people you don't need to ask. You can see their situation. And you feel the pain.'

I arrived back home in Turkey and set to work. I wrote project outlines and grant applications. I applied for scholarships and research awards, one of which a non-profit anthropology foundation decided to fund. I would spend a year in Doha. It wasn't a great expanse of time, but it was long enough, I reasoned, to seek out some of the complexities. As the World Cup approached and all nuance was lost under the waves of promotion and condemnation of Qatar, I wanted just to listen – to the stories of people who have made it their home.

In all of my preparation, I hadn't come across a book that did this. Academics have produced works analysing Qatar's economic and foreign policies; journalists have investigated allegations of corruption in its World Cup bid; both camps have scrutinised the nation's purported link to Islamic extremism. What was missing, I felt, was a book about what Qatar is actually *like* as a place to live. How does it feel to move around Doha as an Indian, a Briton, a white man, a brown woman, a cleaner or a minor royal? What are the hopes and dreams of those living in the skyscrapers and the labour camps? Do any of them ever encounter each other for more than a fleeting moment?

This is a book written by an outsider, for outsiders. As such, it is necessarily selective. The book is also, despite my best efforts, male-dominated – a consequence of Qatar's lopsided gender ratio and the conversations opened up (or closed down) by being a man. But as well as limitations, there is under-appreciated utility in being an outsider. I faced a steep learning curve, yes, but being fresh to Qatar was in some ways a blessing. It allowed me to assess the lay of the land before I became too habituated to its idiosyncrasies, too bogged down by its baggage.

I arrived in Doha in the midst of the country's biggest modern crisis. At dawn on 5 June 2017, Saudi Arabia, the United Arab Emirates, Bahrain and Egypt announced that they were severing all diplomatic ties with Qatar. Land, air and sea routes were cut. It was the biggest disruption in Gulf relations in a generation.[†] There had long been simmering tension between Qatar and its neighbours, in particular over Qatar's support for Islamist groups that were seeking to topple Arab dictators. But the severity of the action came as a surprise. Reliant on other Gulf states for everything from concrete to cow's milk, Doha had to scramble to adapt. The blockade hit the real estate and tourism sectors particularly hard. But it also forced companies to seek out new markets and stoked national pride as locals – and even foreigners – rallied round Qatar's leader, Sheikh Tamim bin Hamad Al Thani.[‡] The embargo would come to a partial end in January 2021. But being in Qatar in the years prior to this point felt a bit like walking into a bar after a particularly brutal brawl and wincing at the destruction.

Even against that troubled backdrop, the Qatar I got to know felt like a modern-day boom town, a global Wild West, with both the promise and the iniquity that the historical parallel conjures. I want to do justice to the diversity that I saw and experienced around me. That of course means telling the stories of the people who wished they had never come: those cheated

---

[†] There is much debate – driven by petty nationalisms – over the name of the region we are talking about. Should it be called the Persian or Arab Gulf? I don't want to get involved and so will just call it 'the Gulf'. I trust the reader to know I'm not talking about the Gulf of Mexico, the Gulf of Alaska or any other Gulf.

[‡] The name of Qatar's royal family, the Al Thani, has no hyphen because the 'Al' means 'house of' rather than 'the'.

out of livelihoods, abused, deported, exploited – these stories should be told until the day that no one suffers them. But not everyone's experience of Qatar is negative. And so it also means including the tales of the hustlers and the lovers, the do-gooders and bullshitters, the preachers and armchair philosophers, the entrepreneurs and adventurers whom I also encountered. 'Qatar is like sweet poison,' a Pakistani businessman once told me, capturing the country's mix of allure and danger.

Looking back, my despair on that first trip to the Industrial Area was overcooked. I did get to meet many interesting people: labourers, cleaners, engineers, nannies, IT consultants, bureaucrats, taxi drivers, DJs, teachers, priests, public relations managers, football coaches, hoteliers – all living variegated versions of the Qatari Dream. I also met Qataris, the privileged few who struggle to make sense of the conservatism, opulence and diversity that is all around them. The sum of their tales is not some exotic cabinet of curiosities but a glimpse of life on the coalface of globalisation.

The people of Qatar have much to teach the rest of us. They show the corrosive effects of inequality, the insatiability of hope and the fallacy of believing that you will be judged by your individual actions alone. They show how good people perpetuate broken systems – and the bravery required by those who want to change the status quo. But perhaps most of all, the people of Qatar force us to reflect on many of the global problems – of unfettered capitalism, growing inequality and climate change – that concern us all.

2 'Now, everybody they like falcon'

Nasser* is talking to me as we rush out of Doha in his four-by-four, down eight-lane highways paved in immaculate tarmac.

'What you think for yourself, the falcon is thinking the same,' he says with the cadence of someone used to being listened to.

'The falcon, he don't like to look at the sun direct. The falcon is like a child from the beginning ... if he's tired he will be crying; if there is any pain he will cry. Many things about the falcon—' Nasser seems to feel a rush of sensation. It overwhelms him, causing him to stop speaking.

'It's very difficult to talk with you everything at the same time.'

Nasser likes falcons. He owns twelve. I've just watched his Bangladeshi helpers rush around loading three of them into the jeep. And now we are heading to the desert, where Nasser trains his birds.

Nasser turns to check on the falcons sat in the back. He has a Roman nose that takes up most of his face, the rest of his head being closed off by a tightly wrapped white headdress. 'Tah!' he exclaims.

Nasser trains his birds to perch on the seats of the car facing backwards, in order to protect their long tail feathers from damage if he drives over a bump. But one has spun itself forward. Taking his right hand off the wheel, he leans back and gently nudges the bird back round. Its tail drops into the footwell where it oscillates gently, like a toddler's wiggling legs.

'This one is new,' he offers by way of explanation.

The trip is my first time going to watch falcon training. In my initial months in Qatar I have tried hard to befriend Qataris. I've attempted to muscle in on conversations, injected myself into proposed trips and plans. The reactions have all been the same: unfailingly polite, but invitations have not been forthcoming. Until, that is, I started to become interested in falcons.

Historically an important part of Bedouin life, falconry has recently undergone a renaissance in Qatar, as it has across the whole Gulf region. These birds of prey have become a hobby and status symbol, a source of bonding among men (women are conspicuously absent in the falconry world) and totems of the nation. There is a society in Doha dedicated to their development, the headquarters shaped like the hood that owners place over the heads of their birds to keep them quiet. Qataris race their best specimens in competitions where the prizes are brand new Land Cruisers. When they are unwell, there is a state-subsidised falcon hospital that can handle 1,000 birds a week. If you watch any promotional video of the country – and if you are here for a year, you will see many – there will be the metamorphosis of something into a falcon, or a falcon into something. Lush computer graphics of birds and shots of the desert confirm that they are one and the same.

I want to understand what it is about these birds. Why are they so revered? Helen Macdonald, author of the bird-memoir *H is for Hawk*, has noted how encounters with animals are really encounters with ourselves – who we think we are and who we want to be. Qataris and falcons: in my head, the two have fused. Understanding falcons will help me understand Qataris: citizens of one of the wealthiest nations in the world by GDP per capita;[†] a people who make up only 11 per cent of the population of their own country; custodians of possibly the most rapid development of anywhere on earth, now struggling to carve a role for themselves out of the swirling vortex they've set in motion.

'Now, everybody they like falcon.'

We race out of the city. Past the old palace at Al-Rayyan, past the intersection with the shopping mall, past the turning at Al-Shahaniya for the camel racing track, heading west.

'Maybe before, with the life it's very difficult, the falcon is for the rich people,' Nasser tells me. 'Now, *alhamdulillah*, thanks God, everything gets good. Everybody they are working, they are with salary, they can buy. But, still, if you have a lot of money you can buy very nice falcons.'

[†] From 2002 to 2014 Qatar was *the* world's richest nation, according to one particular measure: the catchy GDP per capita adjusted for purchasing power parity (which accounts for global differences in the cost of goods and services). It has fallen from the top spot in recent years but it still came in at third place by the same measure in 2020 – just behind Luxembourg and Singapore – with adjusted GDP per person of close to $97,000.

I clarify what a lot of money is. Over $100,000, I am told.

'But also here, the people they like each other. Sometimes they buy the falcon and send it, like a gift,' adds Nasser. He gestures to one of the birds in the back, which was given to him by a friend. He knows precisely how much it cost: 128,000 rials, around $35,000. I quip that he must be a good friend and Nasser shrugs. 'This is normal between the people here.'

Until the mid-20th century, Qatar was one of the poorest places on the planet. With a climate unsuited to growing almost anything, it had an economy based around pearl diving, an industry that collapsed in the space of a decade as a result of the development of Japanese cultured pearls and the 1929 Wall Street crash. By 1940, the population of Doha – never particularly big – had sunk to less than 16,000. The situation was so parlous that the ruler at the time, Sheikh Abdullah Al Thani, had to take out a mortgage on his own house. Then after the bust came the boom. Geologists working for the Anglo-Persian Oil Company discovered oil onshore at Jebel Dukhan in 1939. In 1949, oil exports began and Qatar commenced the journey from poor backwater to modern entrepôt.

The road is becoming more spindle-like. The traffic has thinned out. Instead of buildings we are now flanked by desert – not the large sand dunes of the imagination but a plain dotted with scrub. We pull off the tarmac road and onto a track that bumps and winds across the flat land. All this time, the falcons have been sitting patiently in the back. They are so quiet that I am only reminded of their presence by the occasional nibbling of the seat cushion or puffing out of feathers.

The short-wave radio suddenly crackles into life. Nasser picks up the mouthpiece and replies. We are within range of his brother and friends.

Training our eyes forwards, specks appear. A couple of four-by-fours, maybe a kilometre apart, move in tandem across the land. As we get closer, I begin to see two dots in the sky ahead of the jeeps. They keep rising and falling, occasionally crossing paths. Nasser straight away picks out that it's a falcon closing in on a pigeon.

'You see the wing? He's *very* strong – this is the peregrine.'

Globally there are more than 60 species of falcon, ranging from small kestrels to hulking gyrs. Despite the superficial resemblance to other birds of prey, such as hawks, eagles and vultures, the falcon family is distinct. In the Gulf, two kinds of falcons dominate: sakers and peregrines, known in Arabic as *saqr* and *shaheen*. Both subscribe closely to the classic idea of the falcon: large, regal, with a fierce beak and tapered wings. In both species, females are a third larger than males. Consequently, all birds used for hunting are females, despite Nasser's persistent use of the male pronoun.

Falcons used to be exclusively caught from the wild. Then in the 1970s, in response to near-extinction, humans worked out how to artificially inseminate them in captivity. The process involves elaborate choreography whereby a handler builds a bond with a male bird by bowing and chirping like a courting female falcon. If successful, the bird copulates with a latex hat worn by the handler. Its sperm is taken up in a pipette and deposited in the female. Nasser isn't so keen on the farmed birds.

'If you are going for the top falcon, it's from the wild. From the wild, he's learning with his mother and father, flying with him in open area. But from the farms, he cannot fly too much. Only in the pen.'

The trade in wild birds is discouraged but still rampant. 'In Qatar there are no regulations, it's open season,' a French breeder once told me. I ask Nasser about the legality of purchasing wild falcons. 'Sometimes it's illegal,' he answers enigmatically.

The rise of falconry in the Arabian Gulf is normally given a functional explanation: it was a necessary means of survival, a way in which nomadic people could add a bit of protein to their otherwise sparse diet by using the birds to catch small mammals. But this prosaic rendering overlooks the clear spiritual and social importance of falconry in the Middle East. Falconry appears in the Quran, which says that believers can eat 'what you have taught your hunting birds and beasts to catch'. In the 9th century a whole genre of hunting poetry emerged, called *tardiyyat*, in which the birds are frequently mentioned. Falcon imagery has been incorporated into objects as diverse as rings, coins, statues and religious standards. Clearly, for many centuries, falconry has fulfilled both sustenance and spiritual needs across the Islamic world.

As we join the entourage of vehicles, the falcon succeeds in its chase. It grabs the pigeon and both hit the ground. I expect a tussle but as we pull up next to it, the work is done. The falcon is stood upright as if posing for a photo, the pigeon pinned under its talons, already dead.

A man hops out of the other car. He is in his fifties, all wrinkles and smiles, carrying an air of the countryside due to the worn, beige-coloured jacket he wears over his *thobe*, the white, ankle-length garment that all Qatari men wear.[†] Nasser's brother, I assume (we are never formally introduced). A halo of feathers, mostly pigeon, surrounds the birds. The man levers his gloved arm under the falcon and manages to pull the prey out of its talons – no mean feat as the bird's toes have a tendon mechanism that operates like a ratchet. The falcon quietly observes him as he produces a pocketknife and hacks off the pigeon's head. He then places the body of the bird in the fist of his glove and holds it out. Without hesitation, the falcon hops onto his hand and dives its beak into the cavity where the pigeon's head once was. There are crunches and cracks as it hungrily eats. It lifts up its head, red entrails smeared across the tip of its beak.

'Doctor! What you say?' he calls cheerfully to me.

'... It's good!' I find myself spluttering, a bit unsure of what I've just witnessed.

Everything in Qatar changed when the oil – and later gas – began to flow. So profitable is the income from hydrocarbons that the Qatari government has no need to tax individual citizens. Qatar jealously protects its wealth by making citizenship by birth or naturalisation next to impossible to obtain. Mechanisms have

[†] In public Qatari women wear an *abaya*, a full-length black cloak, and a headscarf called a *shayla*. Only the most conservative cover their face with veils.

been created for distributing the largesse in the form of free university education, generous gifts of land and well-paid jobs in the state sector. Politically, the wealth has tempered demands for democracy (Qatar is an autocratic monarchy, political parties are banned and its constitution gives near-absolute powers to the emir – the head of state). Socially, the change in lifestyles has been destabilising. Elderly Qataris who remember having no running water watch as their grandchildren race Ferraris down Doha's streets. There has been a huge influx of migrants who came firstly to work in the extraction industries but then in construction, hospitality and retail. The population of Qatar has roughly doubled every decade. In November 2021 it stood at close to 2.7 million, of which Qataris were believed to number between 300,000 and 350,000.

It is within this context of rapid change that contemporary falconry should be understood. Every day in Qatar, a battle is being waged within the small community of nationals over the question: who are Qataris and what do they stand for? Hawking, its proponents argue, is one of the few shared cultural touchstones, a thread linking present and past, and consequently an important receptacle for passing on Qatar's traditional values of thrift, self-denial and egalitarianism. Flying falcons is an easy, visual way of marking oneself as Qatari. It is a hobby not open to the other 89 per cent of the population.

It's now Nasser's turn. Or, rather, the turn of one of Nasser's falcons.

He goes to the back of the jeep and takes out a silver box half the size of carry-on airport luggage. The clasps open with a snap. Inside is expensive-looking electrical equipment padded liberally with foam. Nasser extracts a delicate antenna, perhaps fifteen centimetres long. With the help of his brother he attaches it to the tail of the bird.

'Very dangerous with the wind now.'

He gets his phone, swipes and taps and it starts emitting a bleep. He's activated a tracking app.

'If the falcon moving somewhere, you leave him here but you cannot catch him in maybe 50 kilometres.' Nasser mimics with his hand an object being swept away. 'The wind will take him.'

I think of how precarious the human hold is over these birds. You shell out a small fortune and attach transmitters but still an unanticipated gust or a moment's inattention can see them gone.

The other man removes the bird and drives away with her. Here at his car, Nasser opens the bonnet. He then takes a falcon glove and a piece of raw pigeon – all red, pink and bulbous – and places both on top of the engine.

'It's better if the pigeon is warm.'

Nasser then gets out a piece of rope perhaps eight-foot long with a lure tied on the end, a codpiece of feathers known as a *tilwah*.

The feathers on the *tilwah* come from the houbara, a sand-coloured bustard native to the region, although no longer living in the wild in Qatar due to overhunting. Pigeons are the main prey for falcons but that's only due to their abundance; what most Qataris want to catch are houbara. So keen are they to hunt the birds that groups from the Gulf organise hawking trips to lands where they are more plentiful – Azerbaijan, Iraq, Pakistan. These trips can take on lavish proportions, costing millions of dollars and involving hundreds of people camped out in a mini city of tents. The desire of Gulf men to hunt with falcons can even have geopolitical implications. During a 2014 hunt in Pakistan, Saudi Prince Fahd bin Sultan bin Abdulaziz killed 2,100 houbara over 21 days, about twenty times more than his allocated quota, sparking a diplomatic incident. The following year, nine members of the Qatari royal family were kidnapped by Iranian militias while hunting houbara in Iraq. To get the hostages released, the Qatari state is reported to have paid $360 million in cash and forced the proxies they were support-ing in the Syrian civil war – who were fighting Iranian-backed forces – to make several battlefield concessions.

A crackle of radio informs us that the bird is about to be released. Nasser readies himself, twirling the *tilwah* and making high-pitched yelps.

At first, I can't see anything. Then, emerging out of the wind and the fading light is a small black object going at a clip. Falcons are the fastest beings on the planet. When they dive, they can reach speeds of over 160 miles per hour. Every detail about these birds seems scarcely credible: a kestrel can see a two-millimetre-long insect at eighteen metres away on account of eyes so large their backs press into each other in the middle of the skull; when a falcon pulls out of a dive it experiences gravitational force equivalent to over 25Gs (human pilots black out over 7Gs); they migrate so far that Siberian peregrines have been found wintering in South Africa (during their annual migration, birds often land on ships and hitch a ride). Given all this, today's training must feel rather tame for the bird.

Nasser's falcon is honing in on the *tilwah*. Nasser gives it a yank, shifting its direction and the falcon suddenly zips past and banks away into the sky. She then takes another dive from the opposite angle. Nasser tugs the *tilwah* again and the bird arcs back into the sky. After doing this four or five times, Nasser lets the lure rest on the floor while he goes and grabs the glove with the meat from the car engine. The falcon swoops in and grasps the *tilwah* in a tangle of claws and feathers. Nasser then crouches down and substitutes the glove and the pigeon meat for the lure. The crunch of bones and sinew follows.

When we climb back into the four-by-four, Nasser is visibly more at ease.

'Now he will relax. If he's relaxed, I'm relaxed!'

The bird rides up front, on the armrest between Nasser and me, the plume on her hood looking faintly ridiculous. There's something about Nasser's smiles and the falcon's carriage that make the journey feel like a regal procession – the victorious hunter returning home.

Our destination is barely a kilometre away, a group of objects that Nasser keeps calling his camp. But 'camp' evokes too bucolic and rudimentary a scene. As we pull up, I count ten trailers parked in a large square. There is a scattering of service tents surrounding a larger entertaining tent modelled on a *majlis*, a lounge where guests are received and consultations happen among men. This tent has the added benefit of a fireplace and a 60-inch flat-screen TV. The compound is crisscrossed by paths of elaborate decking, so that you don't have to tread in the sandy scree, and lit by heavy-duty spotlights that are starting to flicker into operation. It is not something you could fling up in a day.

Sat in a collapsible picnic chair in the middle of the compound is a younger Qatari man in his twenties. In his hands is a large remote control, like the kind a small kid would use to direct a racing car. In front of him, on the ground, one of the Bangladeshi helpers is setting up a drone. He folds out the six legs, each with a propeller on the end.

No one introduces me to the four Bangladeshi men who are working at the camp. Nor did Nasser introduce me to the three men who prepared the jeep for our trip. Yet the entire endeavour of falconry – like everything in Qatar – rests on the labour of these people. It is Bangladeshi home helpers who feed, water and lock the birds up at night. Indian veterinarians and anaesthetists give them endoscopies and injections when they're unwell. Sri Lankan and Nepali cleaners patrol the tents at festivals, wiping up their shit. Falconry is presented as a solely Qatari pursuit. The political geographer Natalie Koch believes that the erasure of non-Qataris from falconry is a coping strategy 'to assuage the anxiety of citizen-nationals about their minority status'. If outsiders must be acknowledged, then it is only in ancillary roles: as servants helping make it happen or, like me now, as guests cooing and clucking their appreciation.

The Bangladeshi guy takes a piece of wire or string maybe fifteen feet long. Halfway down its length is a small, deflated parachute with something at the end which looks like a pigeon. I peer closer. It is a pigeon, but a pretend one, a cuddly toy. He checks everything is secure and then backs away.

The man in the chair jams back the joystick, sending the drone whizzing angrily into the air. It pulls the string with the parachute and the pigeon after itself. A falcon is let loose and immediately starts going after the pigeon.

'*Habibi* yes! *Yalla*!' shouts someone. Baby, yes! Come on!

Then, a groan. The falcon has had its attention diverted by a real-life pigeon that flaps across the sky perpendicular to the drone.

Contrary to my expectations, it's actually very difficult for a falcon to catch a pigeon. The pigeons in Qatar are not the obese vermin that you accidentally kick when leaving a London branch of McDonald's, but rather sleek racing pigeons. They often have too much gusto and stamina for falcons which, like highly tuned dragsters, burn bright but then give up after a few minutes. Close to two-thirds of young wild falcons die in their first year, mostly from starvation, a fact that seems completely contrary to their legend as the world's most successful hunter.

The bird grows tired of the real pigeon. Chasing the fake one is a less strenuous prospect, given that it's bobbing invitingly under the drone around a kilometre up in the sky. After some simulated dogfighting impelled by the man in the chair, the falcon grabs the doll pigeon, the line detaches and bird and toy go twirling together to the earth, the parachute lending the descent a slow grace.

After retrieving and feeding the bird, Nasser gives me a tour of his camp in the rapidly fading light. He gets most excited when showing me the place where they have their campfires.

'We are in the desert,' he declares theatrically, a twinkle in his eye.

'The sky—' he can't find the word and so gestures at the encroaching night.

'Then we start talking. Talking about the past or talking about anything in life. This is night in the desert.'

If the falcon is an object used to quell anxiety over what it means to be Qatari, then the backdrop for this performance is the desert. The Qatari state plays a role in the mythologising. At the National Museum of Qatar they have an exhibition detailing how, in old times, families would spend winter in the desert herding animals, and summer on the coast taking part in the pearl harvest. There is an easy omission of the histories of the non-nomadic inhabitants of the peninsula, such as the businessmen with familial links to India or the Iranian ship builders. That would complicate the narrative. The way the past and present are discussed seems to manufacture opposites – desert/city,

original/new, Bedouin/urbanite – with the lingering sense that the former might have been better.

In the way Nasser talks, I begin to understand that his camp takes its cue from this mythologising. It is a redoubt. An escape from the city, with its capitalism, consumption and cosmopolitan churn.

'Life is difficult ... You have to work hard to keep your money. Money like blood for the humans, really. You cannot move without money.'

I find myself conflicted. How much political and ecological damage is done in pursuit of the chimera of an authentically 'Qatari' space? If feels less like the desert is being respected and more like it's being conquered. The peninsula is dotted with hundreds – possibly thousands – of these camps, making true wilderness hard to find. Another popular pastime is 'dune bashing' – using four-by-fours or buggies to drive fast up and down huge sand dunes. On weekend afternoons the mounds of Khor Al-Adaid, a UNESCO nature reserve, echo to the roar of engines. Maybe it's not the desert but the technology that is the star of the show. This expanse of barren land totally shaped life on this peninsula for millennia. Now, with air conditioning and four-by-fours, it feels like people no longer have to respond to its diktats.

Then again, a few months after my day of falconry I had the chance to spend a night in the desert with another Qatari. Driving in, the land looked like something out of a Neil Armstrong photograph. On the horizon, other camps were small clusters of light. They maintained a magical allure, glistening like ships on a sea. In the morning we awoke to fog so thick the driver lost his way and we got stuck in a sand drift. It was a reminder that the desert is not wholly passive. It can shred car tyres and make you drive around in circles. Falcons often fly away, never to be found.

On the drive back to Doha, Nasser shares his views on how Qatar has altered.

'It changed very quickly, *very* quickly.'

Some of this change has his approval. He likes the latest technologies. But other elements cause him concern.

'Everything is free now, I don't like everything to be free ... Like women, too much free. Children are free.'

Qatar is not as restrictive a country as Saudi Arabia. Women have been allowed to drive, albeit under certain conditions, for several decades. They're encouraged by the state to work. Three times as many Qatari women as men graduate from university. Yet at the same time, most Qataris adhere to various schools of Wahhabism, an austere, ultra-conservative movement that eschews even music and shaving as part of the return to a 'purer' form of Islam. The country is shaped by highly patriarchal notions of family. Women require the approval of a male guardian – usually their father or husband – to marry, study abroad or, in many cases, even to obtain a driving licence.

'Now, if my son he need to go and drink alcohol, I cannot stop him,' continues Nasser. 'Before I can stop. Now, the government, they say, "No, this is not your responsibility. After eighteen, he's responsible for himself."'

Faced with the proliferating number of paths available to them, Qataris fracture along different lines – and not simply by generation. Within families, liberal fathers despair at their sons' religious zealotry; twenty-something daughters chafe at having to obtain written permission from their fathers before being permitted to leave the country. Nasser marvels at how his fourteen-year-old son behaves.

'When he's sitting with you, he speaks with you about the politics, he speaks with you about the business. *All the time*, the child— they *like* the business!'

The world his son inhabits is miles away from Nasser's life with his safe government job – good hours, no hassle – and even further away from his own father's.

'With my dad it was different. My dad was too much strong,' he chuckles. 'We were afraid of him too much. In that time, if you are not listening to your father he will hit you. Now he cannot hit you.'

Despite acknowledging the fear he felt, Nasser sounds rueful. 'Different life. Different 100 per cent.'

Our journey to the desert is being re-wound – from track to spindle road, spindle to highway. Wide horizons and stars morph back into overpasses and streetlights. We drive past a man stood next to a parked car. In a flash Nasser flares up.

'See, this is Indian. He is stopped and doing something wrong in the street.'

I failed to see what happened, although I flinch inwardly at the instant racial profiling. Nasser tells me angrily that the man was urinating by the side of the road.

'I can make trouble for him ... I can stop, call the police, "Come, please, take this man."'

It's a terrifying glimpse of the power that Qataris feel they have over others. Non-Qataris live under this shadow constantly, afraid that it will be brought to bear on them. And then, like a storm cloud on a blustery day, Nasser's anger passes.

'I'm not going for trouble.'

We are back in the suburbs, driving past gated compounds with villas poking over the tops of walls. Pulling up where we started, the Bangladeshi helpers approach the car. With a wave and a sharp tongue, Nasser gets them to unload the boxes and the birds. The falcons are brought to their home, a small outhouse maybe fifteen feet by eight, with sand on the floor and an air conditioning unit thrumming away. Each bird is tied to an individual perch set at distances across the floor. Their hoods are taken off. One helper is ordered to go and produce large saucers of water for them to drink. Qataris are perpetually worried about their birds becoming dehydrated, a not unreasonable concern when nursing an animal that breeds in Siberia through the Qatari summer.

Nasser then takes me on a tour of his compound: the outside seating area, the patriotic rock garden ('I do the rocks, from *my* culture. My country, I bring these rocks') the long bench, like a carpeted balancing beam, used as a perch for the falcons of his guests. The tour culminates in tea and dates in the *majlis*, a large structure reminiscent of a tent but sat on a concrete plinth and with doors, air conditioning and a thick carpet.

'The *majlis* for the men,' I am told. 'For any man. It's coming like your home.'

I am excited. Many people have told me about the importance of *majalis* (the plural of *majlis*) in Qatar. They are framed as the social centre, where men hang out and chat about life, politics, the universe. If you want to understand Qataris, people say, you need to be here. This is the first time I have been invited in. I excitedly wait to learn the secrets.

Inside, the room feels hangar-like. At one end, a huge TV screen is playing a Turkish soap opera. A stuffed houbara sits underneath looking on angrily. Two petrified Bangladeshi men are crouched on the floor by the stove in the corner preparing a constant supply of tea. Nasser leads me to the opposite end of the room – so far away that the sofa edge partly obscures them, giving them the appearance of being sat in a pit.

A procession of Qatari men turn up. First is an old guy who isn't very friendly, then a man in his early forties, tall, with a neatly clipped beard and incredible English. Prompted by my last name, he wants to talk about Scotland.

'How many Scottish tribes are there?'

'Er ...'

The word 'tribe' sounds odd in the Scottish context. The question, though, is revealing.

There are numerous tribes in Qatar, extended groupings

tens of thousands of people large, to which individuals view themselves as belonging. Most important is the Al Thani (House of Thani), whose members have been de facto rulers of Qatar since the 19th century.[†] The rest are ranked and ordered by various contested categories and histories, including those who trace their lineage to the Bedouin tribes of the Qatar peninsula, those whose families come from settled communities, those who map their ancestry to tribes from elsewhere (Iran, Saudi Arabia, Kuwait, Yemen) and those who are the descendants of slaves. Despite a national Qatari identity now beginning to exert a pull, tribe and family remain key to how Qatari politics, business and society functions.

We move on from Scottish tribes to kilts. Can I confirm that a true Scotsman doesn't wear anything underneath?

All eyes on me. I would ruin everything by saying that I have no idea. I feel I can't point out that, despite my Scottish granddad, I've been to Scotland fewer than half a dozen times in my life and have never worn a kilt. Instead, I nod. Nasser's face exhibits shock.

Yet maybe it's not so ridiculous having an Englishman pronounce on Scottish traditions. After all, kilts were invented in the 18th century by a Quaker from Lancashire called Thomas Rawlinson, and that other central element of Scottish culture – the differentiated 'clan tartan' – is an even later invention. It

[†] The Al Thani tribe are so important to the working of Qatar that one PR firm sells an 'Al Thani family tree'. For $6,000, you can follow which members of the tribe dominate which businesses and ministries.

is only retrospectively that these objects have come to stand as symbols of Scottish culture in its entirety.

The kilt is a perfect example of what the historians Eric Hobsbawm and Terence Ranger term the 'invention of tradition'. Many traditions that appear to be old, they argue, have often been recently manufactured. The reasons for their creation are various: to establish social cohesion, legitimise institutions and authorities or inculcate certain beliefs and value systems. Crucially, they suggest that such inventions occur more readily in societies undergoing great social flux and change. When everything is slipping and sliding, an invented tradition gives an anchor point, an illusion of unchanging life to hold on to.

It's not hard to see the resonance with falconry in Qatar. Yes, people who inhabited this peninsula in the past hunted with falcons. But today's hunters are less their direct descendants and more the proponents of new traditions: of displays of status linked to consumption; of a class of people divorced from worries about income, wondering instead what to do with their leisure time. The example of the Scottish kilt serves as a reminder that manufacturing tradition isn't unique to the Gulf. It is a universal game that humans like to play.

After a few more questions from my inquisitor about Scottish tribes, the conversation moves on. More men join, including a young guy who Nasser tells me has a motorboat moored in the marina downtown. An offer is made for me to go out on the water. I express strong enthusiasm but suspect it will never happen. As the time passes, my presence in the *majlis* has become less novel. The percentage of Arabic spoken increases, the stretches of time where I don't know the topic of conversation grow longer. My hope that this experience was going to crack open the gilded life of Qataris seeps away. It's clear their hopes, dreams and grievances will not be revealed by one evening hanging out with half a dozen guys in a *majlis*, falcon or no falcons.

I feel I have overstayed my welcome.

I try to make my own exit but Nasser insists on getting one of his helpers to drop me home.

Shadman* has broad shoulders and deep-set eyes. He gestures for me to climb into an oversized pick-up truck before jumping into the driver's seat.

'London – my dream city!'

I have mentioned that I'm from the UK. Everyone in Bangladesh wants to go to London, I am told. Shadman was supposed to go to Italy. He had filled out all the paperwork and paid for the visa, but the Italian embassy never granted it. His sister's husband was working in Qatar and so he followed him here. That was eight years ago. I look at his face – there's not a wrinkle on it. He must have been in his teens when he arrived.

Shadman talks me through a typical day. He rises at 5am, drives various members of Nasser's family around Doha and turns in around 1am. Sleep is topped up during any downtime, but not today:

'No sleep today because a cricket match – watching cricket.'

If I am honest, I want a narrative of discontent. Of anger towards Nasser and Qatar. But it never materialises.

'Best thing about the work is you are free,' Shadman says decisively, before moving on to describe a situation that doesn't sound very free.

'Here you can get a call, "*Baba* is going out," "*Baba* wants you to pick up daughter," and you go.'

His use of *baba*, 'father', to refer to Nasser hits me with its paternalism and I think back to an utterance of Nasser's on the drive home: 'If you are go to Bangladesh, you will say, "Oh my God, how this people live here?"'

Shadman goes on to say that Nasser is a good man and that he likes him. He talks to me about all the money and the electronics he gets given when Nasser comes back from a trip abroad. His pay is 1,800 rials a month ($500). This is actually high for Qatar, almost double the minimum wage.

Once home, I do the sums.

Shadman's wage amounts to 1.4 per cent of the cost of the falcon that Nasser received as a gift.

3

'I know I am the driver. I can't take my family here'

Kumar* picks me up.

There's no place to park where I suggested we meet, a coffee shop near the Sheraton hotel. It's full of well-dressed families enjoying their Friday. My botched suggestion reveals two things: I clearly don't own a car in Qatar and I'm terrible at sticking to my own rules. Let the other person decide where to meet; make them feel comfortable, I remind myself yet again.

Kumar drives us round the Corniche, Doha's waterfront promenade, to the spit of land that serves as the harbour for dhow boats. These mid-sized wooden ships at one time transported goods and people around the Indian Ocean, from Madagascar to Malacca. Now they're employed to whisk bored weekenders on a tour of the bay. The promontory is mostly car park. At its far end, people sit on the rocks or fish into the waters, which are turning from turquoise to sheet-metal grey as the sun dips towards evening.

This seems to be where the low-income workers hang out. There are crowds of men sitting, walking and crowding the tea stand. From here you can stare across at the Museum of Islamic Art or the skyscrapers of West Bay – look but don't touch. How do workers know to be here and not over there? Maybe through run-ins with the police in the swankier parts of the Corniche. Or perhaps through that feeling I am experiencing now: when you scan a crowd and realise that you are somewhere where you do not belong.

Kumar was my taxi driver a week earlier. It was his wide, smiley face that drew me in. That, and the better-than-average English. Now I also notice the leathery skin and silver-flecked stubble that prematurely age a man who must be in his thirties. Kumar has been in Qatar for ten years, the last two and a half of them driving taxis. But he's had enough. He's flying home in three days' time.

From the overcrowded tea stand Kumar fetches us two cups of *karak*, a milky, spicy tea that is Qatar's national drink. We clamber up and sit on the concrete wall that separates the car park from the rocks. From here you can just about make out our original meeting place in the shadow of the oblong hotel across the bay. I take a slurp of tea and we begin.

'Main reason for the peoples coming to Qatar – not only Qatar, all Gulf country ... their country is not developed much.'

With my eyes I implore him to go on.

'They don't have any jobs in their country. They cannot earn money in their country, even me. We can earn money but it's not enough. It's not enough for our family maintenance.'

He breaks off and hesitates.

'Now, world is going very fast. Before the 30 years or 50 years, peoples ... they need the important items only. They want house, they want food, they want dress. Now peoples needs lot of items … washing machine, car, television. And air conditions. The varieties of the dress, you know? And education – education is very important now.'

Kumar hasn't grasped that I want *his* story. He's speaking for all Asians: representative to the white guy from the world of brown folk.

'I am thinking, everybody's thinking, about the family.'

As Kumar speaks, a singular point of view never holds. 'I' becomes 'we' becomes 'everybody' as he struggles to bridge the gap between his view on the world and mine.

'My daughter, my son. We want to do something for them … but it's not enough in my country. *Yani*,' he draws out the Arabic filler word that is akin to 'like' or 'you know'.

'Not only me, the *all* peoples – you can ask all peoples.'

He pauses, as if wanting me to do as he says.

'They not like to work here, but it's— it's a situation.'

Kumar tells me about his life in Sri Lanka. He worked in sales for a biscuit manufacturer, but it didn't pay enough to support his wife and two children. They never considered the prospect of his wife working – her job was looking after the children. Kumar's best friend was working in Qatar as an office supervisor. They would chat every week. If Kumar wanted, he could arrange a visa for him, said the friend. Kumar thought about the house he wanted to build, about the school fees, the car that the family had their eyes on.

'Yeah, I need to come.'

When he first arrived in Qatar the temperature floored him.

'Forty-seven to 50 [degrees] means it's half-boiled! We can boil the egg, it's a half-boiled, no?'

He was employed at first as a salesman with a food supply company. He spent eight hours a day working with an international cast of characters, sharing a room with seven others – a Ghanaian, an Eritrean, two Indians, two Sri Lankans and an unspecified other.

Sounds difficult, I say on impulse.

'"It's difficult" means it's difficult for *you*,' counters Kumar. 'You don't know that situation.'

A smile in the corner of his mouth assures me that the comment is not an attack.

'You don't know that situation. You didn't sleep with eight people ... It's difficult for you, it's not difficult for us. We know that.'

Kumar is warming to his task of explaining.

'My ear knows I want sleep. He is closed, the ear. Automatically it will close. You know? You are talking, other man, but I am sleeping.'

I feel a prickle of annoyance – I'm not unaware of the privations of people here or my own privilege. But it passes when I correct myself: I am *aware*, but I don't *know*.

Kumar likes the variation of life in Doha, the different foods, languages, colours.

'I feel I am in the world,' he says with a smile.

'Before I am only Sri Lanka. I feel I am in the world now ... My right-hand side is Nepal, my left-hand side is

Africa. My front side is India, back side Pakistan. I'm around. I feel it.'

But Kumar wasn't making enough money at the food supply company. However high the salary, costs at home seemed to exhaust his funds. Fed up with the office job, in 2017 he changed his visa and became a taxi driver.

Doha is crawling with taxis. The heat, cheap fuel and urban sprawl render it a car city. Public transport exists but only a handful take it. Attempts to walk anywhere will usually be curtailed by the heat, the lack of pavement or very often both. There are official taxis, green and yellow saloons that cruise around downtown, but ride-sharing apps are what nearly everyone uses.

The gig economy doesn't operate like it does in the US or UK. The inflexibility to move between jobs in Qatar means that, legally, you can't supplement work in a supermarket with some extra driving or leave your construction job and give chauffeuring a go. You need to be on a valid driver's visa, issued by what are called 'limousine companies', although there is nothing luxurious about them. Companies rent the cars to the drivers on a monthly basis. Some also supply food and accommodation. Others demand the money made from the apps goes directly to them, with the driver receiving a regular monthly amount like a wage.

In his sales job, Kumar earned 2,200–3,000 rials a month ($600–$825). Driving taxis, he normally makes double that. But it's no easy way to make a living. He has to pay 1,800 a month ($500) to rent the car. The app takes 25 per cent commission. His food, accommodation, petrol and any maintenance costs on the vehicle all come out of his earnings. To get close to his target of 6,000 rials take-home pay he has to work a minimum of twelve hours a day, seven days a week.

It's common to hear people around the world talk about the revealing nature of cities. Dense populations and a lack of space force the private into the public. People break up with each other on the streets or unselfconsciously do their make-up on the train. Doha is the exact opposite. As you drive along highways, past manicured verges, skyscrapers and walled villas, you sometimes never see a soul. The vehicles streaming past are often the only sign of life.

Taxis are perfect for Doha: private commercial transport for a private city. People move through town in thousands of separately enclosed worlds. And yet in the passenger–driver relationship, taxis are one of the few points in Doha where the middle classes of Qatar come together with those lower down the pecking order. You might learn something new, hear a view-point you never expected, perhaps be entertained. Or you might just put in your headphones, driver and passenger alike, studi-ously ignore each other and imagine you are somewhere else. The arrival at your destination can be a relief or a disappoint-ment. You make the short dash from air-conditioned car into air-conditioned shopping mall, ready to tuck into your salmon salad, while the driver goes in search of another eight rials.

Doha used to be a maze of roundabouts christened with great names. There was rainbow roundabout (after the arch in its middle), crazy roundabout (two smaller roundabouts inside a larger one) and smelly roundabout (thanks to a nearby sewage tower). But an exploding population plus too many roundabouts was causing tailbacks and accidents. The government ripped them out in favour of American-style intersections with lights. If there's a lot of traffic or you arrive at the wrong time, you have to sit patiently for up to three or four minutes before you can move.

I have to credit Doha's intersections as being my most helpful research assistant. When you're moving, the lack of conversation can be soaked up by the sound of the motor or the moving scenery. But when idling in a car with another person, the silences just pile up and up, pushing and squashing until someone feels they have to say something.

I have heard all sorts from Doha's taxi drivers. A Pakistani driver told me the story of how he fell in love with his Filipino passenger, got married and had a son, only for his father to shun him. A Bangladeshi chauffeur declared with a straight face that the reason Vietnamese people no longer receive Qatari visas is because they once cooked and ate a Nepali worker.

There are the wily drivers, like the guy who showed me how he switches between two ride-sharing apps to circumvent their twelve-hour limit on work. There are the desperate drivers, such as the Keralan illegally working on the spare account of his friend ('This isn't me! I'm not Abdul!'). There are the exploited drivers: the one fed only rice and vegetables; the one whose employer makes up imagined deductions and takes them from his pay; the one whose compensation for working twelve hours on his day off is a grand total of 50 rials ($14). And there are the lonely drivers, like the diminutive Nepali who works overtime because otherwise he sits in his room, crying about being away from his wife and baby girl. A driver so alone that, when I give him a tip, he doesn't say anything but gives me a small hug.

There are the political drivers: Indians who deliver panegyrics on Narendra Modi; Tunisians who hate the Arab Spring; Filipinos who don't really like President Rodrigo Duterte but somebody had to deal with the drug dealers. Then there are the positive, breezy drivers, my favourite being the rogue from Senegal who was back in Doha for a second attempt after blowing all his cash back home ('I used my money on the ladies – they finished it!'). Most of those with a sanguine outlook have, not coincidentally, been doing the job for less than a year. A surprising number share an unquenchable belief in the Qatari Dream. Work hard, save enough and you can make this country work for you, they insist, despite the mounting evidence to the contrary.

Then there are the angry ones: the guy who berated me for paying for my journey on a card ('Everyone doesn't have cash! How am I meant to eat? I have no cash!'). The Keralan whose hatred for the ride-sharing companies knew no bounds ('Not any thinking from Uber this is a human, he also has a family ... Uber is selfish. Only his need for the profit.'). I felt that these were the ones who had peered through the entrepreneurial gift wrap and seen the set-up for what it is – a trap, where they can never make enough money, the structure designed to ensure it is impossible.

It's the taxi drivers who understand the city's underbelly. One excitedly told me about the Qatari women who use taxis to facilitate illicit encounters. They wait until their husbands are back from work and having their afternoon naps, he claimed. Then, rather than using their personal chauffeurs, they order a taxi. He drops them at the door of hotels or by flyovers where they get into unmarked Land Cruisers. Another driver told me of the time a woman in a full-face veil got in and started speaking on the phone in Arabic, assuming he didn't understand.

'I'm on my way. What room number did you say it was?'

Most drivers are encumbered with the same petty prejudices as the rest of us, ranking and ordering customers by ethnicity and nationality: the Europeans are respectful but don't tip; Filipinos are fun; the Arabs are the rudest – but never Qataris, they are keen to point out. Yet every now and then you get someone who, via their seat at the meeting point of Qatar, seems to have transcended their status and become a philosopher-king on the Doha experience.

'We are all humans, but we are not equal,' warned one such driver from Ghana who was tired of hearing the same liberal platitudes. Doha gives everyone a chance to reinvent themselves, he conceded, but don't get carried away.

'I am black,' he declared. 'I must be treated differently. You are white, you must be treated differently. We cannot be treated the same. No—'

At this point he broke off definitively.

'It can never happen. Until you die, until I will die – it will never.'

The traffic in Qatar is intense. Highways are constrained by endless building work. Lane markings are interpreted as suggestions. Indicating before moving is distinctly optional. Afternoon rush hour starts at 2pm and sees half the city grind to an ill-tempered, fume-ridden crawl. Driving is a dog-eat-dog experience in which timidity is sniffed out and crushed, leaving the uninitiated to waste ten minutes trying to cross an intersection. Top of the food chain are the tank-sized SUVs and Jeeps driven by the rich. At traffic lights and in queues they tower elephant-like over regular-sized cars. Like Qatar more broadly, you should know your place in the traffic hierarchy and get out of their way.

All taxi drivers are scared of the locals. 'I give way to these people,' one told me after slamming on the brakes to avoid hitting a swerving Land Cruiser. 'Because if not – no job tomorrow.' Ferraris, Porsches and Maserati liberally pepper queues at traffic lights. At weekends, their five-litre engines are audible all night. When the lights change, it's best to hang back. Another driver told me of a Qatari who got so incensed with his inability to move out of the fast lane that he rammed the back of his car. 'Not big damage,' he recounted. 'I stopped, but he didn't stop, he gone ... He never stops.'

Recent years have been rough for taxi drivers. The Saudis and Emiratis, once so plentiful, vanished after the 2017 diplomatic crisis. The opening of the metro in 2019 siphoned off a few more passengers. And don't get them started on coronavirus. By 2020, there were so many drivers that the market had become saturated. The waiting list for becoming an Uber driver was hundreds of people long. The minimum fare had dropped to eight rials ($2.20).

For many drivers I met, the World Cup in 2022 was their focal point. A month of good custom shining like an oasis on the horizon. But most of them planned to leave after that. This isn't Dubai, I was told repeatedly. Once the football show moves on, what tourists are going to come on holiday to Qatar?

D o your family understand what you do here?
   'No, no,' says Kumar with a mournful chuckle. 'They don't have any idea.'

He then nuances his answer.

'They know my *jobs*, but they don't know how I am living here. How is my life is going, how is my entertainments.'

It is not fully their fault. Kumar shields his family from worrying about him. He lies when he's sick and conceals that he sometimes skips meals to send more money home.

I ask Kumar what he likes most about living in Qatar.

He pauses.

'We can earn more money ... first in mind is earn money.'

Of course it is. He's not here to understand more about Qatar, escape with his family from cold, rainy Europe or play

out any of the other fantasies and indulgences that draw people like me.

'It's different ... you don't know that mind,' Kumar tells me gently.

'Asian peoples different, European different and American different, I already say you.'

I hesitate and Kumar continues.

'I mean, everything – we are doing *everything* for our family only. Not thinking about us, our entertainments ... We don't know that mind. That is why I cannot explain you.'

Is that frustration creeping into his voice? Whatever it is, it disappears as he tries one final approach to make me understand.

'Our body's only here,' he says, lightly touching the rock we are sitting on.

'Our spirit and our mind and our heart [is] in our family.'

Will he miss anything about Qatar?

'I miss wealth!' I hear him say and we both laugh. It seems a clever way of underlining how he'll be earning a lot less. But I've misunderstood.

'World. World,' Kumar corrects me. 'All nationality people, they are living here. When I go my country, only Sri Lankans. I will miss world.'

He'll also miss the freedom.

'When I'm with family, I am – same like house arrest, no?' He laughs. 'Can't go anywhere. Daughter will ask, "Where are you going father? I am coming with you. Why you going?" Hah! Lot of questions. Here, nobody's questioning.'

Across the Gulf, millions live this pseudo-bachelorhood. They are married – and are often fathers – but have lived apart from their wives and children for so long that the single life of the Gulf has become their default. Countless pictures, videos and phone backgrounds have been pressed on me by proud drivers. I have cooed at images of babies gurgling on colourful rugs, marvelled at small children clutching bikes and expressed admiration for young adults in graduation robes. I lost count of the number of times I heard over speakerphone the cry of a toddler or the tired tones of a partner forced to chat in her early hours due to the time difference.

The presence in Qatar of a 'bachelor' class is not simply the result of personal preference. Visas for low-income work don't allow the holders to bring dependents to Qatar. There seems little need for such aggressive immigration policy: even if they could, most low-income workers wouldn't bring their families. Their hard-won money would evaporate on Doha's prohibitive rents, private schools, even basic groceries.

Kumar is cognisant of all this.

'I know I am the driver. I can't take my family here.'

The sun has now set. Kumar stares out across the water. The lights on the skyscrapers are on, doing their hyperactive, seizure-inducing dance into the darkening sky.

Dusk seems to prompt a shift in his register to something more reflective.

'Now is lot of change. Before, I think Sheikh Hamad was the king of the Qatar ... At that time, no any development in Qatar, not *big* developments and roads and buildings and education sites and the metro stations ... I cannot identify the areas now. It's a lot of change.'

Doha years are like dog years. I have to remind myself that the ancient past to which Kumar is referring is 2009.

'Old Qatar is nice. New Qatar is busy.'

Kumar seems to be following the thread of something comforting.

'Everythings old is nice. Not only Qatar. *Everything*,' he says with emphasis. He tells me he loves to ponder how people lived 100, 200 years ago. When he has to choose a film to watch, he always selects one set in old times – with a kingdom, a king, no motor vehicles, only horses.

'I like old,' Kumar reaffirms.

'Then why are you in Qatar?' I joke.

Kumar laughs. 'Yeah, yeah. It's true ... Do you have any more questions?'

A polite way of wrapping it up. I take the hint, reach over and turn off my recorder.

'Now we can talk free,' says Kumar.

My heart skips. I prepare myself for juicy revelations or strident criticism. Kumar leans across and looks at me forlornly.

'How do you stay so skinny? I used to be 48 kilos ten years ago. But now I am very fat.'

4 'In media yes, very very good but in the reality nothing. Zero'

The location is a large villa.

This is the embassy for a middling-sized country in Asia. A couple of men wait outside in the small wedge of shade created by the wall. There are no gates, buzzers or passport checks, simply a security guard who waves me through when I mention who I'm meeting.

I enter a reception hall with a picture of the nation's leader and a sweeping staircase. When I reach the top, a brass plaque on a door announces that it is the office of Mr Rahul* – Labour Attaché. I knock.

He looks more middle-aged and more bald than when I met him the previous week at a conference on labour. Mr Rahul's room is sparsely furnished. It contains a desk with an old computer, some cupboards, a couple of sofas and a coffee table. He gestures for me to sit in front of the desk and goes around behind it. An air conditioning unit blows down on us in an irritating fashion.

'So this report you are compiling, where will it appear?'

The tone lets me know the question is asked for arse-covering purposes rather than interest. I remind him that I'm not writing a report. Mr Rahul opens his eyes further, perhaps with relief. He gets up, goes to the bookcase and returns with a lever arch file stuffed to overflowing.

'This is the records of a case with just one company.'

He points to the company name at the head of the cover sheet. Let's call them Bad Company.

'The company was in Qatar for thirteen years but went bankrupt,' Mr Rahul tells me. 'Its owner fled the country, leaving the salaries unpaid.'

I look more closely. The coversheet is a neat table containing the names of 46 men, their ID numbers and contact details. In the final column various five-figure amounts are written in pencil.

13,560.

20,038.

And one for 129,000.

'What are these?'

'This is the amount of money [in rials] that each worker has been denied.'

If there's one thing most outsiders know about Qatar, it is that the country hasn't treated its migrant labourers very well. Amnesty International, the *Guardian*, Human Rights Watch, the German broadcaster Westdeutscher Rundfunk (WDR), Migrant-Rights.org and the UN special rapporteur on racism have documented a range of abuses, from passport confiscation and unpaid wages to overcrowded accommodation, unsafe working conditions and unexplained deaths. Along with the International Labour Organization (ILO), these organisations have performed an invaluable service by raising awareness of abuses, giving voice to the powerless and lobbying the Qatari government to improve conditions. The poor treatment has gone on for decades and is prevalent across the Gulf region, but the World Cup has shone a light on the abuse. What is it like for those on the front line who are dealing with the fallout and working to make things better? I came to see Mr Rahul to try to answer this question.

According to Mr Rahul, workers filed a case against Bad Company with the Ministry of Labour, where it languished with the Disputes Settlement Committee. When it was eventually taken up, the company manager had long left Qatar. The committee eventually tracked down the company's Qatari sponsor and asked him to make good on the unpaid wages. He refused to pay them in full but offered the workers 10–20 per cent of what they were owed. From a citizen of one of the richest countries in the world it was an insulting suggestion. Still, the majority of the workers agreed to take it. Mr Rahul paraphrased their stance for me: 'We have been suffering more than one-and-a-half years. If it can be done immediately, then we can agree.' That agreement was a year prior to our meeting. Mr Rahul tells me that some of the claimants have yet to be paid. Most people can't tolerate such a long wait. Often in debt, with families reliant on them, delays in justice are existentially crippling. Most of the people in the case against Bad Company had to return to their home country.

'Can the embassy step in to help?'

'It's an internal procedure of Qatari government. We cannot directly intervene,' Mr Rahul tells me.

'But you're not intervening,' I respond. 'The decision has been passed. All you're doing is chasing up to make sure that the decision is implemented.'

I get a shrug. I sense the powerlessness of being the representative of a middling power in Qatar. Decisions are made and conveyed to you. Stamping your foot doesn't work so well without the passports and privileges of more powerful nations.

I'm in need of greater context. 'Is this sort of thing common?'

Mr Rahul turns to his computer and clicks on a few folders. A minute later, a spreadsheet pops up with 'July 2019' written in big letters at the top. Mr Rahul scrolls to the bottom of the spreadsheet (which takes some time) and then reads me the numbers.

'Ninety-one non-payments of salary. One-hundred-and-thirty-five instances of non-preparation of Qatari ID card [meaning that the employee is in the country illegally, he explains]. Fifteen exit permit issues.'

I ask if this is a typical month.

He closes the sheet and opens another for June 2019. He reads me the stats at the bottom.

'One-hundred-and-ten non-payments of salary. Ninety-six non-preparations of ID cards. Nine exit permit issues.'

And then before I can speak he opens one for May.

'One-hundred-and-fourteen non-payments. One-hundred-and-twenty-one ID card issues. Six exit permit issues.'

Mr Rahul gives me more examples: a young woman hired as a cleaner and abandoned; a labourer who has been in Qatar for eighteen months without the company issuing a Qatari ID. If workers complain, sponsors have a battery of measures they can deploy, including filing a complaint that their employee has absconded or accusing them of theft. The threat alone is enough to terrify most into silence. Mr Rahul stops reading and turns to fix me with an angry glare.

'They play with their privilege.'

This is one embassy. I think of the other Asian and African countries in Qatar, of India with its 700,000 or so citizens here. There will be thousands of examples of mistreatment – and these are just the ones we know about.

When discussing the root causes of worker abuse in Qatar, it is common to hear mention of *kafala*. Used in this context, the term refers to a system of sponsorship-based employment found across the Gulf region. Every non-citizen in Qatar – from an American management consultant to a South Asian labourer – needs a *kafeel*, or sponsor, in order to be resident in the country. Private individuals, rather than the state, have the responsibility for workers' status. Workers are bound to their sponsors in arrangements that make it difficult to raise complaints, change jobs or leave the country without permission.

But the contemporary idea of *kafala* is very different to the traditional Islamic notion. *Kafala* was designed to protect the weak and the vulnerable by making it religiously incumbent on guarantors to offer their patronage and protection. Historically, the concept was widely applied to any situation where an assurance was needed, such as guaranteeing a business contract or turning up at court. An essential element was that the guarantor shouldn't demand any benefits – they were supposed to provide their services free of charge. It's important to make this point because for some critics *kafala* is seen as embodying the inherent illiberality and restrictiveness of Islam. It is deployed as a strange, foreign term that 'explains' the problems that workers face while serving to further exoticise the Gulf as a place unlike anywhere else.

In fact, it was British colonial rulers who instigated the shift in the meaning of *kafala*. When Britain started to deepen its control of the Gulf in the early 20th century, *kafala* was widely used for financial and legal assurances, such as providing bail in criminal cases or guarantees for debt. It was the British who chose to extend the same logic of surety to labour. Beginning in the 1920s, they set up the bureaucratic system of work sponsorship – entry and exit visas, valid work permits, non-objection certificates – that would be familiar to visitors to the Gulf today. The discovery of oil triggered an explosion in migration to the region. Small colonial bureaucracies were overwhelmed and consequently delegated responsibility for sponsorship to the local rulers. They in turn passed the authority for the entry and control of migrants to locals. The association of *kafala* with migrant labour, then, is not a barbaric ancient Islamic custom but, as historian Omar AlShehabi notes, an early British foray into outsourcing – a way to control labour and police empire 'on the cheap'.

In the modern-day Gulf, *kafala* has lost all vestige of protection or support. Voluntary cooperation has been replaced with contracts. Punishments for non-compliance that once targeted sponsors now punish the workers themselves (if your employer forgets to renew your ID, you'll be the one dragged before the police and deported). The academics Ray Jureidini and Said Fares Hassan have compiled multiple religious teachings showing that the practice of sponsors profiting by selling visas conflicts with the tenets of Islam.

The contemporary *kafala* system is the underpinning structural factor in the widespread exploitation and abuse faced by workers in Qatar. From there, the injustices leak out and suffuse the entire arc of migration to the Gulf. To work in Qatar, most workers pay fees to a recruiter, despite laws that prohibit charging individuals in this way. These fees are usually around $1,000–1,500, although they can sometimes be three or five times that amount. Many workers can't pay that kind of cash up front and so take out loans or arrange for the amount to be subtracted from their wages. Given the salary in Qatar for a low-paid labourer is $220–330 a month, any repayment happens slowly, locking them into a situation where they don't see any of their earnings for months, sometimes years. The size of the fee bears no resemblance to the actual costs of the visa, flight and other elements of recruitment. It is deliberately inflated to ensure that all the people along the employment chain, from company HR manager to recruiter in the home country, get their 'taste'.

When workers arrive in Qatar their passports are often confiscated, despite laws prohibiting an employer holding on to passports without written permission. Many workers are also subjected to contract substitution, where the contract that they signed in their home country (if they signed one, many don't) has disappeared and is replaced by a new agreement with less favourable terms. Once in Qatar, no longer in possession of their passports and with no money to book a return flight, most workers have no option but to sign.

Workers then go to live in labour camps – securitised, self-contained compounds on the outskirts of Doha. Much of this accommodation is in a lamentable state. The sociologist Geoff Harkness provided a vivid account of one camp he visited in 2011: 'Each bedroom was crowded with four metal bunk beds, topped with thin mattresses ... The kitchen was almost unrecognizable, caked in what appeared to be a decade's worth of charred black grease and cooking oil ... the toilet was a faeces-smeared five-gallon plastic bucket, located next to a hole in the ground.' Other similar accounts abound, including in reports by the BBC, Amnesty International and German broadcaster WDR.

Low-paid construction workers ordinarily work for eight to ten hours a day, six days a week, although a 2018 audit on World Cup sites by the consultancy Impactt revealed many working twelve- or fourteen-hour days. One poor soul had gone 148 consecutive days without a day off. Many workers receive their wages late – or not at all. I lost count of the number of people I spoke with who had not been paid on time. Some had backlogs of over half a year's salary. In 2020 alone, the ILO assisted over 9,000 workers in submitting complaints to the Ministry of Labour, with unpaid wages being the most common problem. Most workers provide the sole source of income for their families. Late or non-payment consequently doesn't just affect them – it results in missed meals and unpaid school fees half a world away. NGOs rightly refer to the abuse as 'wage theft' and, despite government attempts at regulation, it remains, in the words of Amnesty International, 'rampant in Qatar'.

No subject, however, has drawn more international attention and condemnation than the deaths of migrant workers. As I began looking into the issue, I wanted to approach it with an open mind, conscious of how polarised the matter has become. Migrant worker deaths seemed to be *the* issue that both football fans and football agnostics know about the 2022 World Cup. And who could fail to be touched by the stories of men from developing countries, miles from their families, losing their lives in the pursuit of building sports stadiums. I interviewed experts and spent many hours reading reports. I also spoke to construction workers myself. And I have to conclude that, ultimately, Qatar comes out wanting.

It's extremely hard to come up with a number for how many people in the country have died as a result of working conditions. In February 2021, the *Guardian* reported that over 6,500 migrants had died in the decade from 2010 to 2020, with

37 of them directly working on World Cup projects. The huge number drew outrage, but this includes all deaths in the migrant population over these years, not simply fatalities in the construction industries. That being said, the available evidence suggests that Qatar's extreme climate could be playing a role in a significant number of these deaths.

Summer temperatures in Qatar frequently pass 40 degrees Celsius with suffocating humidity. For a third of the year workers are 'potentially performing their job under significant occupational heat stress', in the words of a report that Qatar itself commissioned. One in three workers in that study were found to have become hyperthermic (with an elevated core body temperature) at some part of their shifts in summer. Other research is more forthright. A 2019 article in the journal *Cardiology* showed a correlation between heat and the deaths of some 500 Nepali workers in Qatar. 'There is no reason to doubt this link, as it shows that the death toll follows the peaks in the annual heat waves,' Professor Dan Atar, one of the study's authors, told Amnesty International. 'My conclusion as a cardiologist is that these deaths are caused by heatstrokes.'

In Qatar, the *Guardian* story about thousands of deaths provoked cries of sensationalism and misleading reporting. Doha did not dispute the figures but argued that it was proportionate to the size and demographics of the migrant workforce. Yet arguing over the precise number of deaths is ultimately a fruitless endeavour. As the ILO has reported, the lack of sufficient data renders it impossible to come up with a categorical figure.

'This is the wrong argument,' I was told by Nicholas McGeehan, director at FairSquare Research and Projects, a consultancy specialising in labour rights in the Gulf. 'It shouldn't have been about how many people were dying. The argument should have been about the rate of unexplained deaths.'

Statistics from the Bangladeshi, Indian and Nepali governments – based on the repatriation of deceased citizens – show that the majority of the deaths of their nationals in Qatar are recorded as being the result of 'natural causes' or 'cardiovascular disease'. Given most migrant workers are young men who have passed health checks to come to Qatar, such explanations trouble many experts. 'These are phrases that should not be included on a death certificate,' the pathologist Dr David Bailey told Amnesty International for their report into migrant deaths. 'Everyone dies of respiratory or cardiac failure in the end ... the phrases are meaningless without an explanation of the reason why.'

But finding out why is difficult. Qatar prohibits postmortems, unless to determine if the death was caused by a criminal act or if the deceased had a pre-existing illness. Responding to criticism of this practice, the Qatar Government Communications Office stated that families must first approve an autopsy before it is carried out and that they refuse 'in most cases'. But in six deaths investigated by Amnesty, the families of those who died were never contacted about having an autopsy conducted. In a wealthy country, there isn't anything particularly difficult about investigating and recording accurate death

information. 'We have the know-how to properly certify deaths in all but less than 1 per cent of cases in the UK,' said Peter Blair, Professor of Epidemiology and Statistics at the University of Bristol, in the same Amnesty report.

With the help of the ILO, the Qatari government is moving to improve the quality of information on deaths, training staff and creating a centralised system for data collection across government agencies. But there are huge gaps: the National Trauma Registry, which tracks deaths and severe injuries in hospitals in Qatar, doesn't include fatalities that occurred before the person arrived at hospital; deaths are not disaggregated as work or non-work related; and Qatar's 'list of occupational diseases' does not include deaths resulting from heat stress. Whether intentional or not, these inadequacies have the same result – they disrupt the ability to tell definitively if the deaths of these young men stem from their working conditions. This in turn triggers a cascade of malign consequences: it prevents families from knowing what really happened to their loved ones; it lessens the sense of urgency to develop adequate safety procedures for construction workers; and it denies families from receiving compensation from employers or the Qatari government. '*That's* the scandal,' says McGeehan. 'That is what is entirely unacceptable about this issue.'

The poor treatment and abuse of workers in Qatar did not begin with the awarding of the FIFA World Cup. The tournament, however, has brought a new level of attention to the plight of labourers. In 2014, after a series of high-profile reports about the dire conditions, workers' groups lodged a complaint against Qatar at the ILO. The ILO presented Qatar with a choice: you can continue to stonewall, drag your feet and we will prosecute you, or you can let us in and work with us to help you improve the situation. Qatar chose the second option. In November 2017, the ILO began a technical cooperation programme with Qatar. The organisation agreed to open an office in Doha in return for a commitment from the government to change its labour laws. Top of its demands was the abolishment of the *kafala* system.

'Mate, it was terrible.'
Tarik* chats to me in the back of the car as we leave central Doha.

'You would see maybe eight to ten people sharing one room ... there were payment issues, not providing salary for months and months.'

Tarik works for a big international auditing firm. In his thirties, bearded and a bit overweight, he has an air of cannot-be-arsed that translates into a bored-sounding voice and a general slowness of movement. But as we get chatting he begins to perk up.

Since 2017, his job has been auditing companies that have been awarded contracts to work on World Cup projects. Stung by the international criticism, in 2014 the Supreme Committee for Delivery and Legacy – the entity tasked with preparing Qatar for the World Cup – established what it called its Workers' Welfare Standards, a set of principles designed to protect workers by making its contractors abide by them. It is Tarik's responsibility to check that these guidelines are being followed. 'We are there to ensure each and every worker gets proper meals, three meals a day, the salaries on time, plane tickets ... that they have proper rest,' he tells me.

We are on our way to just such an audit. I have been invited to observe a 'Workers' Forum' – one of the Supreme Committee's innovations to monitor working conditions in the face of international scrutiny and pressure. Workers on World Cup projects elect representatives annually. These representatives meet once a month with the contractor that employs them, raising complaints and bringing forward suggestions. The contractor listens. And Tarik – on behalf of the Supreme Committee – oversees the process. I want to know whether these joint committees are just PR fluff or if they are making a difference.

We pull up to a gate. A guard in a hard hat comes over. Tarik passes our ID cards through the window and continues talking.

'First, we go and talk to the workers ... We see if they're facing any issues ... they discuss it with us and we keep their identity confidential. We then go to the contractor's office and we see the documentation ... if we find an issue we give them some time to fix it. Because it's not a one-size job, it's a collaboration.'

We drive through the gate. Immediately in front of us looms the half-finished bowl of one of the World Cup stadiums. The car takes a left, pulling into an elaborate compound constructed entirely of prefabricated buildings. We go into an office where Tarik greets a few people warmly in Hindi. They briefly gather some paperwork and we head across the road, up some stairs and through a first-floor door.

The room is clinical, with polystyrene roof tiles, lino floor and bright lighting. Seven men are sat on chairs facing two tables. They are dressed in a range of styles – bright orange reflective overalls, *shalwar kameez*, shirts and jeans. Tarik goes and takes a seat behind the table along with a representative from the company and his clerk.

Today's business begins with Hussein* – a labourer from Bangladesh with a square face and a serious demeanour. None of the men speak in English, leaving the company representative to translate.

'So basically he has two complaints. Where they go to eat, outside the mess hall, we have got these wash basins. Stainless steel, huge. So it is like when people are washing their hands, the rice and everything is getting choked in that and it is getting overflow.'

He says something to Hussein in Hindi and then turns back to me.

'So we'll close this complaint of the overflowing of water within the next two days.'

That's brisk, I think to myself.

'The second is, like, in previous month they used to get biryani twice a week. Now it's again back to once a week.'

He turns to face the clerk who is poised to write down what he is about to say.

'We'll resolve this. We'll change the menu and bring biryani twice a week.'

Ravi* speaks next, reading from the notebook open in front of him. He says that he has brought a complaint from some of the workers about snoring. When you sleep four people to a room, one heavy snorer can have a disproportionate impact, he explains. Ravi wants the welfare officers to round up the snorers and make them share rooms.

The company representative nods briskly. He turns to the clerk and says aloud that he'll put the welfare officers on the case.

'Thank you, sir!' says Ravi and gives a small round of applause on his own.

We continue in the same swift fashion for another fifteen minutes. One worker wants the company to provide an ATM machine on-site. Another raises a problem with waste water outside an accommodation block. One worker spends a good three minutes explaining a point in Hindi. He looks very serious. The others are chipping in. Tarik and the company representative are speaking back. I get increasingly frustrated that I'm not following what is clearly a matter of grave concern. Then Tarik turns to me to translate.

'So he's complaining about the lentil soup.'

'He doesn't like it?'

'He's saying that the daal they get from the mess hall is a bit thick. What they feel is that they might be adding some powder or something to it, so he's asking to check it.'

They move to the next guy. He says something and they laugh.

'He doesn't have any complaints.'

'No complaints?' I say incredulously.

'No complaints.'

I wonder if this is all some elaborate act for my benefit. But, of course, this particular contractor is competent, otherwise I would never have been permitted to tag along. According to the Supreme Committee, by March 2020 there had been 69 elections to select representatives for these forums involving over 24,000 workers, with an average voter turnout of 84 per cent. 'This is the number that we look to as an organisation to demonstrate confidence and trust in a system,' said Mahmoud Qutub, executive director of the Workers' Welfare programme, at an event I attended in 2020. 'Eighty-four per cent of workers have gone, they have voted and they believe in the system.'

The Supreme Committee's initiatives for workers haven't stopped at joint committees. They have carried out over 6,800 audits. They have also pressured their contractors to retrospectively reimburse workers who paid recruitment fees. Almost 104 million rials ($28.5 million) has been paid or is pending to over 49,000 workers (although that amount still only works out as an average of $580 per worker, about half the typical fee paid by labour migrants to Qatar). It's easy to pick holes in these initiatives. Providing forums for workers is all well and good, but if the Supreme Committee were serious about workers' rights they would lobby the government to allow migrant workers to form or join trade unions (by law only Qatari nationals possess the right to establish unions). Stories of poor treatment on World Cup projects are still emerging – in June 2020, Amnesty International revealed that 100 workers at Qatar Meta Coats, a subcontractor working at the Al-Bayt Stadium, had not been paid for over half a year. Employees were owed amounts that ranged from 8,000 to 60,000 rials ($2,200–$16,500). Clearly, there are still issues. The improvements have been driven by outside pressure and the initiatives are dripping in self-congratulatory trumpet-blowing. But that doesn't mean that the Supreme Committee is lying or that there is no substance to what it has achieved.

The problem is less what the Supreme Committee is doing and more that too few companies in Qatar are following suit. In 2019, only around 35,000 people were employed directly on World Cup projects out of a total construction labour force of over 800,000. In other words, almost 96 per cent of workers in Qatar aren't covered by the enhanced audits, extended scrutiny and media attention that's focused on World Cup projects but just by regular Qatari labour law. It is true that recent years have seen these laws improve. In 2015, the government introduced the Wage Protection System, which offers electronic oversight of salary payments aimed at eliminating non-payment. It has increased accommodation and worksite inspections. To improve worker safety, it is now illegal to work outside between the hours of 10am and 3.30pm in the summer. But all of these initiatives are flawed. Companies still get away without paying their staff, checks aren't as stringent as those done by the Supreme Committee and even at midnight it's still too hot to work outside in August.

Endeavours to improve workers' rights in Qatar face the additional hurdle of an opaque labour market. It is not always straightforward to draw a link between workers who have been abused and those who are responsible. Problems often don't emerge with the primary contractor or even their subcontractor, but the subcontractor below or the one below that. 'I once found seven layers within our own company,' Hans Mielants, the head of HR at QDVC, a joint venture between the construction company Qatari Diar and the French building giant Vinci Construction, explained to me when we chatted by video call. QDVC places great emphasis on ensuring that those working on its projects are treated fairly, Mielants said, while he illustrated just how difficult this can be.

While his company can easily account for workers it employs directly, it's much harder to maintain oversight when working with contractors. 'OK, so how does it work?' said Mielants before starting to explain. 'I call a manpower provider, right? And I call him, and I say, "Joe, please, I need for tomorrow 500 workers." He's not gonna say, "I don't have 500 workers just standing around! What do you mean?" He will say, "Ah, no problem, no problem." But he only has 200, OK? [So] he picks up the phone and says, "Yes! We got a job from QDVC. I need 300 workers, do you have it?" [The person he calls] also will not say no. He only has 100 workers, right? And so, on it goes. Next

73

day, you could have 500 workers on-site, but they're probably from four or five companies.'

Who has responsibility for these workers and their well-being? Companies might audit their contractors but most fail to ask questions beyond that. One labour rights researcher told me that he discovered a security guard at a Western European embassy in Qatar had been trafficked. When he approached the embassy they refused to believe him because the company that they dealt with supposedly abided by a certain standard. 'As far as they were concerned, he didn't exist as a problem because he wasn't on their payroll,' the researcher said.

Qutub, of the Workers' Welfare programme, argues that the challenges are not unique to the construction sector, or even to Qatar. 'Anyone who has a supply chain of any sort, whether it's a very extensive supply chain [or not], they are likely to face these flaws,' he told the audience at an event in 2020. Many businesses see their operations distributed across logistics firms and recruitment agencies that wend around the world. It is possible to acknowledge the difficulty of enforcing accountability without defending bad practice or excusing abuse. In many cases it's not as simple as passing a law.

Given the lack of transparency, the world is almost wholly reliant on the research of academics, journalists and human rights NGOs to highlight abuse and hold employers to account. Those who have been criticised include QDVC who, in 2015, were accused by Sherpa, a French legal NGO, of 'forced labour [and] servitude'. QDVC strongly denied the accusation.

WORKER'S COMMUNITY - ASIAN CITY

05 Oct-19

NATIONALITY WISE		PROJECT WISE		COMPANY WISE		BED SPACE WISE	
NATIONALITY	NOE	PROJECT	NOE	COMPANY	NOE	NATIONALITY	NOE
INDIAN	32	NOH2	14		710	INDIAN	20
FILIPINO	15	LRT	468	SINIYARI GULF	02	FILIPINO	3
SRI LANKAN	1	PMV	0	MEGATRADE	0	SRI LANKAN	0
NEPALI	62	LUCP	29	ARABIAN PALACE	1	NEPALI	5
EGYPTIAN	0	QDVC-HO	09	TECHNO BLUE	0	EGYPTIAN	0
SOUTH AFRICAN	0	SPP	0	METITO	0	SOUTH AFRICAN	0
BANGLADESHI	184	CP01	0	NEWREST GULF	0	BANGLADESHI	6
CAMEROONIAN	2	NEWREST GULF	0	GEO Company (LRT)	05	CAMEROONIAN	2
PAKISTANI	2	DDAB	69			PAKISTANI	0
KENYAN	0					KENYAN	0
ETHIOPIAN	0					ETHIOPIAN	0
TOTAL	589	TOTAL	589	TOTAL	718	TOTAL	36
NO.OF NATIONALITIES	8						

Mielants says that Sherpa only interviewed subcontractors rather than QDVC workers. QDVC counter-sued for defamation before realising it wasn't a good look and dropping the case. In 2018, the French public prosecutor decided to take no further action on the complaint. But in 2019 Sherpa opened another case, which is ongoing.

The accusation clearly annoyed Mielants. 'Look at all the other construction companies,' he told me. 'There is such a big difference between what we do and what they do that it's absurd.' He said that QDVC goes to great lengths to ensure ethical recruitment, including hiring workers directly from India to ensure they don't pay fees and forcing contractors in Qatar to make their subcontractors adopt QDVC standards. Through this process they have managed to build up a loyal workforce and a 'white list' of contractors. Mielants claimed that behaving ethically is actually more profitable. The average length of time a worker stays with QDVC is six years – two to three times the average length of employment for construction companies in Qatar, according to Mielants. 'It is not just because we are [an] ethical company or we have a good soul or what have you – it also makes big business sense,' he said. 'People stay with us.'

Not all companies share his view. I spoke to the CEO of another construction firm who had 10 per cent of his workforce employed on World Cup projects. He was asked by the Supreme Committee if he would mind extending the stricter World Cup standards to the remaining 90 per cent of his employees. 'I was like, OK, I *want* to, but it's a big cost,' he told me. In the end, he upgraded to the more stringent guidelines, but he claimed that there had been consequences – the sales team were struggling to drum up business because the company are now seen as much more expensive than its competitors. He wanted the World Cup standards to be made the law throughout Qatar: 'Then we are on the same playing field,' he said. 'Just because we want to be good or do the right thing, we shouldn't be penalised for it.'

Mohammed Al-Obaidly, the government minister spear-heading Qatar's reform of working practices, was in a triumphant mood when he spoke at a forum on labour in October 2019. Clutching the microphone, he told the audience that a raft of new laws were soon to come into operation that would make it easier for workers to change employer or leave the country. Not only that, but a non-discriminatory minimum wage was to be introduced – the first in the region. 'There were red lines in the past in the state of Qatar, but we have undoubtedly made a quantum leap in this regard,' he said. 'It is impossible for us to go back.'

The microphone was then passed to Nasser Ahmed Al-Meer, former board member of the Qatar Chamber of Commerce and Industry. The audience sat dumbfounded as he launched into a repudiation of everything Al-Obaidly had just praised. If you completely abolish exit permits, argued Al-Meer, what would stop an employee going to the bank, withdrawing 1 million rials in cash from the company account and leaving the country?

Qatar was a unique case, we in the audience were told. 'My community, my society is different ... we need time to adapt.'

What was so unusual about this exchange was that it made public what everyone knew was happening behind closed doors – extreme battles among Qataris about how far to go with labour reforms. The slow and piecemeal progress on migrant workers' rights becomes more intelligible when you understand the tensions among the 11 per cent of the population who are Qatari citizens.

Qatar has been ruled by one family, the Al Thani (House of Thani), for over 150 years. When family rule is mentioned, my benchmark is usually the British royal family, with power passing from father to son (or the occasional daughter). But 'family rule' in Qatar operates along different guidelines. Historically, there was no tradition of primogeniture. Instead, a family council would be convened at moments of transition. Prominent relatives would bargain, horse-trade and argue – sometimes vehemently – about who should take over. The transition of power in Qatar has consequently been contentious, ricocheting from brothers to uncles to nephews (it remains an all-male affair). It became more heated when the oil and gas revenues started flowing and the benefit of being near the top showed itself to be more lucrative. In the past 70 years there have been two abdications, in 1949 and 1960, and two coups, in 1972 and 1995, with the latter involving a son overthrowing his father. It's only since the 1990s, when Sheikh Hamad bin Khalifa Al Thani changed the constitution to give himself the power to designate his son as successor, that the contention has been smoothed out. And still, power transitions operate differently to European monarchies: Qatar's current ruler, Sheikh Tamim, is the fourth son of the previous emir.

What is true for the Al Thani tribe goes for Qatari society more broadly. Even though there are only around 300,000 Qatari citizens, it is a mistake to view them as monolithic. Not all Qataris are rich. I spoke with a young man who was one of eleven children, raised by a single mother after his dad died. 'There have been times where we didn't have a proper meal. It was only bread and water,' he told me. Qatari society is still shaped by the division between *badawin* and *hadarin* – Bedouin nomads and those who are settled – the former lauded for their presumed uncorrupted Arabian culture at the same time as being discriminated against as gruff, uncouth and too closely linked to Saudi Arabia. People regularly disagree, and no question is more contentious than whether Qatar should open up or stick to its traditions. Nicholas McGeehan, from FairSquare, points out that the huge flows of foreign workers were 'foisted' on Qatari nationals. 'The extent of the immigration – they didn't ask for that,' he says. 'Most of them didn't want the World Cup. And suddenly the whole country, where they live, has been utterly transformed ... you can entirely see where those [conservative] attitudes come from.'

Since Al-Obaidly made his triumphant speech, the situation of workers in Qatar has deteriorated. During the coronavirus pandemic, the non-payment of wages exploded, from 588 separate company violations in January 2020 to 8,756 by June the same year. When the minimum wage was ready to be implemented in late 2020, it emerged that it was to be set at 1,000 rials ($275 a month) – more than some were earning at the time but still a derisory amount for one of the richest countries in the world. The abolition of non-objection certificates, freeing workers to move easily between companies, has not been as transformative as initially hoped. The government says that in the first year of the new law, over 240,000 workers were approved to change jobs. Yet NGOs have documented growing pushback from employers. Some have invented the need for additional written approval, others charge workers a fee to 'release' them and others still file false charges of 'absconding' to stop workers moving – a criminal accusation that is taken up by the Interior Ministry.

The icing on the cake came in early 2021 when the Shura Council, Qatar's legislative body, proposed a list of changes that would water down the newly minted laws. To date, the recommendations have not passed into law but they highlight the strength of local resistance to change. As Amnesty concluded, 'Progress on the ground has stagnated and old abusive practices have been resurfacing.'

Andrew Gardner, an expert on labour in the Gulf, has written powerfully about the gap between the discourse on reform and the reality. 'Discussing potential changes and engaging in the process of proposing such possible changes often eclipses the implementation of actual changes,' he wrote in 2018. The frenetic stream of press releases emanating from the government, the frequent conference panels and think tank reports contrast markedly with what most low-income workers in Qatar experience, which is a sense of stasis. It is striking that, while international media and NGOs are told of the hundreds of thousands of workers who have already changed jobs following the law change, the Minister of Labour is on record assuring the Shura Council that 'the number of workers who requested a transfer is few and that those whose requests were approved are smaller'.

Gardner's assessment is that little has changed. 'The problems that migrants encounter today are, essentially, the very same problems that migrants detailed to me in Saudi Arabia in 1999, in Bahrain in 2002–3, and in Qatar from 2008 to the present,' he concluded. It seems as if the effect of the law on improving lives is less important to the Qatari government than its symbolic function of showcasing Qatar as being modern and on a path to reform.

Even worse, Qatar has responded aggressively to those trying to highlight the many instances of non-compliance. In May 2021, the government detained Kenyan labour rights activist Malcolm Bidali. While working as a security guard, Bidali blogged, tweeted and spoke about the situation of workers in Qatar. He was arrested, held in solitary confinement for 26 days and the authorities refused to reveal his location or what crime he had committed. Bidali was eventually handed a criminal order that said he had published 'false news with the intent of endangering the public system of the state'. After a concerted campaign by human rights organisations, Bidali was finally allowed to leave the country in August 2021, albeit after paying a fine of 25,000 rials (approximately $6,800). 'Outrageous charges, and an even more outrageous fine, for simply sharing our lived experiences and pointing out shortcomings of the specific entities responsible for workers' welfare,' he said after his release. 'None of which translates to "misinformation".'

Vani Saraswathi, editor-at-large at Migrant-Rights.org, believes Qatar is going through the motions. She told me of her experience of dealing with the National Human Rights Committee, the government entity set up with much fanfare to protect the rights and dignity of people in Qatar. 'They're always under-resourced,' she told me. 'The number of cases waiting to be heard keeps growing by the day. The excuse given for the snail-like pace is that they're under-staffed.' She gives an exasperated sigh.

'How can you be under-staffed in the richest country in the world?'

Who deserves the blame for the plight of workers in Qatar? Employers are certainly a fair target. Given the devolved immigration laws, companies are the ones legally responsible for their employees' welfare and work conditions. However, despite being mostly based in Qatar, very few of these organisations are actually run by Qataris. The typical low-paid construction worker has no contact with a Qatari national. They are normally managed by other migrants. The majority of abuse and poor treatment is inflicted by non-Qataris on non-Qataris in a grim sort of migrant-on-migrant bear pit.

Should we blame the government? It is the Qatari authorities who have failed to legislate effectively or commit the resources to ensure that the necessary laws are being enforced. But the government does not have carte blanche. It has to placate a constituency that is hostile to change. It is trying to nudge a group of people into a form of existence they find alien.

What about Qatari nationals? It is surprising that few seem to care that their country is being built on the backs of workers whose treatment is iniquitous and stands at odds with the teachings of their religion. At the very least, they ought to be concerned that the issue is inflicting damage on Qatar's international image. Of course, some do care. There are Qataris such as Al-Obaidly, the assistant undersecretary for labour, who was named as a 'hero' in the US government's annual 'Trafficking in Persons Report' in 2021. It said that he and his team had been 'persistent in the drive to instil real change, even when the task at hand seemed impossible'.

There is also a crucial global dimension. Labour abuse is not somehow exceptional to Qatar or the Gulf region. Qatar is simply a stark example of the perniciousness of contemporary global capitalism. When speaking to migrant workers, I was often struck by the sense of inevitability about their decision to move to the Gulf for work. There was little in the way of regret, because the wholly uneven pattern of global development meant that they felt they had no option but to leave their home country in search of better-paying work. Some of the same problems and systems that bring workers to Qatar also compel people to take rickety boats across the Mediterranean from Africa to Europe or chance their luck with the harsh desert and even harsher border guards at the US–Mexico frontier. The Qatari company that keeps its workers in pitiful accommodation and pays their wages late is separated by degree – not kind – from the men convicted for manslaughter following the deaths of the Vietnamese workers who they had trafficked to the UK in the back of a lorry.

That said, the dynamics in Qatar are particularly laissez-faire. When the reality of global inequality interacts with an immigration system that hands too much power to an employer, the result is the highly exploitative situation found in the country. Even those who believe they are safe from abusive practices can suddenly find themselves ensnared.

In wrestling with the issue of Qatar's worker problem, I kept coming back to the memory of Steven*. In October 2020, I met Steven, who is originally from the Philippines, in his flat in Doha. Sitting on armchairs covered with white doilies, the sound of frying coming from the kitchen, he told me that he worked as a mechanical engineer for a construction company, but his main calling was serving as a community volunteer helping Filipinos with work troubles in Qatar.

Four months later, I heard from a mutual friend that Steven himself was in trouble. I dropped him a line on WhatsApp and he responded almost instantly, telling me that his company hadn't paid his salary for five months. He had been taken to court by his landlord for the unpaid rent on his flat. While waiting for the court date, a travel ban had been issued against him. 'I'm just pray in the corner and cry,' he wrote to me in his idiosyncratic English. 'Why suffer like this? I'm work hard with heart. I'm the community leader helping others for how many years, but now here I am facing same difficulty.'

This is the human impact of Qatar's Wild-West labour market. You can be sitting pretty and then, through no fault of your own, find yourself destitute, penniless, deported. When there's a free-for-all, it is inevitably the most vulnerable who will be hardest hit.

Steven ultimately holds the Qatari government responsible for his plight. He is indignant that officials are seemingly unwilling to enforce their own laws. What angers him the most is their two-facedness – the gap between the image they convey to the world and the actuality of life on the ground for workers.

I wait, looking at my phone. It says Steven is typing but it takes a few minutes for his parting shot to arrive.

'In media yes very very good but in the reality nothing. Zero.'

5 'There are so many people looking for job in this country'

It is a Tuesday evening and I'm hungry.

I walk past faded apartment blocks, scarred with water damage from leaky air conditioners, through the warren of small alleyways that make up the old centre of Doha. Past shops selling carpets and garages fixing cars. Past walls plastered in adverts in Hindi for spare rooms, until I find what I am looking for.

A falafel shop. The attendants are no-nonsense, spooning it into pita, loading it with pickled veg, shovelling in long-past-their-best chips. It's the cheapest and most delicious meal I'll eat all week, courtesy of being in the part of town that houses the lower, less-white rungs of the middle class.

Meal over, I spot the familiar glow of floodlights from across the street. Going to investigate, I find a small municipal sports field. Like all the smaller grounds in Doha, it is left open for the public to enjoy. On the pitch, a man with a whistle seems to be teaching other referees their positioning during corners. In the stands sit various people – players waiting to play, old guys just hanging out.

'This isn't the game, the game will come afterwards.'

His voice is rich, with West African vowels. I turn to see a broad-shouldered man with a boyish face, freckles and camel-like eyelashes standing next to me. He introduces himself as Abu Yusuf* and tells me he lives in an apartment nearby. He often comes to the pitch after dinner to watch the games, 'Even though they're never very good.'

Abu Yusuf tells me that he is currently between jobs but in the past has worked in the construction industry. In 2019, 883,000 people in Qatar – 40 per cent of the entire working population – worked in the sector, the majority in low-paid jobs that are subject to some of the worst transgressions of Qatari labour law. It feels like you cannot go anywhere in Doha without seeing men labouring. They are like modern-day chain gangs, dressed in overalls with improvised face coverings to protect them from the sand and sun. But Abu Yusuf didn't just work in any old form of construction, he worked in oil and gas. The mother industry. The source of Qatar's wealth, from which all other activity on the peninsula originates.

I tell him I want to see inside the camps. Abu Yusuf shakes his head.

'You *can't*. You will never.'

I would need gate passes, permission.

But how to understand what life is like for construction workers? The conditions, the expectations, the realities.

He agrees to speak to me. But not here, not now.

'There's two worlds in Qatar: world A and world B,' he tells me. 'When you come to the world B, then you'll see. You'll see how our lives are in Qatar.'

I meet Abu Yusuf the following week in a coffee shop.
He plays with a packet of sugar on the table as he tells me that, in 2015, an Indian recruiter came to his city.

'They were goin' all over Africa: Ghana, Nigeria, Senegal, Sierra Leone.'

Africans are sought, Abu Yusuf says, because they work hard.

'They don't take bullshit, you cannot just push them, but if you need some labour work done ... they know Africans can work.'

He doesn't mention that they're also wanted because they are cheap.

Most workers in Doha come from South Asia. Because of this fact, people both inside and outside Qatar often overlook Africans, despite there being significant numbers of them in the country. There are North Africans, mostly Egyptians and Tunisians, who have the advantage of speaking Arabic and can be found in a range of jobs in Qatar. There are Ethiopians – I participated for a month in the Ethiopian taxi drivers' weekly football match, courtesy of a friendly Uber driver named Temescan. The Qatari police and armed forces contain many Sudanese nationals. Kenyan and Ugandan men seem to fill every vacancy for private security. Many domestic workers are Kenyan women. And then there are the West Africans, mostly men, mostly working in construction.

'There is nothing in Africa,' Abu Yusuf says matter-of-factly. 'Especially in my country, there's rapid deterioration every day.'

After the approach by the Indian recruiter, Abu Yusuf ended up in a labour camp in Al-Khor, an hour outside of Doha. His job was to work at the huge Ras Laffan gas refinery that dominates the north of the peninsula. The sea north of Qatar is home to the world's single-largest gas field, all 900 trillion cubic feet of it. Ras Laffan is the point where the gas comes onshore. Its pipes, tubes, cabling and tanks – stretching miles – remove impurities, compress the gas and refrigerate it down to $-162°C$, the point at which it becomes a liquid. From Ras Laffan the gas is pumped onto specially designed tankers, which chug down the Strait of Hormuz, pass into the Indian Ocean and set off to fulfil energy needs around the world. In mid-2021, almost a quarter of the UK's total gas imports was liquified natural gas from Qatar.

Abu Yusuf worked an eight-hour day, six days a week for a basic salary of 1,500 rials ($410) a month. There were opportunities for overtime, paid at the princely sum of five rials an hour ($1.35).

'I'm telling you, it's like eight people in your room. Everybody's just with his baggage and he just eat anywhere and everything— it was so ... so ...'

Abu Yusuf runs out of words. 1,500 rials a month. Eight to a room. This was not what he wanted.

He got into conversation with some Nigerian workers doing safety work. Forget labouring, they told him. Just save some money and go back to school.

Abu Yusuf saved until he had enough to enrol in a computer administration course. Every Friday, on his day off, he would travel the 45 kilometres from Al-Khor to Doha to take classes. After he graduated, over a couple of years he worked through health and safety certificates – an alphabet soup of awarding bodies. First was OSHA (Occupational Safety and Health Administration). Then IOSH (Institution of Occupational Safety and Health). Armed with these qualifications, he applied for, and was accepted into, new jobs. Timekeeper. Health and safety officer. He went from an eight- to a six-person room, and then from six people to four, four to two. His salary also inched upwards – from 1,700, to 1,900, to 2,000 rials a month.

But being a health and safety officer in the gas industry is not easy.

'Some people will not follow safety procedure. You understand? For example, you need gloves before doing anything – they will not. You need to use a grinding machine at work, you need to wear a high protection? They will not.'

On most projects, the majority of labourers were South Asian. To be understood, Abu Yusuf delivered his toolbox talk every morning in a mixture of English and Hindi.

'You are just forced to learn,' he says when I express amusement. 'You just have to be like them for them to understand you exactly.'

The joking fades away and is replaced by something colder and harder.

'You know, in a construction field, in the morning people are stressed ... We don't have our families, our wife and kids. Sometimes you just pick up a call and something will get you upset ... people wake up in the morning with so many things in their [heads].'

Abu Yusuf is looking away as he speaks.

'If you're in this field working, you just have to be the same as people. If they are crazy, you just have to be crazy. If they go easy with you, you just have to be easy ... Like this Egyptian, they will jump down a 2.5 metre excavation. Or maybe while the excavator is working, they will be *very* close to the excavator. You just have to protect your job, man. Negligence— you can't tolerate negligence in your job.'

He seems to be replaying events and conversations in his mind's eye.

'Some foreman, some superiors ... they just want the work to be done. Because they have targets. They just want to meet them; they don't even *care* about safety.'

Abu Yusuf is braver than most. Even if pressured, he stands his ground.

'I will be there stopping them, they will come and shout, we will just shout, shout, shout.'

Abu Yusuf pauses and looks at me.

'It's very crazy.'

In such a context accidents happen.

'Someone was trapped inside a gas pipe.'

Abu Yusuf registers my look of surprise and continues.

'You know those 32-inch gas pipes? They were doing some welding inside ... not knowing that the H_2S already inside.'

Hydrogen sulphide. Similar in toxicity to carbon monoxide

but easier to detect due to its strong smell of rotten eggs. The first symptoms are eye irritation, a sore throat and cough. Significant doses lead to a loss of smell as the olfactory nerve is paralysed. Then it's fluid in the lungs, collapse and death.

Abu Yusuf speaks quietly.

'One of them died, he was a Nepali I think.'

He returns to his favourite phrase, uttering it multiple times while shaking his head.

'It's risky. To work in the oil and gas field is very risky.'

After almost five years, Abu Yusuf had seen enough to understand the rules of Qatar. He needed to dispense with the labour visa. Governed by its logic he would remain confined to Qatar's lowest rung. So, he went home and applied for – and received – a new visa category: administration. This would provide greater flexibility and the chance of earning much more money. But it meant returning to Qatar without a job. He would have to live off his meagre savings while he tried to line one up. It was a gamble. When I first met him, four months in with still no work, he was getting twitchy.

Abu Yusuf was attending school when the civil war broke out.

'Everything was up and down ... There was no school, *nothing*.'

We have met up again over coffee in a shopping mall. His story keeps being interrupted by the whirr of the coffee grinder and the whack of the barista emptying used grounds into the bin.

'If your family's wealthy enough you can go to Ghana or Nigeria and have an education, but if you stay ... you can't learn anything 'cause every day there is problem. Fighting, killing and everything. So you were scared, you always home. So it was very, very difficult.'

I ask about his family back home. He tells me he is one of nine children his father has had with three wives.

'They're just primitive.'

He scans my face for a reaction.

'That's the right word, primitive.'

Whatever he sees, he decides to double down on his assessment.

'I only plan to have two kids, that's all.'

His wife and four-year-old daughter live with his father and five brothers, he tells me. A temporary state of affairs, he's quick to point out. Just until he can get earning again and then he'll save up enough for a house of their own.

'My dad didn't want me to go to school. He just wanted me to learn Arabic,' says Abu Yusuf. Abu Yusuf's father ran a bakery. He wanted Abu Yusuf and his brothers to work in the shop, checking stock and supply. It was his older sister – by then married and moved out – along with his mum who helped him to attend school. His family are Muslim but he went to a Catholic school.

Where he's from, he explains, the only prospects are 'fishing and football'. 'You go to the bankside and fish or you play football ... So I was lucky to go to this Catholic school and I met a lot of friends with ambition,' he continues. They were from wealthier families, ones with relatives overseas. Abu Yusuf absorbed their drive, their desire to leave at the first opportunity.

Abu Yusuf breaks off his narrative to tell me that he was offered a job the previous week but didn't take it. The salary was too low. It included accommodation and food, but he is done with living in camps outside of Doha. Nonetheless, it's been months now and still no work. He puts on a brave face.

'I knew it would always be difficult ... you can't just come with your own visa and say, "Tomorrow I start working."'

If he were willing to settle for 2,000 or 2,500 rials a month, he says, he would have got a job a long time ago. But Abu Yusuf has a house he wants to build, a child about to start school. He's holding out for at least 5,000 rials.

'Sometimes I just go for walk around the Corniche,' he tells me.

'What do you think about when you walk?'

'Just *think* man! Just free your mind!' He tells me about his wife. 'She understands exactly what I'm going through ... I don't have to make it to her like I am stressed, stressed, stressed, you know?' He can't relate every detail. 'If you tell exactly what is happening, she will definitely be so stressed.'

'You hide it from her a bit?'

'Not everything. But some things you just have to.' He pauses before launching with more weight into the next phrase.

'You just have to be a man.' And like testing a rickety rope bridge, he decides it's safe to proceed. 'I'm the man. I will just be a man.'

Abu Yusuf may not have told his wife about his daily routine, but he tells me. How he tramps all over the city – from West Bay to Najma, Old Airport to Mansoura – looking for work. He rations his dwindling resources by eating a big breakfast and then nothing until dinner. He saves money by avoiding all buses and the metro, instead walking everywhere. Abu Yusuf estimates that he has handed his CV to more than 1,000 companies. But this is all information his wife cannot know.

'Yeah 'cause she will feel more and more depressed. So you just have to be a man.' He pauses.

'I just hope by the end of this month I will grab one.' He means a job.

I'm not sure how to do this subtly. It is the reason Abu Yusuf dropped me a line. The reason I'm meeting him tonight.

I hand him the money.

'God bless you, man. Thank you *so* much, man. God bless you, man.'

It's 500 rials, around $135. A nice dinner for two or a week's worth of taxi rides for me. I'm caught between two worries: that I should have given more and that I shouldn't appear too obnoxiously rich. I fear the gesture has me coming up short on both fronts.

'I'm sorry, you know,' he tells me dolefully.

I'm sorry too.

'And what about you, how's your wife?'

To escape the awkwardness, Abu Yusuf has asked me a question.

It takes me by surprise. What about me? I say that I find it difficult being away from her. I don't mention that I see her once a month, with either me flying home or her coming to visit. Or that I'll be back with her properly before the year is through.

'Yeah, man, it makes you sick. Makes you sick,' he concurs. 'With my status I can bring my wife here. But not now. In the future. And she will come to visit but not to stay.'

'Why?'

'Expensive, man. If the kid stays here, then she has to go to school also.'

'But then you'll be together all the time?'

'Huh?'

He doesn't understand the question. I try rephrasing it. 'Don't you want to be together all the time?'

Abu Yusuf looks at me with amazement. Like I'm missing the most obvious thing in the world.

'But what about the expense? She's not working, she will be at home all the time.'

'She could get a job as well.'

Abu Yusuf pauses. 'No.'

'No?'

There's a silence. 'Because she doesn't want to or you don't want her to?' I worry I've pushed it too far, been too aggressive in my questioning. Abu Yusuf replies with a tone somewhere between annoyance and exasperation.

'Not because I don't want to, but what kind of job? Doing the babysitting work? What's the job?' he asks me firmly.

She could go back to school – she could get a qualification ...

'Then she need to do that at home, not here,' he says fiercely.

We're talking past one another – incapable of seeing each other's conception of family life.

'She can come for visit, like two, three months and go back. But not to stay.'

A few weeks later, I get an excited phone call from Abu Yusuf.

He finally found a job. Oil and gas work again, but with an employer offering a wage and benefits he could accept. Yet when it was time to process his paperwork there was an unforeseen problem – it turned out he was already registered with an employer.

A month earlier, Abu Yusuf had gone to an interview with a construction firm. When the salary and conditions were made clear he turned them down. Unbeknownst to him, however, the company had started processing his paperwork to add him to their roster. When he found out, Abu Yusuf called them and demanded they stop the process. Too late, they replied. The paperwork had already been sent to the ministry. Abu Yusuf was stuck. The company he wanted to work for couldn't properly hire him without documentation, documentation that the previous company was holding on to.

The story is wearily familiar, laying bare yet again the lop-sided power differential. All control is with the sponsor, the worker is left with only angst and worry.

While Abu Yusuf was assessing his next steps, the corona-virus pandemic struck.

Before borders were closed, I scrambled onto a plane back home. This wasn't an option for Abu Yusuf. He stayed in Qatar and watched as everything shut down. Our mode of interaction changed from chats over coffee to WhatsApp voice messages that started off optimistically but became increasingly anguished.

April: 'The guy was saying ... this coming week. So I'm just hoping for this coming week ... They just need to release my NOC [non-objection certificate] again.'

May: 'There are times, if I keep thinking about what is happening, it's really, really stressful ... These people they can't keep waiting for me. There are so many people look-ing for job in this country. So they can't be waiting for me, waiting for me, waiting for me.'

June: 'It's not been easy for me, but thank God I'm fight-ing it ... I guess this is the last week ... 'cause the guy asked me to call him Sunday... It's not been easy man. It's not been easy.'

Abu Yusuf stopped paying his rent of 400 rials a month for a room he shared with five others. He told his landlady she could

kick him out if she wanted but without a job he was not going to be able to pay. Finally, in July, Abu Yusuf reached breaking point.

'I just woke up one morning ... I showered, dressed up and said I'm gonna solve this on my own *OR ELSE* just go back, 'cause I'm tired.'

Abu Yusuf went to the company offices. He argued with someone in HR.

'I don't have any contract with you, why are you guys keeping me?' he asked them.

They told him to come back in a week, but Abu Yusuf wouldn't budge.

'I've been going more than two months now. So I will not go any more.'

They called the head of HR who came and told him to stop shouting.

'I'm not shouting,' Abu Yusuf replied. 'I'm just trying to make you people understand exactly the way I'm feeling. I've been here almost three months with you guys. I'm feeding myself, I'm paying house rent, I'm doing all this transportation. And you guys don't even know what I'm going through.'

He decided to personalise his appeal.

'If it was your brother, will you do that? Will you allow these things to happen to him the way it happened to me?'

There was a mumble from the head of HR as she washed her hands of the incident. The visa had already been transferred to her company's sponsorship, she said.

'How can you transfer my visa without informing me, without *no* contract?'

In the anger and pleading, something shifted. The woman looked at Abu Yusuf.

'We'll see what we can do. Just give me some few days.'

October 2020. I'm back in Qatar after seven months away due to the pandemic. Abu Yusuf and I are chatting over tea in Souq Waqif, the touristy faux-old town close to where he stays.

'Maaaaan, I was dying in this country!'

Abu Yusuf makes a sucking noise through his teeth.

'Things was not easy man ... I was so stressed, running up and down like a *mad man.*' He emits a chuckle. 'You know I needed to hustle to survive.'

He pauses and looks around. It's a warm night. The usual waves stream past our table – families out for a walk, men in Qatari dress clutching arms, groups of teenagers having loud conversations. Abu Yusuf scratches his head and tuts.

'It's really not easy in Qatar.'

The company finally cancelled his paperwork in August, allowing him to sign on with his new employer. He's been working for two months now. Health and safety again, but this time in Dukhan, the centre of the oil industry, an hour or so west of Doha. The schedule is punishing. Abu Yusuf is picked up at 4.30am every day by the company bus. He works a full day before getting home between 7 and 8pm. His evening schedule is normally a shower, dinner and sleep, the exception being today when he has met with me.

The man I last saw in March is transformed.

'Now I know I will sleep and wake up in the morning and have a job,' he says with a brightness in his eyes.

'And in the end of the month, no matter how the money is, I know I have a salary, I can pay my bills and send some money for my family. That's the most thing, 'cause I have to take care of my wife and my kid.'

He's barely been in the job two months but already he's planning how to move forward.

'I already registered for NEBOSH [the National Examination Board in Occupational Safety and Health],' he tells me. I'm handed a slip of paper out of his wallet. It's a 200 rial down payment on the next health and safety qualification.

'I start 15 November.'

Abu Yusuf tells me that the certification will make him eligible to apply for jobs with the big firms: Qatargas, Qatar Petroleum, Shell. They pay salaries of close to 10,000 rials ($2,750) a month, I am told, with two days off a week. He's planning on moving out of his current shared room to some-where quieter to allow him to study.

For all his drive, he tells me his end goal is modest. 'I just need an average life. I don't need to look for billions of dollars' worth of work. I just need to take care of me and my family, that's all.'

It sounds perfectly reasonable. And it shouldn't be forgotten that Qatar can facilitate Abu Yusuf's goal. For all the stories of exploitation, there are many thousands from the world's poorest regions who make the country work for them. They see Qatar's impatience to grow, grow, grow and they offer themselves up. They're the ones fortunate enough to avoid the charlatan brokers. They are blessed with a sponsor who pays them on time. They work, they save and, as a result, they transform their own lives and those of their families.

But Abu Yusuf has done something beyond merely subsisting in Qatar. Through sheer force of will, he has risen from the bottom of Qatar's hierarchy. He has managed to lever aside the wider structural factors – wrong passport, wrong qualifications, wrong skin colour – just enough to be able to slip through to the next level. And then done it again. And again. In doing so, he has not followed a planned route or got lucky. He has hot-wired the entire logic of Qatar, and it is nothing short of remarkable.

Which is why it is all the more disappointing when he gives me his explanation of why so many others are struggling.

'Because they're lazy, no? That's the word, lazy.'

I didn't expect this assessment.

'There are so many things you can do! It all depends on you.'

Ah, the great lie. We can be whatever we want to be. No matter our backgrounds, if we grit our teeth and are determined, we can all be successes. I'm struck yet again by the invasiveness of the idea. It is laced liberally through so many national dreams – American, Chinese and now Qatari.

I push back. 'Sometimes the social environment doesn't let people succeed.'

He jumps in, quick as a flash. 'But you have to force yourself out from that social environment,' he retorts.

I could continue in this vein but I don't want an argument. I just want to hang out with ... my friend? The word somehow seems too presumptuous. The person I've spent more time with than anyone else in Qatar? More clunky, but also more accurate. I can't really hide that, for all the fun and warmth, we are worlds apart. We can spend time together but, clearly, still not really know each other.

I drop the current line of conversation. Into the gap jumps Abu Yusuf's whirling mind.

'Working in oil and gas, you just have to develop yourself.'

Here he goes again. Forever planning, scheming, forging ahead. I don't know how it doesn't tire him out.

'I will.'

He seems to be talking more to himself than to me.

'I just need a licence and my NEBOSH and I will get a better job here.'

'I will get a job.'

'Yeah, I will.'

6

'I've got an S-Class Mercedes picking me up in the morning and taking me to work'

I meet the policeman at a British embassy trade event.

In the bar of a hotel, waiters circulate with canapés. The audience is mostly men, most of them middle-aged and working in the defence and security industries. The policeman is in his fifties and maybe six-foot-four. He was another person stood awkwardly, sipping a beer.

A figure ascends the stage and introduces himself. He talks about bringing 33 companies on a two-day World Cup fact-finding mission and praises the response he's received from locals. 'The affection towards our own country is a really positive signal and sign that we are welcome here as a country and also as businesses.'

Britain's trade with Qatar was valued at £6.3 billion in late 2019 – part of a wider relationship of cooperation between the UK and Gulf Arab monarchies. British power (and weapons) help prop up governments in the region. In return, Gulf fossil fuels keep the lights burning and Gulf investment keeps the economy purring. The trenchant criticism of Qatar from UK-based newspapers and NGOs is only half of the picture. Plenty of British people and companies are eager for a piece of the Qatari pie.

The policeman has ridden the wave of interest all the way to Qatar, along with an estimated 22,000 other Britons. He's newly retired and, compared to the standard Brit I meet here, seems more thoughtful and honest. 'I haven't come here for the sunshine,' he tells me sardonically. 'I've come here to earn more money than I could earn in the UK.' His job will be working with the Qatari security forces as part of the preparations for the World Cup.

He begins to outline the ins and outs of his role when we're interrupted by another man, also in his fifties but razor-thin and with Rod Stewart hair. After introducing himself, he mentions that he owns a media production firm in the UK that has Qatari clients.

'For a while we used to fly over but the Qataris made us set up an office here,' he says. I prepare for a moan but he surprises me. 'It was the best thing that happened actually. They decided – not unreasonably – that they didn't want us Europeans coming in with all our film equipment, filming and then leaving.'

His clients include many of the oil and gas companies in Qatar, for whom he produces flashy productions as part of their corporate social responsibility mandate.

'It's a bit of a charade,' he concedes. 'It's done to show that they're helping Qatari society so that the emir looks favourably on them when the next oil or gas contract comes up.'

He shrugs.

'But it pays the bills.'

Not every migrant in Qatar is being exploited. The country plays host to many thousands of high-income workers. The professional class of Qatar comprises a multiplicity of characters. South Asians can be found in industries ranging from banking to engineering. There are many professionals from elsewhere in the Middle East – Lebanon, Tunisia, Jordan, Palestine – whose knowledge of Arabic means they are found in government, education and legal jobs. Nursing is dominated by Filipinos. But the group that fascinated me the most, perhaps because I am one myself, was the Westerners.

In the Doha hierarchy, Westerners are second only to Qataris. They comprise around 5 per cent of the population and yet, along with Qataris, they are highly visible, especially those who are white. Most of the city's spaces, in particular its malls, golf courses and high-end hotels, are designed for their use. In the vocabulary of Qatar, Westerners are 'expatriates' and never 'migrant workers' – that term is reserved for low-income Asians, Africans and Arabs.

I expected the behaviour of 'expats' to be distinct from that of Qataris, and on the surface it is. Socialising frequently revolves around alcohol, clubbing or sunbathing in mixed-sex groupings – all activities which you will rarely, if ever, see the locals doing. But Westerners join Qataris in forming a privileged elite. Consequently, they share in many of the vices that stem from that privilege, including poking fun at other classes of people, not paying their domestic workers on time and generally enjoying the pleasures of Qatar while disavowing their complicity in the racialised segregation that defines the place.[†]

As the reception goes on, I find myself increasingly appalled by the guests. All the clichés are being rolled out. There is much talk of exotic holidays. The racial stereotyping is in full force, as is the preternatural ability to feel superior to Qataris while engaging in an obsequious chase for their patronage.

Towards the end, a confrontation breaks out at the bar.

'YOU CUNT!'

The viciousness of the word is like a gunshot.

'YOU FAT FUCK!'

Heads turn to see a man with a British accent cursing at another person who is goading him. The bouncer intervenes, holding back the swearer and instructing the man provoking him to leave. As he makes his way out, the man at the bar continues to scream obscenities at his back.

This is my second night out in Doha in as many months, and on both occasions I've witnessed drunk Brits getting into fights and being chucked out. Rule Britannia.

The organiser of the event turns, embarrassed, to the remaining guests.

'They're not with us! They came later!'

She tries to smooth over the incident with a joke. 'I arranged it so that the fifteen security companies in the room could show their stuff. But they had all already left!'

[†] Of course, Qataris learnt the trick of racialised hierarchies from the British empire.

It was 1949 when the first ever police officer arrived in Qatar. Ronald Cochrane was a Glaswegian put in charge of a new colonial force comprised almost entirely of foreigners. In those days, Qatar was little more than a small British protectorate. Despite (or maybe because of) this, Cochrane struggled to establish his authority. The Sheikh at the time, Ali bin Abdullah Al Thani, preferred to settle disputes with his Bedouin forces rather than the new British-led outfit. Locals looked on Cochrane with indifference. When a slave belonging to the nephew of the Sheikh nearly ran over the wife of a British diplomat in a truck with faulty brakes, Cochrane had the vehicle impounded. Rather than accept the decision, the nephew turned up armed with a sub-machine gun and stole it back. The stress of his role drove Cochrane to have a nervous breakdown, and in 1953 he went on extended leave. He later returned to Qatar, became a Muslim and changed his name to Muhammad Mahdi. He went on to spend decades in the country, overseeing the establishment of the new nation's army.

Cochrane/Mahdi was the first of many people from the British security sector to operate in Qatar. 'Rich, repressive and vulnerable governments have turned to Britain, as well as to the USA, and France, for the techniques they need,' wrote the historian Fred Halliday. 'Within this general flow of arms and "advice", large numbers of service and ex-service personnel are involved.' Halliday was writing in the 1970s, but his words are no less relevant today. Modern Qatar has built its security firmly on the basis of support from the West. It is a significant purchaser of arms from the US, France, Germany and the UK. It hosts the largest American base in the Middle East, Al-Udeid, with over 10,000 US troops. For Britain in particular, the Middle East is a vital market for its defence companies, especially Qatar and its neighbours in the Gulf Cooperation Council (GCC).

But the sale of arms and security expertise is not solely for economic gain. As the academic David Wearing has noted in his book *AngloArabia*, it is as much about building strategic and political connections. The current emir, like his father before him, was educated at Sandhurst, the famous British Army officer training school. Numerous Qatari soldiers spend time training in the UK, including a young man I sat next to at a Qatar vs. Oman football match. At half-time he waxed lyrical about his experience, flicking through photos on his phone of himself in army gear, grinning on a wet and windy Brecon Beacons in Wales. For Wearing, the personal connections between the Qatari elite and the British military lies behind the uptick in British defence sales to Qatar. Lagging behind the US and France historically, Britain has in recent years begun to catch up.

Security and defence may be significant sectors, but they are far from the only business bringing Europeans and Americans to Qatar. Oil is the ur-industry, without which nothing and no one would ever have come. There have been foreign oil workers in Qatar since the 1920s, but it was towards the end of the century, when the natural gas started coming online, that the numbers really took off. 'The biggest community here was Scottish,' a Brit who arrived in the early 2000s told me. '*Bags* of Scots.' As the UK's North Sea oil industry began to decline after its production peak in 1999, hundreds of workers swapped Aberdeen for Doha. Qatar was an unknown entity and those willing to come could command a premium. 'It was the old fixed-term packages – six business class flights home a year, the kids have all gone through private school,' continued the Brit. 'People have gone home as millionaires,' she added, with what I thought was a hint of jealousy.

Qatar's appeal was obvious. 'I lived in the Sheraton [hotel] for the first two years,' I was told by a British man who arrived in the 2000s to work on Doha's infrastructure. 'And I've got an S-Class Mercedes picking me up in the morning and taking me to work and membership of the health club.' Combine that with a hefty tax-free salary and over 300 days a year of sun and the end result is a lifestyle impossible to create back home. 'I've stayed ever since,' he continued. 'And very happily so.'

So rapid are the cycles of development in Qatar that everyone's perception of time has been compressed. Hearing talk of early 21st-century Doha reminds me of listening to an elderly person reflecting on life in pre-war Britain. 'I liked Qatar years and years ago, because all socialising was in people's houses,' remarked the female professional. 'You could walk your dogs along the whole of the coastline that is now Lusail,' she recalled, referring to an area now buried underneath a city of skyscrapers and cranes. Her fond recollections even stretched to a dating scene that more closely resembled a meat market. 'There were five men to every woman,' she told me. 'Apart from on a

Wednesday night when the rigs changed and it was eight men to every woman,' she added with a chortle. 'You could go anywhere as a woman on Wednesday night and drink for free.'

And then the boom came.

In 2003, the population of Qatar was 700,000. By 2008, the figure had doubled – and then increased by a further 50 per cent over the next five years. People were flooding into Qatar. Locals were too few in number and often lacked the expertise to oversee development. Qatar needed architects to design the buildings and engineers to oversee their construction. Lawyers were required to draw up employment contracts. Consultants were sought to advise on expansions of government. As Qatar looked to enact its 'diversification' strategy, the ripples were felt further out still – the country needed academics to staff its new universities, TV producers for its news channels, coaches for its growing sports infrastructure.

'I saw all the masterplans,' the Brit who worked on Doha's infrastructure told me. 'We were doing population growth, demographic modelling ... And we saw the plans for the hotels, we saw the plans for the shopping malls, we saw the plans for the petrol stations all over the place and we said, "But there's not enough people here for all of that!"'

'And what did they say?' I asked.

'"It will come! It will come!"'

Every old-timer I spoke to agreed that it was in the late 2000s that Qatar changed irrevocably. Amenities started coming online for all the new arrivals. Beach clubs exploded in number.

Supermarkets began to stock Tesco products. High-end restaurants with famous chefs opened in the hotels. And at the heart of expat life was a new, exciting and slightly bonkers urban development project.

The Pearl is Qatar's most exclusive district: 4-million square metres – a thousand acres – of artificial islands built on land reclaimed from the sea. It contains apartments, five-star hotels, high-end shops, man-made beaches, private islands and even a section of canals modelled on Venice, complete with a replica Rialto Bridge.

Pearl inhabitants are almost exclusively well-remunerated foreigners, many from Western countries. They can be glimpsed waiting for taxis in the marble-clad lobbies of their apartments or carrying their shopping into pastel-coloured villas. Their children are walked to nursery by Filipina nannies, past perfectly manicured streets resembling a pastiche of an American town with Spanish names ('Malaga Way', 'Porto Arabia'). They eat and drink in faux Spanish and Lebanese bars, buy air-freighted Dutch tomatoes from the French supermarket and go for sweaty jogs along the marina boardwalk. The first time I visited, a handful of people were sunbathing on an artificial beach, studiously ignoring the two South Asian men with brooms raking the sand.

The lavishness comes at some expense. Rents are London-level or higher (a one-bedroom apartment on the Pearl will set you back around 8,500 rials, $2,330 per month). Imported food costs many times what it would at home – I once paid $10 for a

jar of peanut butter. Alcohol prices in Qatar are the most expensive in the world. The average price for a 330 millilitre bottle of beer is $11.26. The cost is inflated by a 100 per cent 'sin tax', albeit one that doesn't really stop people from drinking. Indeed, the highlight of the stereotypical expat week is the Friday brunch. Hotels across Doha offer lavish spreads of food and unlimited alcohol at prices north of $135 per person. Starting in the late morning, people go to drink, pick half-heartedly from tables serving everything from sushi to pizza and then drink some more. The brunch at the St Regis hotel has a map on hand to guide its 700 diners to one of sixteen 'food stations' – and still this was not good enough for one TripAdvisor reviewer: 'Come on guys ... more cocktail stands and dessert and less food. It's a booze brunch now!'

A frequent complaint from Westerners is that Doha is boring. Once you've been to a brunch and driven up the sand dunes in the desert, what else is there to do? Well, a lot actually. Qatar is forever hosting some event or another. Tellingly, the 'boring' criticism is rarely heard out of the mouths of educated migrants from elsewhere on the globe. 'It's a country where you feel safe, it's a country where you can really plan your life,' a Lebanese hotel manager once told me. Months before we met, over 200 people were killed, more than 6,000 injured and half of downtown Beirut flattened when thousands of tonnes of ammonium nitrate, fifteen tonnes of fireworks and five miles of fuse left in a hangar at Beirut port exploded. Investigations revealed years of neglect from a government more concerned with bribery and graft than public safety. It is hard to imagine something similar happening in Doha.

The Pearl is also frequented by Qataris. The Maserati and Bentley showrooms are aimed at them rather than the British primary school teacher working at an international school. But few Qataris, if any, *live* there. In the unwritten segregation of the city, the Pearl is the wealthy 'expat' zone. Indeed, so complete is the insularity of the Pearl that the well-paid foreigner can carve out a life where their only significant interactions are with people like themselves. The whole place carries the whiff of a European Disneyland. Or perhaps a low-security detention centre – a contained world, landscaped and populated so that its residents, if they squint, might be able to convince themselves that they're not in the Middle East.

And what of the work? The stereotypical image of white-collar employment in Qatar is of a Qatari boss doing nothing while a frazzled foreigner runs the show. This is not wholly fair. There are many competent, hard-working Qataris, including Khalid*, who eschewed a cushy public sector job to work long hours as an engineer with an oil company. 'Sooner or later, the world will get tougher,' he explained to me. 'And if you are not skilled enough, then it will be really hard to survive. And for me, having two of the international oil companies on your doorstep – why you are not taking the chance?'

But the stereotype of local work habits is not entirely without teeth. In recent decades, the Qatari government has operated a policy of 'Qatarization', which involves populating the high ranks of various industries with its own citizens. Government statistics, however, show that only 110,000 Qataris are in work, meaning there isn't a lot of talent to go around. Oil and gas is too existentially important to allow for significant inefficiency but in other sectors you don't have to look far to find over-promotion, incompetence and general malaise. 'I don't think you understand the extent of it,' I was told by one former employee at beIN Sports, a global sports channel run out of Doha. 'You write the emails for them [Qataris] when they have to send an email internally to someone else, knowing that you're probably going to have to write the response for that someone else as well.' Doha is littered with foreigners frustrated at having had promotions blocked or work reduced to letter opening as a result of nativist labour laws.

While in Qatar I met a broad array of high-income foreigners: mercenaries for sale, alcoholics unable to hold down a job back home, veterinarians who delighted in treating falcons and researchers overjoyed to have the time and money to write a book on 8th-century Mamluk rugs. Being in a place where the normal employment rules don't apply can open up a wonderful flexibility to research what you want, be promoted far higher than is sensible or pursue a side career on a whim. It has to be said, however, that those who seize such opportunities are outnumbered by those happy to coast along, collect a pay cheque and avoid rocking the boat. 'I mistakenly thought people would be doing what I was doing, trying to get ahead,' one British woman working in media told me. 'In fact they weren't. No one was.'

'I find some of the rudest people out here are the expats.'

It is the police officer again, this time speaking with me over coffee.

'I think some of the expats who have been here for five, ten years have got into the lifestyle of the rich and famous,' he tells me. Newness means his eyes are still sharp to the strange milieu that is wealthy Doha: the legions of domestic staff, the curt, clipped tones of interaction, the expectation of everything being done for them. He gives the example of getting petrol.

'I feel quite lucky that I can roll up at the petrol station and somebody will come and fill my car,' he tells me. 'But there'll be other people who start tooting after 30 seconds because the guy's busy filling someone else's up.'

While he talks, my mind flicks to an incident that I had recently witnessed. A foreign woman at the supermarket checkout was being indecently rude to the South Asian man bagging up her shopping. He was too petrified to make eye contact, let alone complain.

'It's that service-led society here,' the policeman continues. 'Why would I do anything if I can get someone else to do it? Rather than be thankful for that, it's almost seen as obligatory.'

Of course, many Westerners don't mind the inequality as they benefit immeasurably from the status quo. Vani Saraswathi, editor-at-large of Migrant-Rights.org, often saw this first-hand when working with low-paid migrants who had faced exploitation. 'Some of the most discriminatory language and practices

were from Western expats who liked the privilege they had ... Salaries are based on where you come from, what passport you hold. So the ones most privileged are not gonna question that discrimination, they're gonna go with it,' she explained to me. Most are oblivious to what the academic Katie Walsh has labelled the 'undeclared history' that accrues to the actions of Britons in the Gulf courtesy of imperialism. Giddy with the privilege and perks, they slip into their pre-ordained place in the hierarchy without stopping to consider how it originates.

Those with a better understanding deploy different tactics for justifying their inaction. Some retreat to cultural relativism: 'Of course I don't agree with the labour situation but you have to respect Qatari culture.' The more self-aware point out the similarities between exploitative arrangements in Qatar and those back home. 'Lots of people have said to me, "I don't know how you could go there and work for the World Cup. They're treating the workers really badly,"' the policeman told me. 'And I say, well, you know, in the 1990s when the Poles came over, you were happy to pay them less than the British bloke to come and build your house. They were living in rooms of six, sending all their money home. It's no different to out here.' But in general, there is a lot of delusion flying around. Many Westerners I encountered considered themselves more egalitarian and intelligent than the locals. Many cling steadfastly to the notion that they are being judged on their skills and experience, when in reality the colour of their skin and the ability to bullshit the role of 'expert' often matters more.

Of course, not all foreign professionals in Qatar are rude, racist and simply out for themselves. Wardah Mamukoya, who is Indian, was disturbed by the amount of food she saw being wasted in Doha and so co-founded Wa'hab, a business that redistributes surplus food to those in need and recycles food waste for compost. 'Given that most of us don't even know our next-door neighbour, how are we to ensure that others are not hungry?' she said, outlining their mission when I spoke to her. I also met Americans who founded environmental charities, South Asians organising literary festivals and Europeans giving natural history seminars. With many volunteering programmes and community events in Doha, it seems to be outsiders who provide the impetus.

It is often people who have lived around the globe, or whose backgrounds encompass different cultures, that provide more subtle or playful points of view on the Qatar experience. 'In Qatar I can choose who I want to be,' I was told by an Arab–British man called Ibrahim*. 'If I want to be an Arab I can be an Arab. If, on the random occasions I get in an altercation with a Qatari on the roads, or if a policeman stops me, nobody's more British than me.' An Argentinian woman told me that it's a real boon to be Latin American. 'We don't look that different [to Middle Easterners]. When I go out, people speak Arabic to me.' I felt a pang of jealousy when such individuals told me how they moved between Doha's different worlds in a way that I never could. 'I have seen what maybe 1 per cent of foreigners in Qatar see,' boasted the Argentinian. She gets invited to hang out in the *majlis* with her Qatari male friends but also attends the female-only parts of Qatari weddings. She describes for me her shock at what goes on in the latter. 'There will be women with cleavage down to here,' she gestures low on her chest. 'Can you imagine a Qatari woman dressed like that?'

Muslims from Western countries offer another take still. People told me how they were relieved to have left behind a general climate of Islamophobia: to be able to wear a headscarf without fear or follow a work schedule that makes it easier to pray and fast. Ibrahim was particularly grateful for having dispensed with the awkwardness surrounding alcohol. 'I always felt weird when the guy would be holding a pint and I would be holding a coke or a Red Bull,' he told me of his UK life. He felt that not drinking hampered his relations with work colleagues and deterred bosses from promoting him. Many people don't drink in Qatar. 'It'll be absolutely fine for one or two people to order wine and everybody else not to,' he explained. 'It's normal. As opposed to "pints for everybody!"'

It's not fashionable to get the violin out for wealthy foreigners in Qatar. But for all their privileges, beneath the bonnet they share an important similarity with the less-fortunate: just like low-paid labourers, they require a sponsor to be in the country. As a result, their lives are still shot through with precarity. 'There's a feeling that you're completely expendable,' recalled the former beIN employee. Contracts are nearly always short-term, lasting a year or two. They are often extended but this is never guaranteed, even for decades-long service. High-end workers can find themselves suddenly sacked during downturns, as two friends of mine discovered when they were summarily fired during the coronavirus pandemic.

Even as a wealthy foreigner, if you break the wrong law or fall out with the wrong people you can be on the first flight home. I am still haunted by the experience of Dave*, who was accused of arguing with someone in traffic and giving them the finger. Dave didn't do it, he knew that it's a criminal offence to swear. 'But it's my word against a Qatari,' he told me grimly. In a months-long investigation, as the case went from the traffic department to the public prosecutor, Dave wasn't allowed to leave the country (standard practice while all criminal and civil cases are open). After eight months and many thousands of rials in costs, Dave decided to get a Qatari at his work involved. The colleague called his buddy at the Ministry of Interior, who in turn called a friend at the public prosecutor's office to get the number of the complainant. One well-mannered phone call later, the plaintiff agreed to drop the case. After telling me the story, Dave said, 'Now, if that doesn't *screw* you and your opinion about this place, I don't know what will.'

Many professional-class foreigners accept the rules of the game. If you're a gambler, a chancer or simply someone who has a high tolerance for risk, then living with the perpetual insecurity can be a price worth paying. Get the right job or meet the right people and Qatar can transform your life. 'I came here to pay off a mortgage,' a British lawyer told me. Other people – sports journalists, curators, academics – use Qatar as a stepping stone allowing them to transition back to the West with a higher status and burnished reputation. Even Dave decided, ultimately, that he was happy with the deal he's made with Qatar. 'I still like this country,' he said. 'I've come back voluntarily.'

But if you're someone craving consistency and security, or you want to try to establish a deeper sense of belonging in Qatar, then it can be dispiriting. 'We have people parachuting in and out for some short period of time,' the European founder of a Doha environmental group told me. 'That's just the nature of this place. Which is sad, because you feel all the time that you start over again.' Even Westerners who simply want to do something unexpected frequently end up disappointed. The British policeman told me he was taking Arabic lessons but was sad at how little opportunity he had found to practice. Ibrahim said that when he first arrived in Qatar he would chat to everybody – the security guard at his building, random people in the mosque – before realising that it was seen as weird and made people uncomfortable.

Tim Newnham is chairman of Doha Rugby Club, a fixture among British workers in Qatar with its men's, women's and youth rugby teams, not to mention the fact that it is the only non-hotel in Doha to have a liquor licence. 'Two weeks ago, I actually had an email from an Arabic guy who likes rugby,' Newnham tells me when we meet at the club. 'He emailed me and said, "Look, I know it's a Western club but are Arabs allowed to come down and train?"' It really depressed Newnham. 'Of course you can come,' he replied. 'You have this perception, "No, that's a Western club, you guys can't really go there."' It's not true, he tells me, 'But it comes across that way sometimes.'

These lamentations all hint at a deeper, more unpalatable, truth: Qatar doesn't *want* the country's relationship to its migrants – or their relationship to each other – to be anything other than transactional. Exhibit no. 1 is the near impossibility of outsiders acquiring citizenship. Other examples include zoning laws that prevent low-income workers from living in certain neighbourhoods and a puzzlement – sometimes bordering on hostility – to those who step outside of their prescribed bubble. Newnham gives the example of being taken to go and watch a falconry competition by a Qatari friend. 'I hope you're not bringing too many of these guys down,' said a compatriot to his friend. 'This is our culture.'

To some extent I can sympathise with Qatar's reluctance. Holding back citizenship from the many freeloaders, carpetbaggers and opportunists attracted to the country is understandable. Furthermore, the sheer size of the migrant population relative to locals is difficult to comprehend. Look at the response to immigration in the West – Brexit, Trump – when only around 14 per cent of the population in both the UK and US was born abroad. For Qatari nationals, being hugely outnumbered is an objective truth. That must create a strange dynamic in a place that's meant to be 'yours'. I was surprised how many high-income foreigners, despite being disadvantaged by the stance, seemed to sympathise with Qatar's dilemma. 'I'm not trying to defend it because basically I don't like [it],' one Syrian engineer close to retirement said of the country's stand-offish attitude to foreigners. 'But try to have 10 per cent Britishers [British nationals] in Britain and see what laws will be issued.'

At the same time, I can't help but feel it becomes a self-perpetuating circle. If Qatar made it more appealing for those who want to settle for the long haul, might it not play host to more meaningful businesses and charities and fewer cowboy companies? This was the view of one high-income professional I met called Bilal*. Bilal believed that Dubai had siphoned off the high-calibre foreign talent in the Gulf. He told me that Dubai provides good schools and allows non-citizens to buy land and property. In Qatar, by contrast, 'You were never thinking about Qatar further than the duration of your contract,' says Bilal. 'There was no reason to put your kids in school and think of it as a second home ... They made it unappealing for you to want to stay... there is a certain ceiling to how [far] you can reach, because we're never gonna have a CEO that's an expat.' Qatar does allow foreigners to hold property, but only in limited areas.

Bilal lived in Qatar for seven years but is now back working in his home country. In his words I can sense a bitterness borne of affection, like a relationship that turned sour.

'They just didn't allow people to feel like this is somewhere that I want to spend time. In Dubai it's the opposite. People who live there *really, really* like Dubai. They speak very well of it. Doha? Anyone you speak to from there will be like, "Get the fuck out!"'

By 2020, there was a sense of anxiety among many in the professional class that boom time in Qatar was over. In the preceding seven years, Qatar had been hit by three large shocks: a collapse in the global oil price, the 2017 blockade and the coronavirus pandemic. Each caused significant belt tightening by the government, triggering a wave of redundancies and salary cuts through public and private sectors. Rents had slumped. Commercial properties stood empty. Towers on the Pearl had little-to-no occupancy. The rugby club had seen its membership shrink from around 2,000 members at its peak to 1,500 in early 2020.

Low-income workers I spoke with felt that they had no choice but to remain in Qatar. They had to keep food on the table or kids in school. But for the professional class, deciding whether to stay wasn't accompanied by such existential angst. They could go home. They might have to downsize on housing and ditch the domestic help, but it wouldn't be the end of the world. As perks were removed and salaries trimmed, it seemed that more people were contemplating saying goodbye.

Among them was Ibrahim. He liked Qatar but worried about the impact on his two small children of growing up in an 'uber-materialistic environment' that could leave them out of touch with reality. 'I'm finding it more and more difficult to say no to my kids for things,' he told me. 'I found that I cannot win the argument when it comes to materialistic things in Qatar. I can never win the argument because the argument is "all of my friends have it".'

Not long after speaking to Ibrahim I found myself – as I often do – on the Pearl.

I went to a public toilet inside one of the towers. There was a bored-looking worker on hand to show me how to start the water on the touch-sensitive tap and then offer a hand towel when I was done. He looked young and crushed.

I can't decide whether I agree with Ibrahim's take. I certainly get his point that Qatar is a hyper-strange environment in which to bring up children. But I can't stop wondering if, on the subject of inequality, Doha is weirdly more honest. The world is divided into such distinct spheres – separate and unequal. You might come to understand very well the inequality within a particular society or country but, especially in Europe, that pales in comparison to inequality globally. You can't see global stratification with your own eyes. There is no personal interaction with the Bangladeshi woman paid pennies to make your T-shirt or the Congolese mining the cobalt for the battery in your phone. But it feels like, in Qatar, the extreme wealth and the poverty coexist. The iniquity has no place to hide. Might that be a good lesson for a child?

As I left the Pearl in a taxi, I passed a bus of construction workers coming the other way. Maybe they were coming to construct another high-rise to be occupied by rich people they might see but never speak to. Or perhaps they were coming to douse the bougainvillea and tulips in desalinated water, pumped from the ocean, treated at great energy and environmental expense, to make sure the area looked and felt like Surrey in 45°C heat.

Ibrahim told me of the moment the inequality of Qatar truly hit him.

'It was early in my stay ... and I found myself a little bit late to the *asr* prayers, to the late afternoon prayers. So I run into a little mosque that I found. And it was just me. So I started praying by myself and then somebody tapped me on the shoulder.' Ibrahim explained that congregational prayer is prioritised in Islam and that if someone encounters you at a scheduled prayer time praying alone they will take a position alongside or behind you, tap you on the shoulder and follow your lead.

'So I was praying by myself. Somebody tapped me, so I figured, OK, maybe a couple of people came in. And then when I finished the prayers, I looked behind and I realised it was a minibus-load of about twenty to 25 labourers.' The bus had pulled over on its way back to the camp. They had been working under the sun all day and were sweaty and smelly. 'It wasn't pleasant,' chuckles Ibrahim. 'But the thought that rushed through my head was not that—' He pauses for a good three seconds. 'I came into this country as a foreigner and they came to this country as a foreigner, but I thought about it. I was earning the equivalent of those 25 people put together. And this is when this schism, this gap, hit me.'

He looked at me thoughtfully.

'In the UK, it is very rare where I will meet a billionaire – or a multi-millionaire or whatever – who earns twenty, 30, 40 times what I earn ... but *I was that to them.*' He had a look of awe, as if this realisation still blows his mind today.

'When you see that, you think, "Wow." In comparison, wealth is a very, very relative thing.'

7 'It's like Leicester winning the Premier League with homegrown players'

Which of these statements is true?

> *Qatar has fewer than 7,500 registered footballers.*
> *Qatar's national team is the current football champion of Asia.*

If you chose both, congratulations! From an impossibly small pool, Qatar has managed to craft a football team that cowed a continent of 4.6 billion. When talking of Qatar's accomplishments, both outsiders and locals mention the ambitious architecture, the burst of new universities, the logistics of hosting a football World Cup in a place the size of Yorkshire. But if we're going for improbable things Qatar has achieved, I would suggest that winning the 2019 Asian Cup has to be close to the top.

That's certainly how it's viewed by one of the coaches who made it happen.

'If you take out the ones who cannot run, the ones who are overweight, the ones who don't care enough, [the number of good players left] might be 500. So this is a *miracle*.'

The coach is in his mid-forties, tanned, charismatic, from

a European country with a strong footballing tradition. The words are spoken with wonder but he decides it isn't enough. He repeats the line, this time enunciating every syllable separately.

'What we have done here is a *mi-ra-cle*.'

How was the miracle achieved? You might reasonably expect it to have something to do with the 2022 World Cup. But although that certainly lent weight to the initiative, the plan started much earlier. It involved a Sheikh, an air-conditioned football dome, an army of European football coaches and lots and lots of money.

Anyone who has spent more than five minutes in Qatar knows it is a place that likes football. Shisha bars are packed whenever Real Madrid or Barcelona play. Football talk shows run late into the night, dissecting refereeing decisions and debating teams' fortunes. One of the Qatari government's investment funds, Qatar Sports Investments, bought French club Paris Saint-Germain and has since pumped in billions in an attempt to make them Europe's best side. Most Qataris I've met have been to more Premier League stadiums in the past decade than anyone I know in England. It is important to shoot down the canard that the 2022 World Cup is going to a nation that doesn't know or appreciate the Beautiful Game.

It is equally true, however, that local football in Qatar is rather limited. The first club in the country was formed in 1950. For a lot of its history the Qatari league has been dominated by teams comprised of army and police employees.[†] There are a few storied clubs, such as Al-Rayyan, Al-Arabi and Al-Sadd. A sprinkling of world stars have been tempted to Qatar at the tail-end of their careers. They include former Barcelona player and the world's most famous coach Pep Guardiola, the Argentinian great Gabriel Batistuta and Spanish midfield maestro Xavi Hernández. But despite huge investment and promotion, professional football in Qatar remains an underwhelming affair. For an average league game, 1,000 people would be considered a decent crowd.

Tickets to top division matches are a steal. In 2020, it cost 10 rials ($2.75) for the regular terrace. If you want to sit on leather seats and be brought water and snacks on a silver platter, the VIP section is still only 50 rials ($14). 'We have beautiful stadiums, we have everything you need to enjoy the match. But then you have external elements that you cannot control,' I was told by Ahmed Abbassi, executive director of competitions and football development at the Qatar Stars League, the country's top division. 'The lifestyle here. Everyone is busy with working, with doing something other than going to the stadium and watching.'

Most of Qatar's inhabitants are in the country for one reason: to make money. For many, it's inconceivable to waste time and cash on watching football, especially matches between little-known teams. Even Qataris, for the most part, prefer to watch the games on television with friends and family. The stadiums

[†] The clubs in question are Lekhwiya and El-Jaish. In 2017 they merged and became Al-Duhail.

are left to be populated by a rump of more fanatical locals, a scattering of Westerners and the few dozen 'super fans', who are normally paid by the club to sing, dance and drum some sort of atmosphere into existence. 'It's a pity sometimes because we do have beautiful football,' Abbassi lamented. 'We have a lot of big players ... and it's a pity when you see such a match and there are not that many people watching.'

Away from the professional game, it is rare to find Qataris playing football. Those you see running around in the caged five-a-side pitches or entering teams in the Qatar Community Football League are nearly all foreigners. The climate is no doubt an important impediment. From May to September, even at night, it is impossible to run outside without the heat feeling like an elephant on your chest. Qatari youth face another hurdle, one that is shared with many other countries: the reluctance of families to allow their boys to play sport for fear that it will come at the detriment of their formal education. Until very recently, there were no role models of famous Qatari sportspeople, no poster boys (let alone girls) to inspire people to be more active.

The approach to top-level sport in Qatar used to follow that of the country's development more broadly: buy in the necessary expertise from abroad. That tactic frequently ruffled feathers. In 1999, the Qatari weightlifting team was disqualified from the Arab Games over the presence of four Bulgarian-born weight-lifters in the squad. In 2003, Kenyan runner Stephen Cherono became a Qatari national and changed his name to Saif Saaeed Shaheen, reportedly in exchange for a large lump sum and

$1,000 a month for life. Shaheen didn't let the criticism get to him. In 2004 he ran the fastest-ever steeplechase, a world record that still stands today.

Football fitted the same pattern. The national team contained many foreigners who had been granted Qatari citizenship. In the space of one week in 2004, Qatar tried to naturalise three Brazilian footballers, Ailton, Dede and Leandro. The move so infuriated FIFA that it prompted football's governing body to tighten eligibility requirements for all international footballers. For a country as fiercely patriotic as Qatar, the negative headlines and derision started to sting. There was need for a different tack.

Rising out of the western suburbs of Doha is a huge air-conditioned dome. It is so large it would be capable of housing the Eiffel Tower if it were lying on its side. When the academy was established in 2004 by emiri decree, this dome was the centrepiece of a new sports strategy. Christened the Aspire Academy, it was a state-of-the-art facility for training athletes, containing a full-size indoor football pitch, gyms, basketball courts, an Olympic-sized swimming pool, a fully functioning school and two wings of accommodation.

The Aspire Academy's goal was to produce athletes for Qatar that could go toe-to-toe with the world's best. After the country was named host of the World Cup, the academy was given the task of ensuring that, when the Qatar men's football team took to the pitch during the contest, the nation would not be embarrassed. Boys who showed promise (they were not so interested in girls) would be plucked out of their school or local club. They would be housed in the Aspire Dome – training, eating and sleeping there – and follow a tailor-made educational schedule, all under the watchful eye of some of the world's best coaches.

Overseeing the operation was Sheikh Jassim bin Hamad Al Thani, the eldest son of Sheikh Hamad, Qatar's ruler from 1995 to 2013, and his second wife Sheikha Moza bint Nasser Al-Missned. Sheikh Jassim loves football. He is frequently glimpsed at the stadium of his favourite Qatari team, Al-Sadd. He supposedly has a full-size football pitch in the royal palace complex and, according to an almost certainly apocryphal tale, used to suffer from insomnia caused by watching endless football games on televisions lining his bedroom walls. Having such a prominent figure at the helm of Aspire signalled that support for the project went right to the very top.

Aspire Academy is one plank in the wider strategy of making Qatar known throughout the world for sport. Since the mid-2000s, Qatar has endeavoured to host more and more international sporting events. By the time I arrived, it felt like something was taking place every other weekend, from World Athletics Championships to Swimming World Cups to the World Beach Games. Qatar has sponsored football clubs in Europe, including Italian team AS Roma and German club Bayern Munich, via its airline, Qatar Airways. A state-of-the-art sports medicine hospital that was established in 2007 has treated stars ranging from Barcelona's Ousmane Dembélé to World Cup-winner Kylian Mbappé of Paris Saint-Germain. The Qatari channel beIN Sports, launched in 2012, has become a leading global sports broadcaster. The reason for the hyperactivity surrounding sport is two-fold. It is seen as an important part of the country's economic diversification. But perhaps more importantly, and as the example of Sheikh Jassim shows, the emir and his brothers are huge sports fans.

From the moment it opened its doors, Aspire started to recruit and train young boys living in Qatar. Deep pockets and perfect facilities were only half the battle. Staff were tasked with generating an elite performance culture from scratch. 'I don't think Qatar and Aspire was prepared to have a world-class programme from day one,' I was told by Juan Delgado, formerly a youth coach at Valencia and Villareal in Spain, who worked at Aspire for 13 years from 2007. Coaches would have to double up as scouts, going to watch the youth teams of Qatari first and second division clubs after work. If they saw a player they liked, they would invite them in for a trial. The learning curve was huge. 'Technically speaking, we had a lot of room to improve,' he told me.

In 2011, Juan was tasked with helping set up a dedicated department comprising five scouts, four analysts and three data administrators. They had a simple goal: to make sure every football player in Qatar was scouted. 'We couldn't miss anyone,' said Juan. 'We needed to know *every* single kid that plays football in Qatar, regardless [of] the level.'

The Aspire scouts visited schools and held trials. A programme was established to discover promising six-, seven- and eight-year-olds. These boys would be directed into feeder teams and go to Aspire to train and play in matches. The data analysts would crunch the numbers and come up with benchmarks. Those who fell just short would be monitored, sometimes for years, in case they were late developers. From this pool, a few dozen twelve-year-old boys were selected annually. They joined with athletes recruited in Aspire's other sports – fencing, squash, table tennis, track and field – all moving into the dormitory and becoming full-time Aspire students.

Ahmad Jad was one such student. Qatari-born, Ahmad joined Aspire in 2006, a year after it opened. Smiley, polite and articulate, he spoke to me at the academy where he now works as a resident educator. Ahmad explained what Aspire is like from the athlete's perspective. 'One of the challenges is to prove yourself. I was good enough to be in the team, but to keep up with the training ...' Ahmad blew out his cheeks and opened his eyes wide. He was recruited as a runner and immediately handed a training schedule of nine sessions a week, double what he was used to. 'It was a *huge* difference to me,' he recalled. 'I was really struggling to get that rhythm with the guys.' The content of the training required adjustment too. It was highly quantified. Runners were made aware of their maximum speeds and coached to run at 60 or 80 per cent of them. In the classroom, boys who had never spoken English were put on intense language learning programmes. 'There were two days in the week – Sunday and Thursday – that you was not allowed to speak in Arabic,' recalled another early student of Aspire, Jamal Abubakar. 'I was hating Sunday and Thursday,' he told me with a visible shiver.

On the football side, the academy faced a problem in getting competitive game time for its charges. 'Why does Argentina produce players?' Juan asked me rhetorically. 'They don't have the best systems, they don't have the best facilities, they don't have the best coaches. They do have an insane. Competitive. Environment.' Devoid of adequate competition within Qatar, Aspire turned outwards. Squads were entered into international tournaments all over the world. Youth teams from Europe's top clubs were flown in on a regular basis to play in short trilateral series.

To improve competition further, Aspire devised an even more audacious scheme. Named 'Football Dreams', and reportedly costing over $100 million, the academy sent scouts out across Africa, South America and Asia in search of talent. It seemed to be a win–win: players from countries with limited opportunity and infrastructure would be brought to Qatar and offered the chance to establish sporting careers; and the local kids at Aspire would improve, courtesy of the more competitive environment. Between 2007 and 2014, a mind-boggling 3.5 million boys from seventeen countries were screened by Aspire. Every year, approximately 50 boys from each country were invited to a week-long trial in their home nation's capital. The best three were then cherry-picked and brought to Aspire for a final test. In total, just eighteen to twenty would be offered scholarships.

Establishing good facilities, strong scouting networks and adequate competition was hard enough. Engineering a shift in attitude among the Aspire charges was even tougher. The children who were recruited would be talented athletes, but they did not necessarily possess the mindset needed to succeed at the top. When I met him, Ahmad's job at Aspire was to help students develop this focus through organising activities for the boys in their downtime. He would arrange talks with former students, informal awareness sessions on topics such as leadership and activities to help them de-stress as part of a team of educators available to the students 24/7. The goal is to convince students that they have the talent to become successes; to feed them with inspiration until they embody it for themselves. For Ahmad, the most important element of the Aspire programme is not the coaching or the English lessons but this attitude shift. 'This is where they start realising ... This talent is gonna be used, my country needs it,' he said. 'Not everyone's talented ... not everyone has the thing that I have.'

While the Aspire coaching experiment was bubbling away in the background, the Qatar men's national team continued an unremarkable run. As late as December 2017, the side was ranked 102nd in the world, behind Sierra Leone and the Faroe Islands. The side was packed full of imported foreigners. Having played in Qatar for some time, these players fulfilled the stricter FIFA eligibility criteria but they were not exactly cutting edge. Brazilian Rodrigo Tabata was 37 years old. The team's top goal scorer, the Uruguayan Sebastián Soria, was 34. Billions of dollars had been poured into Aspire and yet, some people grumbled, it didn't seem to be producing top players.

But change was coming. Unbeknownst to many, in 2014, the Qatar under-19 side became Asian champions. The winning team was packed with graduates from the Aspire programme. They had been recruited before age twelve, housed in the dormitory and trained in the Aspire environment for six years. Juan and others at Aspire were thrilled. It was vindication of their model. In July 2017, the coach of the under-19s, Spaniard Félix Sánchez, was promoted to the top coaching role. His remit was to transition his cup-winning youth team into the senior-level Qatar national team. Yet something was missing.

On its own, the locally developed talent wasn't quite enough. The players were too young and raw. Sánchez was close to Qatar's emir and managed to convince him to naturalise a few players. Step up Miguel Carvalho Deus Correia ('Pedro') from Portugal (of Cape Verdean descent), Algerian Boualem Khoukhi and French-born Algerian Karim Boudiaf. All had been playing in Qatar long enough to satisfy FIFA. All three became naturalised Qatari citizens and slotted into the first eleven. They provided the ballast, maturity and consistency that Qatar was missing.

In January 2019, Qatar set off for the Asian Cup finals.

Up to that point, their best performance in the tournament was reaching the quarter-finals. Those behind the scenes privately agreed that another quarter-final showing would be acceptable, especially in light of the wider political context overshadowing their participation.

The host of the 2019 edition would be the United Arab Emirates – one of the countries that had cut all trade, travel and diplomatic links with Qatar in June 2017. Because the Asian Cup was an international tournament, the UAE were unable to ban Qatar from competing. Still, the country made clear that its neighbours would not be receiving the red-carpet treatment. A ban on direct flights from Qatar made it hard for fans from Doha to get to the contest. The team itself had to travel to the tournament via Kuwait. Saoud Al-Mohannadi, vice-president of the Asian Football Confederation and the Qatar Football Association, was allegedly denied entry before the decision was overturned. A British man claimed that he was abused, assaulted, detained and imprisoned after he wore a Qatar football shirt to the side's game with Iraq (the UAE alleged that he had inflicted his injuries on himself and accused him of wasting police time).

During the tournament, Emirati locals would boo the Qatar team. But this didn't seem to affect their performances. The side blasted through their group with three victories and progressed to the knockout stages. After beating Iraq and South Korea, in the semi-final they demolished the UAE 4–0, prompting a hail of bottles and sandals (throwing a shoe is an insult in the Arab world) from the home crowd. Their rivals in the final were Japan, four-time winners of the tournament. But Qatar were 2–0 up within 27 minutes. They went on to win 3–1, the

Japanese goal being the only one Qatar conceded in the whole tournament.

When the side returned to Qatar, the celebrations were extreme. Crowds clogged the Corniche for three straight days, brandishing scarves and honking car horns. The players became household names and were invited to an audience with the emir. Seven of the first eleven who started the final were Aspire graduates. Juan adopted a tone of amazement when reflecting on what happened. The success of the academy, he feels, is unprecedented.

'It doesn't happen nowhere. It doesn't happen at all.'

Japan, the side Qatar beat in the final, had a population of 126 million to choose from. Qatar, mere thousands of registered players.

'It's like Leicester City winning the Premier League,' I suggested to Juan, thinking of my own side's unlikely 2016 championship victory, priced by bookmakers as a 5,000:1 occurrence.

He furrowed his brow in disagreement.

'It's like Leicester City winning the Premier League with homegrown players.'

When it recruits, Aspire makes no distinction between 'full' Qatari citizens and those born in the country to foreign parents – all meet FIFA requirements. Aspire's non-fussiness, however, obscures a salient fact: the majority of

'Qataris' who go to Aspire are actually not Qatari citizens but residents, or *muqimin* in Arabic.

Seventeen of the 23 players in the squad that won the Asian Cup were *muqimin*. They include the top goal scorer, Almoez Ali, who was born in Sudan, and Akram Afif, their most skilful winger, who was born to a Tanzanian father and Yemeni mother.

'People criticise this but ... if this happened in Spain, they will be Spanish,' I was told by a Spanish conditioning coach with a first division youth side. Across the world, national football teams are full of players who were born abroad or are the children of immigrants. The academic Ross Griffin notes that sixteen of the 22 players for the Republic of Ireland in the 1990 FIFA World Cup were born in the UK. Fifteen members of the France side that won the 2018 World Cup had African roots. Thirteen of England's 26-man squad for Euro 2020 could have represented another nation. Sneering at the Qatari national team make-up can lead to the pernicious game of deciding who is 'really' qualified to represent a country, akin to the 'No, where are you *really* from?' line of questioning that people of colour frequently face in Europe and the US.

Yet the uncomfortable truth is that this perniciousness is encouraged by the Qatari government itself. Its strict laws forbid citizenship by birth or naturalisation, except on a case-by-case basis by decree of the emir.[†] The structure of life in Qatar

---

[†] For the emir to bestow citizenship, the candidate must speak Arabic and have lived in the country for more than 25 years or 'rendered great service to the country'. In accordance with the law, only a maximum of 50 foreigners

revolves around reminding 89 per cent of the population of the impossibility of ever becoming a citizen. Laws, cultural myths, geography – even dress codes – are perpetually invoked to generate a ring fence: either you are born Qatari or you are not. It's not something you can 'become'.

Strict citizenship laws are good for retaining benefits when you are a country of few nationals and lots of migrants. They are less good in sport, which requires large pools of potential athletes. Qatar has hit upon an uneasy solution. Those born in Qatar to non-Qatari parents but who represent a local club or the Aspire Academy can be given a temporary 'mission passport'. This allows them to travel to competitions on behalf of Qatar. But domestically it confers few benefits – holders are still excluded from the land grants, jobs and interest-free loans awarded to full Qatari citizens.

The concept of the 'mission passport' seems to show how Qatar wants to have its cake and eat it. The country hungers for athletes to achieve global success and prestige on the nation's behalf yet denies them the official benefits of being fully part of that same community.

The immigration status of the *muqimin* in the Qatar national team is unclear. There are no news stories or public announcements – the topic of naturalisation is highly sensitive. Regardless of official status, these players seem to be embraced by the majority

each year can be naturalised. Naturalised citizens still do not enjoy the same rights as Qatari-born citizens when it comes to the right to work, housing and participation in elections.

of Qataris. In part this is because they're good footballers. It also perhaps helps that all but one of them are Muslims from Arabic-speaking countries. All are highly active in Qatar, visiting schools and participating in the annual Qatar National Sports Day, a public holiday. There is no discernible difference between them and 'full' citizens in their posts on Instagram showing them in white *thobes*, or in tweets declaring their loyalty to the emir.

After their victory in the Asian Cup, the talk in Doha was that the *muqimin* in the national team had been promised an upgrade from 'mission' to 'official' passports as a reward for their performance. I find the contrast between the acceptance of the footballers and the general disregard of everyone else a bit uncomfortable. Many other residents have contributed to Qatar. What about the Indian businessman whose enterprise makes millions, or the Yemeni officer working in the police for 30 years? Even if they manage to acquire a long-term residency permit (difficult, given the number is capped at 100 annually), such individuals seem not to qualify for similar belonging and acceptance.

Furthermore, there were suggestions that even for the footballers it has not been plain sailing. At one event I attended in 2020, I got into conversation with two athletes – themselves Qatar-born residents – who told me that a year after the victory some players were still waiting for their citizenship. 'They did something for the country: [they] won the Asian Cup for the first time,' said the first.

'Yeah, something *extraordinary*!' said the other. He then shook his head in disbelief. 'And still they're not fully citizens.'

Officially, footballers at Aspire belong to their clubs. The best ones, however, spend little time there. Aspire wants to hold on to them – both to counter the perceived deficiencies of local football and protect their charges from the distractions of wider Qatari society. 'We create this bubble,' Juan told me. The protectionism generates a lot of anger in club football in Qatar. One coach I met – a Southern European – got so infuriated at what he saw as my overly positive view of Aspire that he demanded I come and watch a practice session with his team of under-16s at a top-division Qatari side.

When I arrived at the training pitches on a weekday evening, eighteen or so boys were already going through their warm-up.

The coach walked over and before even saying hello he moaned, 'Here we are, it's 6pm but not everyone is here.'

The coach was being helped by a conditioning trainer, a well-built guy from Eastern Europe. Together they set up an exercise of short dribbling and passing. I was taken aback by how shouty they both were whenever a kid didn't quite get it right.

'Abdullah, how many times I tell you?!'

'You go with him! What were you thinking?'

'No! This cone here, I said! SAYED?! WHY YOU NO LISTEN?!'

During another exercise, the coach wandered over to tell me that there were two new players at training today.

'One is—'

The coach turned to gesture at him. The move was

exquisitely timed. As we looked, the boy in question completely butchered the most simple of passes.

'The other is OK.'

They had open spaces on the roster and so were obliged to take Qatari kids, the coach told me.

'You fight with everyone,' he sighed. 'With the coaches, the management, the helpers.' His whole demeanour resonated unhappiness. 'But this is OK. The biggest problem is the players.'

Halfway through the session, the trainers and players all took a water break, after which they moved into a game played on three-quarters of a pitch where the boys were tightly arranged into rows to practice attack and defence. 'Sometimes the players are very lazy,' the physical trainer told me unprompted. 'I'm European. When I get on the pitch it's like a miracle,' he added, describing his excitement to play. 'But for them, they just seem to want to chat to their friends.'

I instinctively winced at the stereotypes. I have lost count of how many times I heard that footballers – and others – in Qatar were lazy and spoilt. How much of the perceived laziness is just teenage boys being teenage boys? In the short tempers and shouting, I wondered if there might be some displacement of frustration among the coaches. These European imports are mostly not good enough to get a top job back home. Instead, they come here, where they have to deal with what they see as lazy, demotivated kids.

Fifty minutes into the training, a player turned up and approached the conditioning trainer. 'Coach I want a warm up.'

For the first time, playfulness crept into the coach's voice. 'Where have you been? Have you been sleeping?!'

To my surprise, the boy concurred. 'Yeah, I was asleep.'

Perhaps the lack of motivation is not entirely concocted.

Watching the training, I noticed a feeling that often rises up within me in Qatar, which is that I'm in *The Truman Show*. In the 1998 film, Jim Carrey plays Truman Burbank, a man who believes he is living an ordinary life but in reality exists on a large set populated by actors and filmed for a TV audience. This particular iteration is the footballing version. If you're male, born in Qatar and vaguely sporty, chances are that you will at some point play in the youth team of a professional club. You will be coached by a foreigner, often one who has managed at the highest level in Europe. You will have access to conditioning coaches and physiotherapists, you'll know your biometric identifiers and be well-schooled in plyometric training. When, as I'm witnessing now, these resources are being brought to bear on indifferent fifteen-year-olds, the whole thing has the air of an absurd pretence.

'I used to tell this to every player ... the easiest country to become a professional footballer in the world is Qatar,' Juan told me. At football academies in other countries, when faced with players who lose interest or fall short, the staff will just shrug. Then they'll devote their attention to the thousands – millions – of other boys who are desperate to make it. In Qatar, they don't have thousands of other boys and can't afford to let anyone go. 'Players with long-term injuries, they had the time to recover; players that were biologically late maturers, they had a chance

to catch up; players that had a bad year, whether in school or on the pitch, they had a second chance,' Juan explained.

On the one hand, it is a more humane approach when compared with the scandalous way in which young boys are treated by elite academies in Europe. With success rates at the top clubs as low as 0.012 per cent, the vast majority of recruits will be cut adrift – sometimes after a decade – with no academic qualifications and little awareness of the difficulties of adapting to what comes next. Having a system in which coaches can't just discard youngsters but have to patiently work with them is no bad thing.

On the other hand, coaches in Qatar frequently complained to me of students behaving like spoilt little princes. 'You say, "OK, ten minutes running" and they say, "No, no, no, coach. I'm tired. Two minutes,"' the Spanish conditioning coach told me. 'Or when they see that it's the physical part they stay in the changing room, and when you finish the physical part then they join.' The coaches resent a hierarchy in which they're forced to bow and scrape to boys half their age. 'If you decide one day to fire one of the guys ... then the technical director for the club comes,' the coach continued. '[He'll say] "No, no, please— because he's [from a certain tribe], you cannot do that," and then the next day, even if the guy was impolite with you, you have [to say], "Oh, come, please, please, Mohammed, come, come, come."' And then, after all the time, money and attention, at the age of eighteen, boys will often ditch it all for a lucrative job in the public sector. A whopping 81 per cent of employed

Qataris work for the state or a state-owned company. Public employment on a lucrative contract is Qatar's preferred mechanism for passing on its largesse to citizens. A public sector job is a much more reliable vocation, shorn of the effort and vicissitudes of a professional athletic career. 'That's not a good thing for football. But it's a good thing for society,' Ahmed Abbassi, of the Qatar Stars League, told me. 'They get the opportunity to go study abroad ... to work in the army or in the police. So that's what gives them the opportunity to have a stable future, while professional football is the total opposite thing.'

Footballers in Qatar are subject to the same head-turning distractions as Qataris more broadly. In recent years, a culture of extravagance and conspicuous consumption has emerged. Doha is littered with malls devoted solely to luxury brands – bright, air-conditioned caverns that are empty apart from the odd Qatari and an army of shop assistants. The Gulf is a key market for luxury car brands. 'You cannot find a sense of performance because all the role models around are against that,' another European coach told me. 'Parents don't go to work and they have a Ferrari. Uncles go once in a while [to work] and they have a private jet.'

'It's that uncertainty [whether or not] you will make it that makes you work harder to achieve it,' Abbassi told me. 'And this is why you have so many players from Africa, you have so many players from South America and you have less talent evolving in countries where it's—'

He paused. We both understood the country he was referring to.

'... You know, where they don't really need football to make a living.'

It has taken a decade of intense funding, scouting and development to produce players good enough for Qatar's senior national football squad. The country's leadership has already signalled that it isn't prepared to keep this level of investment going.

Recent years at Aspire have seen retrenchment. The same factors that caused belt-tightening elsewhere in Qatar – a hydrocarbon price slump in 2014/15, the 2017 blockade, the coronavirus pandemic – led to budget cuts of up to 40 per cent. Late 2016 saw the end of the Football Dreams programme that brought promising footballers from developing countries to Qatar. The official reason was that it was not having enough impact on improving local players. Some wondered, however, if other motives were at play. 'Could it be that hosting the Football Dreams kids in Qatar made less sense after FIFA made it more difficult to naturalize them for the country's national team?' mused Sebastian Abbot in *The Away Game*, a book about the Football Dreams project. 'It's easy to see how placing the players off-limits could have made the hassle of keeping them in Doha seem less worthwhile.'

I heard of increasing nepotism in appointments at Aspire, of coaches failing to adapt to the more conservative cultural climate in the Middle East, even neglecting their charges. 'It may seem shiny and impressive,' one former employee told me. 'But there's a lot of poor practice and a lack of care for people.'

By 2020, many of the older, established coaches had moved on, including Delgado who went to work in the US as the technical director of the Austin FC youth academy. In their place were a lot of trainers in their twenties. 'Why is that?' asked a technical coordinator at a first division club in Qatar. 'Because they're normally single, so Aspire don't need to pay for flight tickets for family. No kids, so no school fees. They're from South America – Chile or Argentina or something – so cheaper than Europe.' On the pitch, the cuts mean the number of international games played by Aspire students has had to be reduced. Tightened budgets had likely come too late to affect the 2022 World Cup performance; that squad was pretty much determined two years prior to the contest. But they raised an important question mark over the trajectory of Qatar's national team after the event – and tapped into wider worries about the ability of a small Gulf country to put sport at the centre of its plans for creating an economy no longer reliant on hydrocarbons.

Some people I spoke to directed me to the sad case of handball as a harbinger of football's fate. In 2015, Qatar hosted the Handball World Championship. In the lead up to the competition they built three incredible arenas. They pumped money into the national team, making the most of handball's lax citizenship requirements to sign up some of the best international talent. The tournament was a huge success. The Qatari team outperformed even their own best expectations and made the final. But by 2020 it had all collapsed. Budget cuts caused an exodus of talent. Things got so bad that the Qatar Handball Association considered reducing the league from eight to two months in order to reduce payments to players. Since 2015, two of the arenas have stood empty, gathering dust. Despite being World Championship finalists in 2015, the Qatari national team failed to qualify for the pandemic-delayed 2020 Olympics.

It would be extraordinary if the Aspire Academy was to follow the same trajectory. Yet even if it were to regress, the place has already indisputably benefited the Qatar national football team and, in doing so, it has transformed the view of sports both within Qatar and internationally. Parents in Qatar today are more willing to let their sons get involved. Ahmad Jad, the former athlete working at Aspire, would send his sons to the academy in a flash. 'The ideas, the mentality that you have here, you will never have it anywhere [else] in the world,' he said.

Juan argued that, if Qatar is serious about becoming a major global sports hub, it would be a monumental error to abandon efforts to raise its own successful sportspeople. 'They need to move from being a place that is just putting on sports events to one that produces talents,' he said. Multi-million-dollar stadia can only take you so far, he argued.

'We have the rocket. Now we need the astronauts.'

8

'Here we are all expats. So we are all on a journey, on a pilgrimage'

The first thing you see is the cars.

Rows and rows of them parked on the hill, glistening in the sunlight. From a distance it's unclear why so many are gathering here, in front of a complex of unremarkable beige buildings, outside the Doha city limits.

The taxi driver drops me at the bottom and I walk up through the lines of vehicles. Every space is taken, forcing those running late to park on surrounding scrubland.

As I get closer to the gate I'm joined by trickles of people. Policemen look on as we are separated into two queues – 'males' and 'families' – and follow metal barriers through wooden doors into a hall filled with airport-style security. As I go to retrieve my bag from the X-ray machine, one of the policemen addresses me.

'Where are you from?'

He is not aggressive, but the tone lets me know he is not asking out of personal curiosity.

'The UK.'

'UK,' he says back, neither in suspicion nor exoneration.

In the compound, I move past a man at a table selling calendars and weave through gaggles of people standing around chatting. Someone in uniform has opened a vending machine.

He is replenishing bottles of water while a ring of people waits impatiently for him to finish. The crowds are heading towards the main building – a modernist structure sitting in a concrete ring, its roof sloping upwards to a small tower. On the door, attendants are handing out pieces of paper, inviting everyone to write down the name of a sick person they want to keep in mind.

The main hall has enough space for a few thousand and is shaped like a fan, reminding me of the UN General Assembly in New York. I walk round to where the crowd is thinner and sit near the front. From here I can observe the musicians on the upper balcony. Random notes on a keyboard have already alerted me to their presence. Now I spot a man holding a guitar and people clustered around microphones. A voice sings, a bit too loud in relation to the instruments and not particularly in tune. They are rehearsing the opening.

The space quickly fills. My immediate neighbours end up being an African woman and a Filipino man. Further down my row are a family from South Asia. In front, the people look Arab or maybe Eastern European. Next to the Filipino man there's a guy with a beard and round, hipster glasses – where's he from? I suddenly catch myself: I'm doing it again, playing 'guess the nationality' – Qatar's favourite game. I try to prise the fingers of my mind off the topic and direct my attention towards the front of the hall.

The music strikes up, this time for real. The sound is gloopy, any nuance swallowed by the cavernous reverb. Everyone gets to their feet and sings along to the words projected on two large screens. I turn to watch as a small collective enters from the back. It is an entourage of people in robes, followed by the priest.

Every Friday in Qatar, tens of thousands of Christians head to 'Church City', a complex of nine places of worship on the outskirts of Doha. The church that I visited, the Catholic Church of Our Lady of the Rosary, is the largest. Loud music drew me afterwards to one of the others – the Evangelical Churches Alliance Qatar, a Filipino group that populated a large tent with a vocalist, dancers, a full ten-piece band and a thousand people singing and dancing in various states of rapture. Around the corner, the Anglican church was similarly busy. From behind each door on its long corridors came the sounds of fire and brimstone preaching, music and collective chanting. Other churches on the site include Greek Orthodox, Egyptian Coptic, Syrian Orthodox and Lebanese Maronite.

The reason for the extreme concentration of churches in this remote location is simple: Church City is the only legal place in Qatar for Christians to gather and hold services. The country has passed regulations allowing freedom of worship, but the status of Christians is perhaps best captured in the phrase devised by the political scientist Hilal Khashan to describe the situation of Christians in the Gulf more broadly: limited forbearance.

The state religion of Qatar is Islam. The country is not an Islamic theocracy like Iran where clerics are part of the state apparatus. But neither is it like Turkey, which follows a Western week and where you can easily buy a beer in most towns. On the whole, and there are of course exceptions, Qataris are remarkably religious. Life in Qatar is punctuated by visible displays of Islam. The five-times-a-day call to prayer emanates not only from mosques but interrupts radio broadcasts and even the muzak filling shopping malls. All business and leisure facilities shut for Friday prayers, the most important of the week. The sale of alcohol and pork products is strictly managed. There are notices and pictures in most public buildings reminding people how to dress appropriately.

The visibility of Islam contrasts markedly with the complete absence of other religions. There are no Hindu or Buddhist temples, no synagogues. At Church City, symbols that allude to the complex's function cannot be visible from outside. The tower of the Catholic church, where the roof tapers to a point clearly meant for a crucifix, remains incongruously bare. Even the word 'church' is avoided. Two weeks after opening, it was scrubbed from the road signs and replaced with the euphemistic 'Religious Complex', supposedly to avoid offending Qataris.[†] Physical invisibility is backed up by strict laws governing religious activities. Christians are not allowed to proselytise. They cannot publicly celebrate religious festivals outside of Church

---

[†] There are of course plenty of Western cities where the same invisibility can be said of Islam. Switzerland passed its infamous 'Minaret ban' in 2009. Until a mosque was opened in Athens in 2020, Muslims in the city had no official place of worship.

City and their charitable work is restricted. It is forbidden to distribute bibles or other religious literature.

The hypersensitivity towards Christianity is not solely doctrinal. Concern over imported religion is caught up in the wider insecurity over foreign influence on Qatari citizens. Unlike the rest of the Middle East, historically there were next to no Christians in the Gulf. What little presence there was diminished after the 7th-century Arab conquests that spread Islam across the region. It is therefore quite straightforward to paint Christianity as an alien presence. Foreign religion dovetails easily into the wider worry the Qatari state has of its own customs and beliefs being lost under the tide of foreign workers. There have been small groups of Christians in Qatar since the 1930s, often as part of the petrochemical industries. But it is only in the past few decades that Qatar began to see their numbers increase to almost 14 per cent of the population in 2010, or around 250,000 people.

'I came in '85. At that time there was no church. We hardly went to mass for two to three years.' So says Nery, a stalwart of Qatar's Catholic church. A large man from Goa, he is in his fifties and speaks to me from his office via a blurry video call. 'It was not that it was *illegal* or something like that,' he tells me. 'The authorities knew that we were doing services, but it was in houses.'

Nery explains that some Catholics turned a small villa into a chapel. A priest would fly in once a month from Bahrain to hold services, but there was no officially established church. The same pattern of DIY services was true of other Christian denominations: the Anglican community used the gymnasium at Doha English Speaking School for their services. Because worship wasn't happening in public spaces, the authorities turned a blind eye unless they received complaints from Qataris, usually about parking space or loud music. When the state intervened, however, it would often be forceful. In 1988, an Indian Pentecostal spent two weeks in jail. The US ambassador to Qatar in those years, Joseph Ghougassian, recalled a priest seeking his help to avoid being deported.

By the 21st century, the lack of formal places in Qatar for Christians to worship was becoming acute – and running increasingly counter to the country's efforts to market itself globally as an open, welcoming nation. Under Sheikh Hamad, the early 2000s saw Qatar quickly introduce a range of measures to make Christians feel more at home: the country established diplomatic relations with the Vatican, hosted inter-faith seminars and, in 2005, signed a 50-year lease for Church City.

On 15 March 2008, the first mass was held in Our Lady of the Rosary. The deputy prime minister, Abdullah bin Hamad Al-Attiyah, officially opened the complex in the presence of dozens of diplomats, religious leaders and tens of thousands of worshippers. Nery's description of the day is biblical in its telling: 'They came in different directions walking – because there was no road. There was only one complex in the middle and the whole area is desert. So people parked their car maybe four, five kilometres [away] and they were walking.'

Today, Our Lady of the Rosary is a microcosm of Qatar's diversity. The parish council is made up of over a dozen different groups, including Africans, Arabs, Brazilians, Europeans, Filipinos, Hispanics, Indians, Indonesians, South Koreans and Sri Lankans. The church is administered by seven priests who live together in a villa close to Church City, supporting and delivering masses to the different communities.

Fridays are the busiest. Nery is at the church from 5am until 9pm, ushering visitors, answering questions and coordinating volunteers. As well as multiple services in English, there is worship in Tagalog, Sinhala, Arabic, Korean, Indonesian, Malayalam, Urdu and Tamil. Across all masses, the structure of the service follows a strict order. Shorn of the schisms of much of Christianity, Catholicism has mind-boggling universality – more than a billion engaging in the same ritual every week. It allows someone like me, who went to a Catholic school but has barely set foot in a church since then, to find almost everything about the service familiar. Except the songs, which I'd never heard before. The Qatari church's solution for this issue is to keep hymns in circulation for a long time. Nery tells me that the same ones are sung for a month. By the end of the four weeks, 'You are already a parrot on that hymn,' he says drily.

Nery reflects on the huge changes to the Catholic community of Qatar – from the few hundred who would hold mass in their chapel to the tens of thousands of people who frequent the current facility. He is grateful to the government for the space and just happy to be able to play a role in it all. Some attitudes

of the newer members of the congregation, though, rankle him a little.

'The mentality of people changes. The young generation is not like the old generation,' he tells me with a playful lilt. Congregants of his age wear shirts and trousers to mass but 'nowadays, they come as if they're going to a fish market'. Nery politely suggests that they might want to wear something a bit more formal. Some are embarrassed, others argue back: "This is not your father's property!"

Nery breaks off. When he resumes, his voice has softened, with a tone akin to a kindly uncle watching a youngster make a mistake.

'Don't think that all who are coming to church are holy!'

'I said, "Why me?" I'm enjoying my life as a parish priest.'

When Father Rally Gonzaga was first approached to lead the Catholic mission in Qatar, it is fair to say he was not that keen on the idea. Middle-aged, short, with a smiley face, he greets me in his office, which is full of shiny wood and religious icons, including a shelf behind his head devoted solely to statues of the Virgin Mary.

Father Rally was happily ensconced in a parish in the Philippines. He had visited Qatar before, spending a month filling in for a priest who was on holiday, but he never thought he would be back. Now, though, the applications received for the Qatar posting were weak. His superiors approached him: try it for a year, they told him. If he didn't like the place then he could come back. Before the year was through, Father Rally knew it was where he was meant to be. 'I like what I'm doing here,' he told them. 'And that started it.'

As chief priest of the entire congregation – approximately 30,000 people – Father Rally has a front seat on the cycle of life in Qatar.

'There are so many baptisms here,' he tells me with an amused sigh. 'The most that I have experienced is ten babies on Fridays ... and mostly these are Filipinos, because we are so much blessed with babies.'

There are a lot of weddings too. The church has the authority to officially marry couples. Father Rally has wedded Filipinos and Indians, Italians and Lebanese, Congolese and Filipinos. He has married Catholics to Hindus, Catholics to Orthodox Christians, Catholics to Anglicans. One wedding he jointly administered with a Maronite priest from Lebanon, with Father Rally speaking English and the Lebanese priest Arabic. In these cross-denominational marriages, special permission is needed from the Catholic bishop in Bahrain (he usually gives it). Father Rally also marries Catholics to non-believers. The first time this happened, he was shocked. There are no self-proclaimed atheists in the Philippines, he tells me.

'Sometimes I ask them, "How do you live your life?" [And] he says, "I am free!"'

Father Rally breaks into a big laugh. He doesn't come across as the doctrinal type.

Then there are the deaths. There is a Christian cemetery in Qatar, but it is in Dukhan on the west coast, far from Doha. There are no funeral homes and no public ceremonies for the Christian dead. Father Rally meets the family at the mortuary where they pray and bless the body. Often it is taken to Dukhan alone. Most of those buried are babies. Miscarriages. Stillbirths. If an older child or adult dies in Qatar, families will normally pay to ship the body home. But the process is very expensive and so people don't do it for the babies. I think of my own experience of pregnancy loss: the coffin barely larger than a shoebox, the difficulty of grieving for someone you loved but never met. The thought of children buried in Qatar, their parents half the world away, makes me unspeakably sad.

My conversation with Father Rally confirms what I had already surmised: the Catholic community of Doha is diverse but dominated by Filipinos, Indians and Africans. Westerners are few and far between, reflecting the shift of Catholicism's centre of power to the global south. He tells me it's not sufficient to have the different groups in the church simply coexisting, he wants them to interact. He tries to lead by example. Simple things, like when Indian members of the parish bring him food, he tries it. 'I don't want them to feel that, "Ah, you don't like us, you don't like our food." So I try to eat.' Fortunately, Father Rally enjoys Indian food. But he tries everyone's even – he tells me with a laugh – if he doesn't like it.

At Christmas or on feast days, Father Rally and the parish council divide up the preparations among the different communities: Filipinos take the liturgy, the Urdu community the offering, Arabic speakers the music. For every new feast the roles are shifted. 'Because that is a church,' he tells me. 'We are not separate communities. Although we have differences, but we have to come together.' I want him to explain some of the tensions that must inevitably ensue, but Father Rally dismisses my question with a self-effacing swish of the arm. 'All those Christians who come here, they have the background already of Christianity back home ... all the teaching of Jesus, all the teaching of the Church,' he says. 'My role is now how to motivate them and to refresh all those things again into their own mind.'

Yet his job does have demanding elements. Along with the heads of the other churches, he has to liaise with Qatari authorities about issues such as security and organising special events. As a key figurehead in the Catholic community, people come to him when they're in trouble. Each case requires a different course of action. For people with job problems, the church has a fund that provides support. For those escaping an abusive sponsor, he contacts their embassy and arranges a place for them in a shelter. To help with those who need food, he recently established a new initiative called the St Anthony's table.

'I encourage people to bring to the church. You bring anything you want to bring. Food. Fruits. Bread. Juice. Coffee. You just put there on the table and anyone could get [for] free.'

He pauses, a mischievous look crosses his face.

'So that is why the canteen got angry with me.'

He chuckles but quickly becomes serious.

'I said this is the way, so that people could interact with each other, talk to each other, know each other.'

When we meet in late 2020, Father Rally is coming to the end of his nine-year stay in Qatar. He hopes his legacy for the country's Catholics will be to associate their community with giving. To have helped people to take on board the importance of charity, especially to those from different backgrounds. 'In my seminary days I learnt this from one of my superiors,' he tells me. 'I could still remember vividly his words: "When people come to you, don't let them go without anything for them. Even small things you give, so they would carry along with them when they go ..." and they would say, "This is church."'

He looks at me squarely.

'When they come to us, that is my principle. Anything that I could give, I would give.'

In all my dealings with Church City I can't shake a feeling of unease. Not with the people I meet – they are all lovely – but with the wider marginalisation of their existence within Qatar. It's only upon returning home that I think I have come to understand why.

So much of the discourse surrounding religious diversity in the West is framed around an imperative towards integration. Whether it is debates over wearing a headscarf or eating halal meat (in Europe it is overwhelmingly Islam that is viewed as the 'problem' religion), degrees of difference are indexed to a person's ability to 'integrate'. By this logic, a Muslim who wears a poppy on Remembrance Day equates to a 'success', while someone who refuses to be seen by a doctor of the opposite sex is manifestly a 'failure'. Religious diversity is a current in the wider stream of conversations surrounding multicultural-ism and what it means, in diverse nations, to belong. Even if it's sometimes done badly, trying to make everyone feel at home is the context that I've grown up in and got used to.

In Qatar, no one talks about integration. 'Non-integration ... is viewed as the basis of social stability,' the academic Anh Nga Longva has written about Kuwait, but the statement is equally true of Qatar. Diversity is managed not through integration but segregation. As explained earlier, citizenship – with all the perks it confers – is made near-impossible to acquire. The geography of the country is a patchwork of camps and compounds. The walls and barriers seem to speak to a deep fear: if the elaborate sifting by ethnicity, race or gender is threatened – if mixing is allowed – then what is uniquely 'Qatari' will slip away. And so there's a need to police the boundaries: workers in overalls will be turned away from glitzy malls and white Europeans wandering the streets of the Industrial Area will be reminded it is private property and asked to move on.

A similar logic seems at work in spaces like Church City. Muslims are forbidden to enter the compound, which is heavily monitored with policemen on every entrance. All the Christians I spoke to accepted the premise that the securitisation is for their own good – a belief that it is not without basis. Some religiously conservative figures in Qatar have publicly opposed the building of churches, citing a popular *hadith* (one of the sayings of the Prophet Mohammed) proclaiming that no two religions should coexist on the Arabian peninsula. Even Muslims in the region have in the past been targeted. In 2015 in neighbouring Kuwait, Sunni extremists from ISIS claimed responsibility for a deadly attack on Shia Muslims, who they view as heretics. But playing the security card also has the convenient effect of dampening down any desire to loosen the sense of separation between Church City and the rest of Qatar. There are no Muslim–Christian outreach programmes. The academic John Fahy has written that no Qatari minister has visited the religious complex since its opening, as if they are reluctant to even draw attention to its existence.

To what extent does this matter? In Europe or North America, ethnic or religious separation might no longer be required by law but there are plenty of segregated cities and neighbourhoods. Furthermore, in the Western context there is greater impetus to generate belonging, given that many of those from ethnic and religious minorities are citizens. In Qatar, why bother trying to integrate foreign workers when they are around for so little time? This logic is embraced by foreigners as often as it is by Qatari nationals. 'Here we are all expats,' I am reminded by Nery. 'We are all on a journey, on a pilgrimage ... You come for five years, ten years, twenty years and then you finish and you go.' Maybe it's only the liberal anthropologist that sees a problem in any of this.

But what irritates me is less the segregation and more the resultant tendency to see people not as individuals but as representatives of a group. Anyone who has felt irritated by someone assuming their thoughts and beliefs based on their gender, nationality or race should surely understand this.

Breaking down the barriers between groups is actually one facet of the church that has been aided by coronavirus. The pandemic forced Our Lady of the Rosary to strip back its schedule and only offer mass in English. 'This is the mass that *I like*,' a smiling Father Rally told me. Where you are from or what language you speak dissolves away. 'There will be no Filipino, no Indians, no Malayalam – we come together and this is church.'

At least the church is aware of the harm in always seeing everyone in terms of their nationality or ethnic group. In the rest of life in Qatar, this sort of categorisation is so normal it's hard to escape. The Catholic church is perhaps the best example I've come across in Doha of people truly mixing and learning from one another. Worshipping together. Getting married and having kids. Living and learning. It is religion's desire not simply for community but to be part of a wider universal belonging that, for all its faults, strikes me as one of its biggest selling points. It can function as an antidote – if only for a few hours a week – to the hierarchy, the stratification, the racialisation of the rest of life in Qatar.

When it's time for me to depart from Church City after my Friday visit, I leave by the method I always use in Qatar: a ride-sharing app. While stuck in a huge traffic jam to get out of the church car park, I notice that my taxi driver has a small crucifix hanging from his rear-view mirror. I ask if he's also been to church.

'Yes, sir. I am a Christian,' is his slightly stiff response.

We get talking. He went to the mass at the Catholic church, but not the one I just went to, the 6am service. I ask if it was busy.

He looks at me and smiles.

'Every mass is busy.'

9

'King of the bat'

In the southern sprawl of Doha, my taxi turns off behind the strip mall.

The side road is so new it has no proper asphalt. It is still pockmarked with small craters, formed by the wheels of the trucks that built the villas lining both sides.

I look at the pin on my phone. Which villa? The one on the left, with the four-by-fours and the delivery driver sat outside? Or the one on the right with half a dozen cars parked in its courtyard? I call the number.

'Hey!'

He appears out of the darkness of the courtyard, waving his phone above his head.

Of course. When I first moved to Qatar, an estate agent told me that you can tell the occupancy of the villas by the cars parked outside – multiple Land Cruisers indicates that it's Qatari; a range of more modest cars and it will be divided into apartments, each inhabited by foreign workers.

He greets me and leads us into the compound.

Stretching from wall to wall is a bare expanse of paving surrounding a two-storey building. No lights are on. The man leads me round the back and inside the building, his flip-flops making loud, indecent slaps. We head up an internal staircase and pause outside a door on the left. He opens it and I am shocked at what I see.

We stand in a small room with no windows. The only light comes from a bulb pumping out a harsh white glare. TV noise leaks out from behind a closed door. Large cardboard boxes take up most of the floor space and they are packed and overflowing with cricket equipment.

Cricket shoes in various stripes of fluorescent green and yellow are tied in pairs by their shoelaces. Spring-loaded stumps stand to attention stacked inside each other. Piles of shiny white equipment – wicket-keeper gloves, thigh pads, kit bags – lie scattered all around, glimmering in shrink wrap. But what draws my attention is something else altogether.

A forest of bats covers the room. They range from crisp, white and unblemished to sand-coloured, warped and chipped. Some have holes cut out of the back to reduce weight, others are thick planks of wood, more tree than bat. There are bats propped on their toes, bats wedged together on their handles and bats still in bubble wrap.

Walking over to the nearest box, the man pulls out a bat. He holds it up to me, stroking it and talking proudly, 'These bats, you won't find them in stores.'

This is Ali*. Diminutive, polite. A thickish beard suggests he's in his thirties, but boyish, messily parted hair makes me question if my guess is too high.

Approximately 1.5 million South Asians live in Qatar.

That's five for every one Qatari. They range from millionaires to low-paid labourers, Muslims to Hindus, Sikhs and Christians. They hail from Karachi, Kerala, Kathmandu and Colombo and speak Punjabi, Tamil, Sinhalese, Malayalam and Bengali – the subcontinent in all its extreme diversity. Qatar might be preparing to host football's biggest tournament. But thanks to its huge population of South Asians, the country's best-loved game is cricket. And it's Ali who keeps everyone supplied with gear.

On my first ever morning in Qatar, I got a glimpse of cricket's importance. Arriving late the night before in darkness, I fell asleep to the neon glare and murmur of voices from the barber's opposite where I was staying. At 6am I was jerked awake by shouts and howls. My first thought was that it was a political demonstration or riot. I leapt up and peered out of the window. A hundred metres from the apartment was a large scrub area. Figures were spaced around it. In the middle, I could make out someone running and another person swiping at something with a bat.

Drive around Qatar on a weekend morning and you'll see tens, possibly hundreds, of these games. They take place in empty car parks, abandoned building sites and areas of scrubland. On any evening, you can spot the telltale halo of floodlights in the Doha sky, illuminating the playing fields of schools where cricketers are taking part in training sessions. One day, during the Indian Premier League tournament, I went from taxi to gym to bar with uninterrupted coverage courtesy of workers glued to the game on phones and TVs. Cricket is folded into the fabric of

Qatar because South Asians are part of every aspect of life in the emirate. Most arrive and work for a few years before returning home. But sizeable numbers are long-term residents and some are second-, or even third-generation Qatar-born.

I hoped that cricket would allow me to interact with some of these people. The experience of South Asians in the Gulf is nearly always viewed through the lens of labour. It is a tale of *homo economicus* and his inevitable exploitation and disappointment. Becoming involved with South Asia's favourite game would provide a chance to widen the scope; to befriend people, listen to their stories and, who knows, maybe comprehend, at least in passing, other facets of what it is like to be South Asian in Qatar.

But there was one problem with the plan – I've never been able to play cricket.

'Watch the ball. 100 per cent. Watch. The. Ball.'

I *know*, I say to myself through gritted teeth. It's not as if I'm staring at the bloody moon.

Taking off my helmet, I try to mop up the sweat. Rivulets and streams flow down my forehead and into my eyes. Qatar is the most humid place I've ever lived. Even on an October night, the merest movement causes a crescendo of beads to break out on my forehead, arms and back. Not good weather in which to wear full cricket protection.

Coach doesn't sweat. Not a drop on him. He's from Sri Lankan hill country and makes it all look effortless, sending deliveries down with the mere flick of his wrist then pausing to joke with the players in the other nets. But now there's no joking. He strides down the wicket to bark instructions at me.

'Keep the bottom hand loose!'

'Right elbow out away from side!'

'Your bat at the end of both front- and back-foot defence should be ANGLED, not straight!'

He grabs the bottom of the bat and pushes it back, pulling my shoulder in the opposite direction. His advice circling in my ears, I brace myself as he goes back and fires in more balls, most of which whizz past the end of my nose.

I've told him I want to concentrate on batting. Being unable to bat has been an impediment ever since my first week in Qatar. The nadir was probably the time when I stumbled across a group of Southern Indians who were all from the same church playing a friendly game. My protestations that I was happy to remain a spectator were ignored and I was forced to take the bat and walk to the middle. With every delivery, and each slash at fresh air, their laughs and banter slowly petered into an embarrassed silence.

The cricketers in the nets this evening are a mix of Indians, Pakistanis and Sri Lankans, with one Nepali thrown in for good measure. Those who use the facility are from the small elite. They work as auditors, lawyers, surveyors and backroom staff at Qatar Airways. Only well-paid workers with disposable income can afford the pads and helmets of official cricket. English is the lingua franca. Everyone rubs along.

Wealthy South Asians are not new to the Gulf. For most of the first and second millennium CE, India was an economic and cultural powerhouse, extending its reach around the whole littoral of the Indian Ocean, from Madagascar to Malacca. The country supplied the wood used for building Gulf boats and houses and the cloth in which Gulfis dressed. Indian money lenders called *sarrafin* financed Gulf projects. Merchants from the subcontinent exported pearls out of shops in Manama, Dubai and Kuwait City. With the arrival of British colonialism in the Gulf, Indian influence deepened. British representatives in the region were appointed by the India Office. Low-level Indian bureaucrats were recruited to man the Gulf's proliferating government institutions. As late as the 1960s, the main currency used in the region was not the pound, dinar or rial but the Indian rupee.

Standing in Qatar today, this early history seems made up. The twin arrivals of oil wealth and Arab nationalism cut the cord with the Asian subcontinent. The Gulf underwent a reorientation – inwards across the desert to the rest of the Arab world and outwards to the new oil-hungry markets of East Asia and the West. Indians would still come but predominately as low-paid labourers – outsiders who were tolerated rather than seen as locals. If you know where to look, traces of the previous history linger on, most noticeably in Gulf cuisine where biriyani is a beloved dish and masala chai is drunk by the bucketful (the latter has been transformed into *karak*, Qatar's national drink). But at the government level there is little taste for such multicultural storytelling. South Asians in the Gulf are, in the words of anthropologist Neha Vora, 'impossible citizens' – essential to the workings of the state and economy but never afforded the protections or full benefits of official belonging.

But being undervalued and marginalised doesn't equate to lifelessness.

O n a Friday afternoon I get Ali to tell me his story. We sit in a shopping mall coffee shop. A procession of families come and go, loudly ordering drinks the size and colours of ice cream tubs. Ali is oblivious to it all. He doesn't even open the bottle of water I buy for him, simply rolling it from one hand to the next, engrossed in his excited, see-sawing narrative.

'When I came, I didn't do cricket for two to three years,' he tells me. 'I didn't even see cricket.'

Ali arrived in Qatar in 2009. He had a job working in procurement for a construction company. It served him adequately for five years, during which time he got married and had a son in Pakistan. But he wasn't earning enough – not enough to secure a family visa to bring his family to Qatar, nor enough to buy the house in Pakistan, the one he needed for his dad before he retired. And he couldn't switch jobs. He needed a non-objection certificate from his boss and everyone knows that bosses never give out NOCs.

It was then that an opportunity arose.

An office colleague suggested it. For just 8,000 rials (around $2,200), Ali could become a member of a group selling watches, or maybe bracelets or necklaces. Limited edition. Not available anywhere else. You needed a reference, but the colleague would be willing to provide it. If he was interested, the boss was coming from Canada next week and he could fix a meeting. Ali was interested.

In the meeting they had charts. They had full business plans. They spoke mellifluously of the riches that would accrue – $200 just for signing someone else up. Ali looked at the money in his hand, 8,000 rials, the entirety of his savings, and handed it over.

Ali lowers his voice.

'They have tactics to handle you.'

He was told to pay meticulous attention to his body language – how to stand, how to pull out the chair for new recruits, to offer them tea, coffee or water when they first meet. He didn't understand why he was being trained to withhold information from the newly enlisted when they signed up. Ali's mind kept travelling to their personal lives. What if they couldn't afford it? What if they're going into debt to join?

'My heart was telling from inside. I cannot do that.'

Ali doesn't speak badly of anyone. Narrating incidents that would quicken the pulse of others causes barely a ruffle to this polite and good-natured man.

'I don't want to say "scam",' he says diplomatically. 'But it's not a correct thing, as per my religion.'

It was a scam. He lost all his savings.

'I was literally crying. Like a kid. I'm not— I never cry.'

He confessed what happened to his mother and swore her to secrecy. His father was suffering from heart problems and he didn't want to be responsible for a relapse. It was time for a rethink.

Pakistan, Ali explains to me, is the centre of the global sporting gear industry. Lahore, where Ali is from, was where products would come and be stored before being shipped abroad. He grew up in the warren of streets in the old town, around shops and warehouses piled high with sports equipment. Peter Oborne, in his masterful history of Pakistani cricket, described walking the same streets searching for the houses of old cricketers: 'Every quarter of the old city seems to have given birth to a Test player: Gul Mohammad, Nazar Mohammad, Imtiaz Ahmet and A.H. Kardar ... [and] their legacy continues: I noticed that small boys are still to be found playing against every wall and by every street corner.'

On a trip home, Ali went to buy some cricket shoes and fell into conversation with an old school mate. The friend had begun exporting sports clothes to Qatar. If Ali needed anything he should let him know. Back in Qatar, he discussed having some T-shirts made with the captain of his cricket team. Nothing fancy, just white with the company name and logo. He agreed. Seven days later, the package arrived. The price he'd agreed with his captain didn't only cover the costs; Ali also made a small profit.

Ten days later, the captain came to Ali with an order from

elsewhere, this time for 40 sets of cricket T-shirts and trousers. Other people were asking him for cricket shoes. Some needed bats. One person asked him for a helmet. Then another. There are sports shops in Qatar, of course. But they are all focused on football, full of boxes of Adidas Predators and posters of Lionel Messi. Before I met Ali, I went in search of cricket supplies and finally found one shop – a dusty place in Najma, the old centre of Doha. They had a picked-over shelf of faded white pads in smudged plastic pouches.

By day Ali worked in accounts. At night he would drive around Doha delivering cricket products to his ever-expanding circle of clients.

'I did very hard work, believe me,' he tells with a chortle.

'My son was not one year old and I have the car and my wife she's sitting with me and I was going door to door to sell the balls ... Only 4 rial margin!' He describes driving the length of the peninsula – from Al-Khor in the north to Wakrah in the south – delivering his products. 'I worked *hard* to make my market, personally.'

Ali had many ways of getting his goods to Qatar. His brothers in Pakistan would send things by courier. He would chip in for a friend's plane ticket home, on the proviso that they would bring 30 kilograms of cricket equipment back with them. When his wife came to visit, he'd get her to fill a bag with cricket shoes. The initial plan was to sell cricket products to subsidise trips home. But quickly it mushroomed into something bigger.

'When the first money will come to your pocket with a profit, it will open in your mind a lot of questions,' he tells me excitedly. 'Can I buy ten? Can I buy 50?'

Ali formed a joint venture with a company that had an import licence. His first shipment was 180 kilograms of cricket shoes. Orders started to come in from more and more teams. The next shipment was 250 kilograms. Then 300, 400, 500 kilograms. He advertised on social media but didn't really need to – word of mouth was enough.

Qatar is spending an estimated $8–10 billion on World Cup stadiums. Since buying Paris Saint-Germain in 2011, the sovereign wealth fund Qatar Sports Investments has spent around $1.17 billion on players, including a world-record $262 million for the Brazilian Neymar. By contrast, the Qatar Cricket Association (QCA), the body responsible for organising the sport in Qatar, receives 700,000 rials ($192,000) a year from the government, one of its employees told me.

Cricket doesn't interest Qataris. 'They say cricket is just for Indian or Pakistanis,' lamented Yousef Al-Kuwari, the president of the QCA, when I met him. At a time when Qatar is trying to brand itself as a global sports hub, the riches bestowed on events in golf, football, tennis – even MotoGP – stand in stark contrast to the neglect of cricket.

Qatar has one internationally recognised cricket stadium, opened in 2013 in the Industrial Area. One evening I head to the ground to watch a 50-over match between the Qatar national team and Uganda. It is a bitter February night, with the biting wind that plagues Qatar in the coldest months cutting through anything that isn't a thick coat. Perhaps the weather is one reason why, despite it being free entry and a national holiday, there are barely 100 people in the ground.

I arrive to find Uganda in the field trying to defend a middling score of 266.

Once in the stadium, I walk past the Qatar bench, the next batsman padded up and practicing his cover drives, to the gazebo which holds the third umpire and members of the cricket association. Everyone is wrapped up in coats and hats and looking distinctly unimpressed at the weather.

I get chatting to an administrator with a skeletal look called Abbas*. Abbas tells me that over half of the association's annual budget – 400,000 rials – goes on renting the stadium from the contractors who built it.

But Qatar's rich, I note. 'Why can't they give you a bit more money?'

Abbas lowers his voice

'They're not giving to us ... because cricket is not recognised in their list, that is the problem.'

He pauses. I've grown to recognise such pauses. He is weighing up whether to say the thing he really wants to say or to bite his tongue.

'You know the phrase? All that glitters is not gold. You understand? A lot of money but ...'

His voice trails off. He thought better of it.

I look at the empty stands and dying grass, peppered in the outfield with numerous holes, and think to myself that the public parks in Doha are better maintained than this.

The stadium is the only turf wicket in Qatar. There are a further two grounds in the country with grass outfields, but both have artificial wickets. The paucity of grass means that the four men's cricket leagues, the school tournaments and the fledgling women's operation all play their cricket on AstroTurf wickets with sand outfields. The lack of proper facilities generates continual injuries.

'We were breaking our heads on the rocks ... I broke my bloody leg,' a retired cricketer once told me. 'From here to here. Tendon muscle,' he explained while hiking up his trouser leg to show me the scar. 'Compound fracture. Thirty-two stitches.'

'Because of the surface?'

'No proper grounds, simple as that.'

A shout goes up on the field, 'Heads up!'

A huge six comes crashing over the ropes just to our left.

I take it as my cue to depart.

L ike so many national organisations, the Qatar cricket team is made up of expatriates – in this case Indians, Sri Lankans and Pakistanis. The eligibility requirements are less stringent than football: live in Qatar for three years and you qualify to represent the country.

No players in the national team are full-time cricketers. The QCA only has the money to pay them token amounts for training and trips abroad. Consequently, all the players have day jobs. Cricket-mad South Asian businessmen in Qatar recruit players from the subcontinent to bolster their company cricket teams. They provide them with work at their businesses, but the jobs are definitely not sinecures.

Faisal Javed Khan, a Pakistani who played for the Qatar national team and a club side, told me that he walked ten kilometres a day around Doha as part of his day job. Khan worked for a construction company specialising in interior design. National team training was two evenings a week. On his one day off he would play a 50-over game for his club, before going back to his twelve-hour shifts. The routine left him continually tired.

'I'm working like an ATM machine, 24/7,' he grimaces.

The most fraught issue facing national team cricketers is getting time off work for the frequent overseas matches. When I spoke to Khan in early 2020, he told me that he was one of five national team cricketers from his company fighting to participate in a tournament in Oman.

'If there's a war in Pakistan, I should leave everything and go back to my country to serve them,' he explains. 'As a patriot, it is our duty.'

I nod uncertainly, not sure where he's going with the analogy.

'So if I'm representing Qatar, I'm also a patriot for Qatar

as well. Because they give me respect, they give me money, they give me job. In return, I want to serve them. But if their system won't allow me to serve, what will I do?'

In the past, cricketers used to *lose* money when representing the national team, as the meagre allowance never compensated the wages they lost from not doing their day jobs. That anomaly has been rectified, but national team cricketers still find it difficult to balance training, matches and work. Khan has a wife and two children in Pakistan who are reliant on his earnings.

'The world is run through money, not with the emotions only,' he tells me. 'If I give you a thumbs up all the time, could you survive in your life with the thumbs up only, without money?'

He is upset.

'Nobody can.'

When attributing responsibility for the unsteady state of cricket in Qatar, the QCA is not free from blame. The organisation could be better run. In December 2019, Qatar instituted an international ten-over tournament modelled on the Indian Premier League, involving franchises with corny names (Flying Oryx, Heat Stormers), along with garish kits and a sprinkling of top-level global cricketers. But it was scheduled to take place in Doha at the same time as the FIFA Club World Cup, leading to little media attention and sparse crowds. A local businessman was damning in his assessment: 'I was in charge of organising a football tournament for the alumni of my school. So this is only twelve teams or something, but I promoted it. And we held [the draw] in the biggest room of one of the hotels and it was packed ... So if I can do all that with an *alumni* football tournament, why can't the QCA properly organise a cricket league?' Khan was playing for one of the tournament's teams. By his account, the foreign players were paid but, three months after the tournament, the locals were still waiting to receive their appearance fees. I also heard players complain that they were overlooked because, unlike many members of the QCA, they were not Pakistani (the QCA told me that players are chosen solely on the basis of their performance in the league).

Despite the unfavourable conditions, Qatar has risen in the world T20 rankings, reaching 21st place as of January 2022. The QCA office has moved into the Olympic Tower, a skyscraper in West Bay that houses many of the sport authorities in Qatar. The hope is to qualify for a T20 World Cup.

'It's impossible,' Khan snorts. 'You are giving a banana and you asking from them the performance of lions. How can it happen?' he says. 'If you want to change anything, you need to change the system.' Khan has agitated for central contracts – the practice in other countries where the association pays the wages of the first team, allowing them to be full-time professionals. He believes that, combined with a new board, is the only way Qatar cricket will kick on.

'Otherwise this [current ranking] is the best ever achieved for Qatar,' he states. 'You can write down in your notebook. This will be the maximum rank which we had.'

When he was a child, Ali was fixated on working in a bank. At school he would see the bankers pass by, 'suited and booted and good personality', and longed to join their ranks. Ali took many exams and had many interviews but it didn't work out. He also wasn't a doctor or an engineer and therefore, despite having a master's degree in operations and management, in the eyes of most Pakistanis he was nothing special.

'I wanted to do *something*!'

His voice is getting faster and more excited.

'Then [I had] one idea – somewhere I want my name. My wish is I have some brand. Either it was a clothes brand, or a food brand, something like that.'

On the subcontinent, most cricket is played with tennis balls. In Pakistan, people cover the balls in electrical tape, causing them to fly fast, swing and pitch. In India and Sri Lanka, a special type of weighted tennis ball – often known by the name of the most successful brand, MRI – has been developed to more closely imitate the heaviness of a leather cricket ball. For the majority of South Asians in Qatar, who only have a few hours and no money to spare, tennis ball cricket reigns supreme.

The bat used to hit a tennis ball can be lighter than a regular cricket bat. To achieve greater lightness, some bats have weight-reducing holes cut into their backs – like several I'd seen in Ali's storeroom. The bat can also be longer, allowing players to dig under low balls and scoop them into the air for boundaries. Ali began importing bats specifically made for hitting tennis balls. But he wondered if there was another way.

'You know that FIFA is preparing the footballs from Pakistan?' He asks me. 'We have the best makers and factories there. So I took the initiative.'

Ali went to Sialkot.

He takes my pen. He writes 'SIALKOT' in my notebook in capitals, followed by an arrow and more words in a curly, cursive script that looks almost Hindi: 'Sports City of Pakistan.'

In Sialkot, Ali found a cricket bat maker called Kassim. He stood with him in his workshop, giving him instructions and watching as he went to work:

'I need this much weight.'

'You need to— little bit reduce the weight from there.'

'Make this much profile.'

'Hide this.'

'The handle should be this many inches.'

Kassim would make the bats in batches of 30. He would then bundle them up and drive them the two hours to Lahore where he would deliver them to Ali's brother. 'I did a lot of experiments,' Ali states. 'I spent a lot of money, but it's all from my sports business. I did not spend anything from my pocket.'

The first prototype Ali designed was a flop. Batsmen would complain about the handle and the weight. But he carried on tinkering: some bats were given short handles, others long handles; some bats were pressed hard, some not at all. The cane used in the handle of Indian-made bats comes from Kerala, but Ali decided to use cane from Malaysia, which he says has greater elasticity. Ali also gave his bats a slight curve, making it easier to play cross-shots, hitting the ball to the opposite side to the one it arrives from, a move that would make cricket traditionalists weep. It took another year, but eventually he came up with a model that satisfied him.

When I visited his stash, he pulled out the bat in question to show me. '*Alhamdulillah*, it's very famous,' he said, like an excited schoolboy. 'You can see on my Instagram, Facebook, a lot of people are giving the reviews.'

The bat has blue and grey colouring with Ali's initials in white. There is only space for two further phrases: 'Handmade in Pakistan' at the splice; and in the middle of the bat – at the point from which a ball will rifle off the willow with an effortless crack – the name he has given his creation: Long Sixer.

Ali timed his business to perfection. New tennis ball leagues were sprouting up every month in Qatar: the Nehan Premier League, Qatar International Cricket Community, Cric Qatar, Victory Cricket Club League. Filling any remaining gaps were the tournaments: at Ramadan and on Qatar National Day; the Salwa Monster tournament and the Hanan Premier League, where the prize money is so high it attracts players from India, Pakistan and Sri Lanka. All in all, Ali estimates, around 600 teams – and thousands of individuals – play cricket regularly in Qatar.

An organiser of Qatar's largest tennis ball cricket league, a Keralan called Riyaj MK, tells me over coffee that he is so in demand that he has 474 unread WhatsApp messages. 'It's all related with cricket,' he chuckles while handing me his phone for verification. 'Cricket, cricket, cricket.'

In his Qatar Expat Cricket Club (QECC) league, and more generally, cricket games unfold in car parks or on scraps of land. In some areas, teammates will chip in to hire a cement mixer to lay down a crude 22 yards of concrete so that at least the main wicket can be flat. Sometimes people do it themselves with the squares of padding found on gym floors (these do not make good wickets). The outfield is left as it is, the surface full of sand and stones. In some areas, people will lay a ring of rocks to demarcate a boundary. On other pitches they just estimate it at a certain distance. A ball hit along the ground will jump and roll or sometimes get stuck, encouraging batsmen to go for the big aerial shot. Only madmen dive after balls. On Friday mornings, most available land in Doha is full of men playing cricket.

But open land in Doha doesn't remain free for long. Building work encroaches. Pitches get reappropriated. There are always more players than available space. 'This is the *biggest* hurdle in cricket,' Ali tells me. 'Even if I have my own team, I want to play, I have my equipment but I don't have the place – where will I play?'

During my time in Qatar, I made it my goal to watch as many cricket games as possible. I followed pick-up contests on the car park outside the Al-Sadd football stadium and tennis ball league games in the central clearing in Fereej Bin Omran. I spent an afternoon at the QCA grounds in Lusail watching genteel games in the official cricket league, and caught exuberant ten-over affairs in a labour camp in the Industrial Area. Walking through the neighbourhood of Mansoura one time, I spotted a game through a gap in the wall and hopped over. Another time, I travelled an hour to Mesaieed to watch the final of an inter-company tournament.

Each game was another twist in the kaleidoscope, reveal-ing another sub-community, another grouping. It is there in the different languages the players shout at the crease and in the adverts for local businesses on the team jerseys. One cricket team near where I was staying were sponsored by the local Indian res-taurant. Every Friday, without fail, the players would go for a post-game breakfast, the highlight of which, I can confirm, was the spicy scrambled egg with piping hot chapati.

It's not all cosmopolitan harmony. When I watched a live-stream of a Qatar national team game, the worst of the subcontinent's religious strife was on display in the comments section, where some had taken to posting ultra-Hindi national-ist and anti-Muslim comments. Tennis ball cricket leagues have no female players. The pool of women cricketers in Qatar is tiny – around 70 – according to Shivani Mishra, the coach for the QCA's women's youth and national sides, and a qualified umpire in her own right.

And yet cricket in Qatar is as important for its social func-tions as its sporting ones. Hundreds of people have found work through a system of advertised openings and a CV exchange set up by Riyaj, the QECC league organiser. While teams often start life as mono-ethnic (a group of Sri Lankan friends) or mono-professional (porters who work at the same hospital), players chop and change sides. I met a Sri Lankan team whose star

batsman was Pakistani and an Indian team that included a lone Nepalese player who became involved because he lived next to where they played. All around you can glimpse the democratising effect of sporting talent: 'We don't mind if you're different so long as you make us more successful.'

One Friday, I rise at 5am to go and watch Ali play. When it's his turn to bat, he strides to the wicket twirling one of his own creations. He is not an expansive player. He has a stocky stance, his movements boxed in. But it only takes a few deliveries for him to start hoiking the ball in the air for six.

Seeing Ali with his teammates, joking and bantering, I begin to understand why people do this. Why they get up at the crack of dawn on their only day off to drive across town and either shiver or sweat through three hours of cricket, to accept the bruises on thighs and the grazes from diving.

The overwhelming majority of South Asians in Qatar are here alone. Cricket is the one time in the week when they can throw off the stress of work, the sadness that their families are a continent away and just hang out with friends. It's why millions around the world play and follow sport – that opportunity to lose yourself in something bigger.

As I watch Ali's team whoop and holler after another boundary, I recall Riyaj's self-deprecating answer as to why he spends every free minute nurturing the cricket league.

'It's a basic concept,' he said. 'I know the mentality of the people here. How they feel bad, how they are far from their family. So do something good for them. That's all it is.'

My chat with Ali goes on for almost three hours.

For most of it I've just sat and listened, so effusive and lyrical is his story. He is happy with the life he has created in Qatar. It can be hectic at times, balancing his day job with the cricket business, but he credits his faith with keeping him grounded.

'I don't need to take anything for sleeping,' Ali tells me with pride.

'When I go to my bed, in maximum three to four minutes I will be asleep.' He contrasts this ease with the experience of his bosses. 'I saw my owners. They are millionaires, they have the flats in England, they have the property in Canada, OK?'

He lowers his voice.

'*But they cannot sleep.*'

Ali tells me the aphorism that he lives by: 'The customer and death – both can come any time!' It's important not to try to second-guess the customer, he explains. Sometimes the highest sales are during off-season; someone who comes into his shop without proper shoes could buy 5,000 rials of material in one go.

Equally, a valued customer can disappear overnight. Ali's business offers a reminder of the acute precarity of any operation in Qatar aimed at migrants. 'The peoples who are playing cricket, they are all expats. So we cannot invest in full-time,' he says. Cricket has the misfortune of being popular among the wrong people. 'We can go any time. One year, two years, three years, four years,' Ali exclaims. 'We don't know. We are not permanent here. Permanent is our own country.'

The impermanence stretches right to the top. In April 2020, there was talk that the QCA might have to abandon their playing fields near Lusail as the government repurposed the site to build a military hospital. They were being given a plot of land far outside Doha in Rawdat Rashed. The QCA planned to address some of the deficiencies of the old site at this new location by seeding multiple grass pitches. But Abbas, the QCA administrator, told me he did not expect to be able to afford any permanent buildings nor any floodlights to allow games to take place at night (essential in the summer when hot weather makes it impossible to play during the day).

Ali has no plans to go home just yet.

When he does eventually return to Pakistan, he now knows what he'll do – he'll run a cricket business of course, but one which will export to the Gulf. 'The money's only in Gulf,' he tells me. 'If I sell ten bats in Pakistan, if I will sell one bat in Qatar or Dubai I will make the same money.'

Before we depart, Ali wants to tell me about the Pakistani bat maker in Lahore who has a bat drying room with some 10,000 bats. People visit from as far away as England and Australia, says Ali. They step out of his shop having spent 800,000 Pakistani rupees (around $4,500) in one fell swoop, so good is his equipment.

'I want to be like that,' announces Ali.

'The people will tell [of] me... He is king of the bat.'

10 'I'm not "your maid". I am Maggie!'

As the plane came over Doha, the desert looked beautiful. A vast expanse of flat sand, turning from yellow to copper in the fading sun.

Maggie, however, wasn't under any false illusions. The agent had not lied to her. She knew life in Qatar was going to be hard. She would not be going to church or anywhere else. She would be working throughout.

Stepping through the sliding doors into the cacophonous arrivals' hall, Maggie was met by her sponsor, a grinning white New Zealander. She was put in the car and driven to the house.

The door clicked. Maggie's eyes passed over the furnishings as she took in the size of the place. Her gaze came to rest on the family. It was her first time living and working in somebody else's house. She was afraid.

Maggie was handed a list of tasks. Wake at 5.45am. Prepare the breakfast for son and mother before they leave for school and work. Continue with housework until the three-year-old girl wakes up. Feed her, change her, bathe her – all the while washing, ironing, cleaning.

The girl would not come near Maggie. She recoiled from this stranger, refusing to be fed or washed. The mother would come home and comment on the bit-part cleaning, the unfinished ironing. The daughter would be crying. Maggie would be despairing. Sad thoughts of her own daughter back home meshed with the burden of her responsibility to this new family. The stress was so overwhelming that she felt continually drained.

Maggie never thought she would live and work abroad.

She was settled in Kenya, living in the informal settlement of Kibera in Nairobi where hundreds of thousands are packed into a few square kilometres of makeshift housing. Maggie looked after her young daughter and took care of their home. Her husband worked as a pastry chef, until his unexpected death wrenched life onto a different track.

Maggie now had to earn. She started working in sales for a telecommunications firm. The job required travelling from shop to shop and city to city throughout Kenya and Tanzania. But it didn't bring in enough.

Her brother-in-law had a friend in Doha, an agent recruiting domestic workers. He told her to think about her daughter's school fees, the hairdressing salon she'd always wanted to open – this was her chance.

Before she could set off, Maggie needed to be prepared for entry to the international system. To get a passport she needed a baptism certificate. And to get a baptism certificate she needed a copy of her parents' ID. They lived in Kajiado County, outside Nairobi. It took three months of chasing, requesting and photocopying until she had the right documents.

Her newly categorised self shone back from the photo page of her passport. The visa was obtained and stamped. Now she could leave.

In floods of confused tears, Maggie entrusted her daughter to her deceased husband's family. She headed to the airport and boarded a plane for her new life.

Six years later, Maggie is talking to me from the bar of one of Doha's bland mid-range hotels. She is sat with another Kenyan domestic worker, Caroline*. Dressed in bright reds and greens in African patterns, they look out of place among the pasty-faced Europeans and metallic grey of the smokers' balcony. The women don't know each other – we have all been brought together by a workers' rights activist.

Our meeting was meant to be a collective conversation, but Maggie is stealing the show. In strident, assertive language she is explaining for me what any woman starting a new job in a home in Qatar should expect.

'First of all, they will take your passport.'

A 2020 report by Amnesty International based on discussions with 105 domestic workers in Qatar found that 83 per cent of them had had their passports confiscated.

'If you say you want to go back home they don't care,' says Maggie. 'They will ask you for visa money, ticket money – everything. And it will cost like 8,000 Qatari rials [$2,200].' Money that most don't have.

'You just carry on, you pray hard,' Maggie continues. 'You have to let God intervene in everything.'

There are approximately 176,000 officially registered domestic workers in Qatar, the majority female. Often referred to as 'maids', domestic workers run the homes of middle- and upper-class migrants and also many locals. Their tasks include cooking, cleaning and raising children. Most domestic workers live with their host family but there are some housed in compounds and working for agencies.

I had seen domestic workers in Qatar only on their public outings – the Indonesian woman in her 'uniform' of shapeless pyjamas being shouted at by the family sat across from me in a restaurant; the Filipina nanny at a football match trying in vain to stop the kids kicking the seats. The reasons that made it so hard for me to find and speak to domestic workers are the same reasons that make them the most vulnerable people in Qatar: their work takes place out of sight, beyond the walls of large villas and the concierge desks of towers in the sky.

Domestic workers are subject to the restrictive *kafala* system of labour sponsorship that affects all migrants in Qatar. Unlike others, however, they have been systematically left outside the scope of improvements. They face a high risk of exploitation and a triple whammy of discrimination: as low-income workers, as people of colour, and as women. It is the migrant construction workers who command the newspaper headlines. But at least the men in their overcrowded dormitories have some camaraderie. These women usually work alone.

As Maggie talks, the story takes on the all-too-familiar contours of so many conversations I have had in Qatar. Before coming she was told that she would get 1,100 rials a month, but when she arrived it turned out to be 800 ($220). Some domestic workers are brought to Qatar on the wrong visas: business, family, tourist. Even those with the right immigration status often don't have employment contracts. As with construction work, contract substitution – where employees sign a contract in their home country only to be presented with a different, less favourable one once they arrive – is rife.

Maggie found herself wondering: who was this family that she worked for? Such strange beliefs! The mother would never lock the bathroom door when she was in the shower. Girls could go to the toilet with their father. It was a far cry from Kenya, and it disturbed Maggie. She would look on wide-eyed as the children's friends refused to eat and dress, threw tantrums or screamed at their parents to shut up without a word of condemnation. Such unpunished behaviour meant that Maggie, too, was told to shut up by her charges. Called stupid. Even physically abused.

But it was the objectification that was the most upsetting.

'Most of the people, they will not call you your name ... she will introduce you: "Hey, this is my maid." I'm not, I am Maggie!'

Maggie speaks through barely controlled indignation.

'Of course I'm working as a maid but I have a name! You are a teacher, do I go and introduce you, "Hey, this is a teacher." You see? But a maid, they always introduce us – most of them they don't say, "Oh, hi, meet my house help Maggie," or "Meet Maggie." They just say simply, "Hey, this is my maid." At that time they're not even looking at you, they are just pointing.'

Maggie would tell herself to choke down the humiliation. Put a smile on her face, pray to God and remember the bigger picture: I am going through this so that my daughter will never have to. When Maggie felt bad she would count her blessings. At least her *madam* spoke English. Two other women that she came to Qatar with ended up working in Arabic-only households. They would call up Maggie in tears having been shouted at for misunderstanding an instruction. Maggie would calm them down, but inside she was afraid. 'Because the story we hear is that if you don't do something well, if they don't like you, they will kill you or they will throw you from a balcony.'

The worst cases of abuse from the Middle East are etched in workers' minds: Ethiopian Lensa Lelisa, 21, who jumped from a balcony breaking both her legs to avoid abuse. Joanna Demafelis, 29, whose body was found in her employer's freezer more than a year after she was reported missing. Tuti Tursilawati, 34, executed for killing her Saudi employer after he tried to sexually abuse her.

Maggie looked on with dismay, watching proud, fun-filled individuals objectified and crushed. 'Here you are caged, you are being told to do this and do that ... you see yourself like you are no good,' she says. 'We lost self-esteem and most of domestic worker are always stressed and depressed.'

'You find most of the people who are sick in Doha, in all Gulf countries, are domestic workers,' says Maggie. 'If you go to cancer places, there are many of them. Depressed. Most of them are there.'

While Maggie talks there is no fidgeting from Caroline. She seems equally captivated by the excoriating account in which no one is spared.

'I don't know whether it is only in Africa but people think that we make a *huge* amount of money,' she scoffs. 'It's unbelievable. [They will] text you, even in the middle of the month and they will ask, "Give me 200 rial." At that time you have nothing. Even you don't have 10 rial to buy yourself a [phone] card to check on your family.'

I expected family back home to be a source of succour. Turns out I was very wrong.

'They will *think* you are earning four times of the money you send,' Maggie tells me. 'No matter how you explain to them, they think you are lying. And if you go back with nothing, you are the talk of the day.'

If anything, her criticism of family is more trenchant than that of her employers.

'You expect them to support you. You expect them to understand you. But they don't ... by the end of the month you go on a tree and shake and the money will fall off, that's what['s] on their mind.'

Suddenly the jet of exasperation is switched off.

'I will not judge them. I was thinking the same when I was back in Kenya.'

And why not? In the photos they post on Facebook, domestic workers are dressed well, browsing Doha's malls or posing against the backdrop of its skyscrapers. So, if you ask a relative in Qatar for 1,000 rials and they send only 50, of course you'll take the money. But you'll start having other thoughts: maybe they are being proud; they think they have done well in life and they don't want to share their rewards. When Maggie has her cold chapati and cup of tea for dinner while talking on the phone, her mum laughs. 'No, you're not! You're eating chicken, meat – *nice food* like in the movies in big hotels.'

'I can feel it on her tongue, she did not believe,' Maggie tells me ruefully. 'I try to tell them, "Sometimes we sacrifice for you guys."'

Throughout the conversation there is something I cannot place. Some deeper current driving what Maggie is saying. And then I realise that it is anger. It gently inflames every sentence, like a small pebble stuck in your shoe.

'Try to imagine, back home you have freedom even if you don't have money. Even if you're going to eat *ugali* and *sukuma*,' – maize flour porridge and collard greens, the cheapest food in Kenya. 'Even if that's what you're going to eat from Sunday to Monday *you have this opportunity*. But here you can't.'

She pauses. The next comment comes from an altogether more mournful place.

'You are living in a big house – very beautiful. The country's rich but what you're carrying within you is totally different.'

Caroline, quiet for so long, begins to speak. After Maggie's rapier-like voice, hers feels emollient.

'I realised there is a church. I didn't know there are churches in Arab countries.'

She asked the lady of the house for a day off to go to church. Her sponsors were a Tunisian couple with three children. She would work for them every day from 6am until midnight. They refused her request. But Caroline wouldn't let it rest. She learnt that, as an African woman, she was being paid the least and treated the worst. The Arab domestic workers got at least 1,000 rials. The Filipinas 1,300, sometimes even 1,500, and a day off. Caroline began to push back.

'There are people who are going to church, why not me? So I went, checked Google and then found the labour laws.'

Until 2017, Qatar's labour protections completely excluded domestic workers. In August of that year, the country ratified a domestic workers' law, enshrining such provisions as a maximum ten-hour workday, a weekly day off and annual paid leave. But in a familiar refrain, the issue is not the absence of legislation but the implementation. Three years after the passage of the law, Amnesty revealed that 85 per cent of domestic workers they spoke to still did not have a weekly day off and 86 per cent worked more than fourteen hours per day.

Laws relating to domestic workers have been the last to be enacted and the worst enforced. 'The abolishment of NOCs [Non-Objection Certificates] was much easier than removing exit permits for domestic workers,' an expert in the legislation told me. 'Because you're fucking with their house, with their castle,' he explained, referring to the Qataris who benefit from the labour of these women in their own homes. 'The NOC, it's just money. A business.' There is a weird paradox. No work is more important than domestic work – raising children, looking after a household. And no work is more intimate. It seems, therefore, that it cannot be classified as work, with the state renouncing the authority to reach behind closed doors. An activist who campaigns for domestic workers told me that many employers don't even believe that new laws have been passed. 'You hear comments, "Oh no, maybe that's a scam, it's not for *real*,"' she said drolly.

Caroline read up on what she was entitled to as a domestic worker, getting increasingly angry. She took the laws to her sponsor and demanded that they wrote a formal contract, gave her a day off and raised her wage. They refused. She lowered her demands. 'Just give me some more hours to go to church,' she pleaded. 'Better I have some free time to relax my mind than subject your kids to all my stress.' The husband agreed that she could go to church for two hours on a Friday, coming straight back home afterwards.

In the two years she had been in Qatar, attending church was the best thing that had happened to Caroline. After being cooped up all week in the house, unable to escape from the

family, the two hours of freedom were transformative. She would look forward to it all week. When the time came, the taxi ride was like a spaceship to another world. In the church, she would sing and dance and worship with increased abandon.

But the family were not happy.

'They tried many ways to stop it,' Caroline tells me. Tasks were invented that absolutely had to take place at the same time on a Friday. But Caroline, with a mix of defiance and charm, would sidestep and complete them afterwards. So the *madam* upped the ante. She mentioned loudly that valuable items were going missing. One time she accused Caroline of stealing money.

'She came to my room and told me, "Caroline, I cannot see my 1,000 Qatari rial. So, if you don't get it tomorrow, I'll tell my husband to call the police."'

Caroline was on the phone with her sister, who heard the exchange.

'Make sure your room doesn't have that money!' she hissed.

Caroline rifled through drawers and under the mattress, making sure that the money hadn't been planted in her possessions. A few minutes later, the *madam* came back to tell her, thank God, that she had found the cash. Caroline was seething.

'Thank God? You can't tell me *sorry*? Just, "Thank God, I found the money?"'

Her face is full of animation, as if she's experiencing the gall for the first time.

'I started looking for a plane to go home that night.'

The next day Caroline packed up her belongings and the family escorted her to the airport. She boarded a flight for Kenya, and the first unhappy chapter of her Qatar life came to a close.

After four years with the New Zealand family, Maggie wanted to move on. No longer an ingénue, she now knew how to get a better job with more money and fewer hours. She found a Qatari woman willing to sell a work permit for 3,000 rials a year. Such trade in work permits is illegal but common. As long as you pay your fee, the sponsor leaves you to hustle for your own work. For two years it worked. Maggie rented her own place and laboured for a single father, until the government discovered the sponsor's enterprise and blacklisted her. Maggie's permit expired and couldn't be renewed. The sponsor, seemingly out of spite, wouldn't give her a NOC to move jobs. She was stuck.

Maggie ended up in a deportation centre on the outskirts of Doha. Unable to obtain an exit visa, her only way home was through the centre. The place was messy, crowded with over 60 women. Some were pregnant – sex outside marriage is a criminal offence in Qatar and, for many women from poorer countries, results in detention. Others were in pain. One woman at the detention centre could not open her hands. She had been forced to clean with bleach products without any protection. Every day more people would arrive.

The women would be grilled by the police.

'Your sponsor said you are a runaway,' they told Maggie.

'No, I'm not a runaway. She refused to renew my ID.'

Under Qatari law, you can charge a person under your sponsorship with 'absconding' from their duties. Absconding charges are almost never used for their primary purpose – to report a worker who is not showing up for work. Instead, they are used to limit movement. To flex power and show who is boss. If a worker asks for an NOC to change jobs: file an absconding charge. If they ask for a pay rise: file an absconding charge. 'The very use of this terminology of "absconding" ... points to the indentured or coercive labour conditions that are the reality for too many low-income workers in Qatar,' concluded the UN special rapporteur on racism in a 2020 report on the country. 'It also recalls the historical reliance on enslaved and coerced labour in the region.'

The abuse of absconding charges is a key example of how new laws designed to help workers are often undermined. From August 2020, workers no longer needed NOCs to move jobs. But instead of resulting in employers letting their workers go more easily, the change led to an increase in the numbers falsely charged with absconding, a person familiar with the process told me.

Some workers really do run away. When things get too much, when they've been beaten or sexually abused or feel their life is in danger, they will abscond. They run to embassies. They run to priests. Community organisations offer support in the form of a sofa for a few weeks. If they're lucky, women who flee find a place in an already overfull embassy shelter or receive help after filing a case at the Ministry of Labour. Still, nearly everyone eventually ends up being deported.

But Maggie had not run away. And she would never sign any of the papers the officials at the detention centre pushed at her or agree to any of the things they were suggesting. She was brought in front of a detention officer to tell her story. And again the next day. And the day after that – endless repetitions as the authorities looked forensically for any inconsistencies in her account. If they found one, they would take her sponsor's version of events as gospel. 'Most of the ladies, they find themselves they have been blacklisted from coming back here for *nothing*,' Maggie says. 'For *nothing*. Just because your sponsor came and said, "She was like this and like this, I don't want her back again."'

Maggie was fortunate. She had a contact at the Kenyan embassy who collected her belongings from her apartment and brought them to the centre. Most women can't retrieve their possessions. The bags, the clothes, the shiny passports – acquired at such expense and struggle – stay at their sponsors' homes, where they were often illegally taken from them when they arrived. In those cases, embassies hastily issue temporary passports, women are pushed onto flights and sent home.

'Most of the ladies they go home just the way they enter to the deportation centre ... just like the way I am,' Maggie sweeps her hand across her current outfit. Dress. Sandals. Handbag.

'When they get to Kenya they don't have... even coins to buy phone cards to call their family that I'm at the airport.'

After six days at the detention centre, it was Maggie's turn to go home. The friend who dropped off her belongings had given her 500 rials. Maggie knew her brother in Nairobi would be able to come and pick her up from the airport, so she divided the money and her possessions among the other women at the centre: sanitary pads for some (none were provided by the centre), pants for others, money for three Kenyan women who lived in Mombasa and would need an eight-hour bus ride to reach home.

The guards then escorted Maggie to Hamad International Airport and put her on a flight.

'I used to complain about my life ... but when you went there ...'

She exhales long and viciously. A breath to dispel a nightmare.

That could have been that. Unceremoniously returned home, both Maggie and Caroline could have reverted to their old lives. But they are the ones that pushed back. 'I was not ready to go home,' Caroline states defiantly.

Being back home was made worse by the stigma attached to being employed as a domestic worker in the Middle East. 'When you're at home and you tell someone I'm [working] in an Arabic nation, back of [their] mind it's torture,' says Caroline. Envy for their perceived wealth is mixed with pity – bordering on shame – for the abuse they are deemed to have suffered to acquire it. 'Many women don't mention what they do. Better not to stress their family and friends or leave them wondering if they'll go to work in the Gulf and come back in a coffin.'

But both Maggie and Caroline knew that they couldn't make money in Kenya like they did in Qatar. Caroline went on Facebook and posted in some groups.

That evening, I scroll through the groups that Caroline mentions: Maids in Qatar, Qatar Maids, Home Help. They are full of 'wanted' adverts posted by families in Qatar. Although barely 50 words in length, these ads seem to convey with uncanny prescience exactly how the recruits will be treated:

> *Only duty is house cleaning. Individual room with*
> *bathroom available. Free Wi-Fi of course and Food. She*
> *has to be Muslim Philippine. Responsible, trustworthy,*
> *neat, and easy to communicate with … No day out during*
> *corona pandemic. After that one day off with some rules.*

> *Urgently looking for a live in filipina baby sitter to start*
> *immediately … no fake agents/no run aways.*

Underneath each post, I found replies of varying desperation:

> *Interested madam im here.*

> *Cheek inbox madam pls i have own visa.*

A cursory browse lays bare the racialised hierarchy: Filipinas at the top; Muslims also popular; black African Christians at the bottom.

Caroline found a Lebanese woman needing a nanny and they talked. Caroline told her everything that had happened, warts and all, and outlined her requirements: a day off each week, 1,200 rials a month. The woman was sympathetic and agreed to sponsor her to return.

Maggie also came back. She had lined up a job working at the home of a family with an autistic child, but when it came to obtaining a visa she found out that she was blocked. Her former sponsor refused to sign an NOC, preventing Maggie from working legally for anyone else in Qatar for two years. After some frantic phone calls, she eventually convinced the sponsor to sign the document. All it took was what is normally needed in these situations.

'I paid for it,' Maggie explains bitterly.

Three-thousand Qatari rials, $825. It took all her savings just to obtain the right to work for someone else.

When I meet Maggie and Caroline in the hotel bar in Doha, both are in jobs they like, with reasonable sponsors, earning a fair wage.

Maggie has become a representative of domestic workers in Doha. She is filled with an evangelical zeal to educate women as to their rights to ensure that others don't have to go through what she went through. These are women like the one in Maggie's compound who has worked for the same family for four years without a day off. She doesn't eat well and comes to Maggie's in the evenings to cook with her. The woman is not allowed to go to the shop or to send money home without supervision.

'I tried to remove that fear,' tells Maggie. 'You educate them: this is your right, this is how you're supposed to approach your sponsor. You do this and this.'

Since her intervention, Maggie says, the woman's situation has changed. But not in a good way: they're now accusing her of stealing the son's passport. None of this fazes Maggie.

'She had fear before,' she says. 'Now she's trying to come out of fear and she approached them. Now they're trying to make her fear again ... to make her silent so that she cannot speak.'

Mention the plight of domestic workers to Qataris and they often respond in a prickly fashion – as if the criticism is aimed at them personally. 'The Qatari people ... we have a kind of passion and caring for the others,' the academic Dr Hend Abdulrahman Al-Muftah told a panel discussing migrant workers that I attended. She was visibly annoyed by the negative takes of the other panellists. 'We always deal with our domestic helpers and assistant[s] as one of our family,' she added. 'We shouldn't always look at the negative side of such relations.'

That might be true. The stories of abuse and exploitation I heard from Maggie, Caroline and others involved New Zealanders, Tunisians, Egyptians and other foreign residents. But Qatari nationals can't absolve themselves of responsibility. It was a Qatari sponsor that engaged in the illegal practice of selling a visa to Maggie. It was the Qatari government that refused to include domestic workers in its wider reforms to the labour law, eventually generating a separate, weaker regulation to govern them. Qatar has sought to emphasise improvements to the treatment of domestic workers, but speak to workers themselves or the charities that support them and they will tell you that it hasn't made a difference.

Maggie tells me she is currently supporting a woman who was beaten by her sponsor so hard that they broke her tooth and she developed back problems. Given the severity of the treatment, the case should have been classified as an emergency. But in five months, neither Maggie nor the woman has had any updates from the court, the police or any other branch of the Qatari state.

In the meantime, such women can barely get by.

'Remember, you are not working because you cannot go back to your sponsor *who beat you*,' says Maggie fiercely. 'You have some injury. So you have to go outside. Live on your own. Find how you're going to survive.'

Maggie has come to appreciate that her main task is stepping in for an absent state. 'I have to find her a job to work and to try to survive,' she says. The most important aspect of Maggie's role is bringing domestic workers together to combat isolation and share information. She paraphrases the response of the women to these group meetings: 'Now I went out stressed, and then I will go back home feeling relieved because she has told me something that will help me.'

I think of the other person I know in Qatar who has managed to claw their way into a decent job – the health and safety officer Abu Yusuf. He is also from an African nation. I ask Maggie and Caroline if it is possible for an African to succeed in Qatar.

There is a long pause at the table.

'It could be possible,' says Caroline in an uncertain voice. 'But I've not met someone who has really succeeded.'

Caroline furrows her brow and modifies her answer. If you have a good education, then Qatar could be great – the best place for anyone. 'But coming here as a domestic worker, then moving from domestic [work] to something else ... it's—'

Maggie cuts in. She has no time for daydreams.

'I normally tell them, just take whatever's on the table. Don't look for a title. Because if you find yourself as a domestic worker, trying to be a security [guard] is adding another problem for you.'

Maggie is warming to her theme.

'Most of us, we don't come to terms that I'm a domestic worker ... in our hearts we want to be security, we want to be a secretary, we want to be a waitress.'

Her words are no-nonsense. One day she'll go home. But not yet. There is still much work to do.

Maggie sits up more proudly in her chair.

'Me, I don't hide. I don't hide even back home what I do.'

11

'It's just really sad if this is what news is'

It is a Saturday afternoon.

As is the case with an alarming number of my weekends, I am spending it at a competition featuring falcons.

The morning spectators have gone, the evening ones yet to arrive. Everyone has slumped into the hours of lethargy that the heat scours out of the day.

Muhannad* bumps into me outside of a Portakabin office. Tall and smiley, his response is completely different to everyone else I meet – he actually looks interested when I explain that I'm here to learn about traditional Qatari sports. Then he explains that he is a journalist covering the event and I understand why.

'Perhaps we can do interview?' he suggests.

'Sure.' I grab a brochure produced by the tournament organisers and make myself comfortable on a seat while he disappears into the Portakabin.

A short while later, Muhannad re-emerges. I sit up straight, clear my throat and prepare to pontificate on the day's events. I am somewhat taken aback by what comes next.

'I have quoted you for the story,' he tells me with a smile.

'Oh. What happened to the interview?' I ask. 'You just made something up?'

'Yes, like the championship is good and this and that,' Muhannad twirls his arms, their movement aimed at conveying the insignificance of what he's done.

'Er—'

Perhaps sensing my hesitancy, he says that he'll send the article when it's published.

I ask if I could possibly see it before.

'Oh yes, of course!'

After a few seconds, Muhannad appears again, this time carrying an open laptop. Balancing it on one hand, he scrolls with the other, showing me words on a screen in Arabic and translating:

'Here, you are saying, "The championship is good and I wish all the teams to—"'

He's struggling to find the words in English.

'I wish them luck?'

'Yes, yes, that!'

Muhannad likes my translation of my own words.

'See – just these two lines, no more!'

I weigh up my options. I could make a fuss and demand that he remove it. But it seems benign enough, and anyway I might need him to help me speak to the organisers.

After writing down my full name – we don't want the quote misattributed! – Muhannad turns to go. I ask what news organisation he works for, reckoning that I may as well keep an eye out for the piece. He shouts his answer breezily as he disappears inside.

'All of them!'

For more than two decades, Qatar has been presenting itself as the epicentre of debate, dialogue and discussion in the Middle East. It is home to Al-Jazeera, the satellite news service that shook up global news. Doha has created and hosted a series of frank debates broadcast by the BBC on topics such as freedom of speech, women's rights and religious extremism. It houses prominent global think tanks, the branch campuses of US universities and not one but two huge conference centres that have played host to events including World Trade Organization (WTO) talks and the COP UN Climate Change Conference. Dubai might have stolen a march on tourism and consumption, the argument runs, but Qatar can be the creative hub and centre of intellectual innovation in the Gulf. 'We want freedom of speech for the people of the region,' declared Sheikh Tamim in a 2017 interview with US television.

Just as long as those people aren't Qatar's own citizens and residents. Flick through the papers in Doha or turn on the car radio and the country's stance on openness takes on a very different hue. For all its positioning as an open, global state, Qatar is a place where freedom of speech is highly restricted. Most news organisations are either state-owned or state-affiliated. Qatar's media laws are censorious. The stifling of independent journalism reflects a deeper illiberalism in the structure of the country. Qatar is not a democracy. Freedom of assembly is constrained.

The Romans used to worship a God called Janus, who was the guardian of transitions – of war and peace, of journeys, of birth. He is usually represented as having two faces looking in opposite directions. Qatar's take on freedom of expression seems equally Janus-like: organisations can say what they want externally but face censure if they turn that critical lens on Qatar; media coverage in English says one thing and in Arabic another. My encounter with Muhannad's 'interview' technique was the tip of the iceberg. For many individuals, one of the hardest elements of living successfully in Qatar is adapting to its strange free/not-free public culture and making peace with the ever-changing rules. Some are better at it than others.

'I've said many times, if you work at NUQ you have the longest elevator pitch of any of the universities here, because we're a media school in a country that does not have free media.'

Craig LaMay is a professor at Northwestern University in Qatar (NUQ). A former journalist back home in the US, LaMay taught at Northwestern's Medill School of Journalism in Chicago when, in 2017, an offer came to spend some time at the university's Doha campus.

Northwestern is one of eight elite universities (six American, one French, one British) that opened outposts at Education City, a huge campus on the edge of Doha devoted to learning. It is fully funded by the Qatar Foundation, a non-profit owned by the government and headed by Sheikha Moza and Sheikha Hind – the mother and sister of the current emir. Education is one strand of Qatar's ambitious strategy to build soft power globally, at the same time as preparing Qatar for a post-hydrocarbon future. In return for their outposts in Qatar, the main US universities receive multi-million-dollar consulting fees. While Texas A&M offers engineering degrees and Weill Cornell training in medicine, Northwestern's remit is more problematic: it is supposed to teach journalism and communication in a country with no free press.

Journalistic restriction might not be immediately apparent to the casual visitor to Qatar. Walk into a coffee shop and you'll see a host of daily newspapers in both Arabic and English. But open more than one of them and you'll find that the content is almost identical, consisting mostly of press releases. The one independent news organisation, the website Doha News, found itself blocked in 2016 (it has since been revived under new ownership). Qatar's law governing the media dates from 1979 and contains multiple restrictions, including a prohibition on quoting the emir without official permission. The law gives the government the right to 'delete any paragraph, article, research or comment' that it believes touches these banned subjects. Penalties for violation can be both fines and imprisonment. Qatar ranks 128 out of 180 in the Reporters Without Borders 2021 World Press Freedom Index – behind Hungary, Uganda and Afghanistan but ahead of India and Turkey.

Northwestern University is emblematic of many organisations in Qatar in that it is forever operating in a grey area. There is no state or institutional censorship of teaching. Academics can – and do – get into meaty discussions in their classes, which contain students from all around the world. The gleaming multi-million-dollar campus hosts exhibitions and events in which speakers talk uncensored on a range of topics (full disclosure: I received an honorarium for chairing one such panel on sports media in 2020). And yet Northwestern students can't actually do any real journalism. When they step out of the doors to try to practice reporting, they are frequently prevented. Their public pronouncements on social media – like everyone's in Qatar – are monitored and occasionally subject to hate mobs.

LaMay has been detained twice during his time in Qatar – once trying to visit a football stadium and once interviewing members of the public in Doha's touristic downtown. It's a lot harder for his students, many of whom come from all over the world. 'There is white privilege here,' says LaMay. 'If you're a journalism student from Ethiopia and you get picked up by the police it's harder ... if I'm a Pakistani kid or a Filipino kid I might think twice about going out to film.' Students have also been detained for tweeting comments critical of Qatar. They are pulled in by the authorities, forced to give access to their electronic devices and, if they're non-nationals, threatened with deportation. There are also limits to what Northwestern can do on its campus. In January 2020, a talk with Lebanese band Mashrou' Leila was relocated to the US after an outcry on Qatari social media. The band's lead singer is openly gay, and their lyrics tackle topics such as sectarianism and homophobia. After initially holding firm, Northwestern capitulated when they were informed that, if the band arrived in Doha, their security could not be guaranteed.

I should say that, in researching this book, I faced no serious problems myself, I believe in part because I knew what the red lines were and approached sensitive topics obliquely. Additionally, I could operate with the freedom that comes with not having my job, family situation or long-term plan tied to Qatar. It is also worth mentioning that Western academia – historically and today – is not as free and liberal as it likes to think it is, as evidenced by fierce debates over decolonising curricula, the questionable origin of many university donations and a history of surveillance of students and staff deemed to be dissidents. The scholar Neha Vora has noted that there is a particular brand of Western academic who, normally with no knowledge of the Middle East, looks critically on projects like Education City while remaining oblivious to their complicity in forms of exclusion and orientalism back home. It's hard at times when parsing the criticism of Education City to avoid the whiff of Muslim or Arab prejudice.

Yet there have to be lingering questions over the presence of Western universities in Qatar. 'These governments only want to produce their own narrative and their own knowledge,' said Dr Abdullah Baabood, a visiting scholar at the National University of Singapore, at an event I attended on academic freedom in the Gulf. 'And only if you subscribe to that are you then recognised as someone who can be promoted ... or even get a job at a university.' The parlous state of free speech, combined with the pressure universities feel if their employees stray from the script, begs the question of whether the financial fillip is worth the logistical headaches, reputational damage and moral ambiguity that come with setting up campuses in the Gulf.

This backdrop may come as a surprise to the outsider who only knows Qatar through Al-Jazeera. Launched in 1996, by then emir Sheikh Hamad, the broadcaster put Qatar on the map through its radical departure from TV news in the Arab world. It offered something genuinely different to Arabic-speaking audiences, inviting pugnacious guests and broadcasting arguments that departed from government lines. Al-Jazeera English – launched in 2006 – extended this reputation globally, providing an important counter to the uncritiqued Western stance of 'global' news. Al-Jazeera reported critically on the US-led invasion of Iraq in 2003 and the wider 'war on terror', drawing the ire of American governments in the process. It supported the 2011 Tunisian, Egyptian and Syrian uprisings that came to be known as the Arab Spring. And it has run shows described by commentators as 'sensationalist', 'provocative' and 'controversial'. Its headquarters in Doha house a multinational group of reporters, including many from Arab states, doing good journalism.

But Al-Jazeera is more timid when it comes to reporting on Qatar. When its editorial lines can dovetail with government policy it is happy to broadcast a story, such as during the 2017 diplomatic crisis when one of the demands of the blockading countries was for Qatar to shut down Al-Jazeera. The channel reported widely from a three-day conference held in Doha to decry this external attempt to limit free speech. Yet on matters of domestic press freedom or other thorny internal issues, Al-Jazeera often remains silent. Its foreign coverage is also not as independent as it might seem. While Al-Jazeera loudly supported the Egyptian and Tunisian people in 2011, there was silence on the civil disobedience taking place in Bahrain. It seems that the uprising in the Gulf emirate, which lies just 40 kilometres north-west of Qatar, was too close to home for Doha to support.

'It's naive to think that Al-Jazeera is there to be a beacon for free press,' one PR manager who worked for the company told me. 'That's what they might *say*, but in reality it's a soft power play, 100 per cent. The agenda comes from the government, it's not like they allow them to find news.' He corrects himself – obviously on some matters the journalists have free reign. 'But on specific topics, you get the script just like everybody else: you don't get to report on news, you get to cover what we tell you to cover.'

The more you look across the Qatar media landscape, the more you notice a pattern. Progressive initiatives, from reforming labour laws to establishing think tanks, are announced to great fanfare. Once attention is elsewhere, however, there is little follow-up reporting and many of the initiatives are left unenforced or quietly discontinued. In 2008, the Doha Center for Media Freedom was established, its mandate to support free speech and journalism in the region. But after a year, the director quit in protest at the restrictions on his operations (it limped on in piecemeal fashion until 2019 when it was finally put out of its misery). Part of the issue is that enterprises such as Al-Jazeera or the Doha Center for Media Freedom are conceived and enacted by the elite. They garner no support in Qatar outside of a small cadre and are often viewed with outright hostility by more conservative citizenry. Qatar seems to follow the playbook of getting the PR boost of good headlines internationally, before then pivoting away to avoid grumbles from the local population. 'There's this habit of these rulers making pronouncements of change and they come to nothing. Just nothing,' Craig LaMay tells me. 'They're paper documents at best, pronouncements at worst, but there's no actual change.'

Understanding the government's take on free expression frequently involves submersing oneself in a world of doublethink. The Qatari foreign minister will announce to an international audience, 'We think that keeping independent news and information from the eyes and ears of the people only demonstrates fear and weakness.' But tell that to the student at Northwestern who, in 2012, reported on a deadly blaze in a shopping mall that became a highly sensitive issue after severe failings in fire safety were revealed. The fledgling reporter was arrested and detained for ten days as a result of his work. The contradictions don't just affect those working in the media. A British primary school teacher once told me that he's not allowed to mention Christmas to the students, given its non-Islamic character. This was despite working at a British school whose Qatari pupils would fly to London every December, go to the Christmas markets and visit Santa's grotto at Harrods.

The past decade has seen a steady decline in media freedom everywhere, including in the US and Europe. But in Qatar, as in the Gulf more widely, the nature of the punishment for erring – prison, deportation – makes the stakes much higher. 'It's become extremely difficult as a Gulf citizen,' said Abdullah Baabood, who along with being a professor of Gulf politics is himself Omani. 'There are countries that now you cannot even think of travelling to, because you expressed your opinion in a conference ... or tweeted this or that ... Our safety, our security is being tested at the moment. And I think that is really fearful for all of us.' Given the stakes, it should come as no surprise that a pernicious culture of self-censorship has arisen among academics and journalists. It's better to leave out that name or that risqué anecdote, some feel, in return for a quieter life.

It is this general acquiescence to the presence of no-go topics that most shocked LaMay. In his journalism career he has reported from wars in the Balkans and transitions to democracy in South-east Asia and Central America. 'I've worked in authoritarian countries before, where it's just been a hostile environment for reporters and being one puts you at risk,' he tells me. 'That's not the way it is here. Here you have just this culture of compliance.'

On the 2nd December 2010 in Zürich, Switzerland, an envelope was opened by then FIFA president Sepp Blatter, revealing – to the shock of the world – who would be the host of the 2022 men's football World Cup.

From the moment the decision was announced, voices in the Western media cried foul. How could the tiny nation of Qatar – one whose bid was declared by FIFA itself as 'high risk'– have edged out Australia, Japan, South Korea and the United States, except by underhand means? Suspicions were deepened when, in 2015, US prosecutors opened a sprawling case – still ongoing – that has seen over 50 people involved in global football charged with various crimes ranging from bribery to money laundering. These prosecutions mostly related to media and marketing rights for FIFA games in the Americas, but for a number of years journalists had also reported that it was secret payments by Qatar that landed them the World Cup. Their claims were bolstered in 2020, when US prosecutors alleged that people working for the Qatar 2022 bid had bribed FIFA officials in order to secure hosting rights. Qatar continues to deny the accusations, but the decision to award the country the World Cup became a source of growing anger among fans about the state of modern football.

Initially, Qatar was caught off-guard by the international response to its successful bid. 'It started with "Who is Qatar and how did they win it?"' I was told by one PR consultant who was brought in to assist. 'They started getting called mean things in the media,' she continued. 'Then the spotlight starts diversifying – not just rich Arabs of new money but the Nepalese and the Indians and what's happening to them ... and this interest just picked up to the point that they freaked out in 2012–13 and realised that they needed somebody [to help].'

The past decade has brought a flood of Western advertising and PR agencies to Qatar. They have been hired by various ministries or quasi-government organisations to help them respond to the increased international attention. Hill+Knowlton Strategies, Portland Communications, Blue Rubicon, Grey, Brown Lloyd James – the list reads like a who's who of the London and New York PR world. Doha is awash with consultants. They are the ones occupying the swish towers in West Bay, the men and women dressed in power suits buying $20 takeaway sushi lunches.

This particular PR consultant was hired when her company won a contract to help the Qatari government in its communications strategy. When she arrived in Doha, she was shocked at what she found.

'They had nothing. They had no government communications infrastructure *at all*,' she told me. 'Journalists who wanted comment from the country had nowhere to go. There was no email address, there was no phone number, there were no routes into any of these people.'

In the absence of opposition parties and an independent press, government institutions in Qatar had grown accustomed to never being criticised. Another person who worked in Doha told me gleefully that doing PR with local media was a breeze. 'You have the ability to literally call up any paper and get an interview or a feature article or a press release published without needing to pitch a story, just because you are a government entity – not even a government entity but a local company.'

The challenge was dealing with outside organisations. The *Sunday Times*, the *Guardian*, German broadcaster WDR, Amnesty International, Human Rights Watch and others all suddenly started writing about Qatar, focusing on the allegations of corruption in the World Cup bids, the poor conditions of construction workers and Qatar's illiberal laws on homosexuality.

The job of Doha's spin doctors was made harder still by the Arab uprisings that began just days after the announcement that the country would host the World Cup. Qatar was one of the few states in the region unscathed by unrest as demonstrations engulfed Tunisia, Egypt, Syria, Libya and Bahrain. But the fallout exacerbated longstanding claims that Qatar was a sponsor of extremists. The country was already host to Yusuf Al-Qaradawi, an Egyptian cleric seen as a spiritual leader of the Muslim Brotherhood, an Islamist group that had for decades agitated against the established autocracies of the region. In the years after the Arab uprisings, he was joined in Doha by senior figures from Hamas, the militant group that runs the Gaza Strip. Members of the Egyptian Muslim Brotherhood swelled the ranks when a coup forced them into exile. There were also accusations that individual Qataris and charitable foundations funnelled money to Al-Nusra Front, a hard-line group linked to Al-Qaeda and battling President Bashar Al-Assad in Syria.

Qatar, which denies accusations that it is soft on extremism, is hardly alone among its Gulf neighbours in facing such claims. Nevertheless, the allegations have given ammunition to Saudi, the UAE and their allies in their campaign to damage Doha's reputation internationally. Qatar's connections have also caused tensions with its allies. David Cohen, a senior US Treasury official, voiced frustration in 2014 that the country 'had a permissive terrorist financing environment'.

Faced with this challenging picture, Qatar wanted the PR consultant and her company to solve its image problem with money. 'They paid us, and then they wanted us to pay the *Wall Street Journal* and the *Washington Post*, and they didn't understand that that's not how the world works,' she laughed.

The PR agency did not pay the newspapers. Instead, they helped coordinate international media. Journalists would contact them. They'd log the query, draft a response, run it past the particular ministry for confirmation and send it back to the media organisation, all in time for their deadline. Except it didn't work. Government departments would refuse to cooperate. Emails would go unanswered for weeks. Strategies that the company would organise for one department would be immediately undermined by the actions of another, like the time when police detained a BBC journalist and his team who were on a government-sponsored press trip. 'What we were doing was dealing with bullshit,' recalled the PR manager with a smile. 'We were stroking egos and coming up with ideas that were brilliant but could never be actually taken forward.'

'At no point did we ever go to the government and say, "We will change your reputation, you guys don't have to do anything,"' she told me. 'We can't. The only thing we can tell them is that the *Guardian* and Amnesty International will not leave you the fuck alone until you abolish *kafala*. That's it. You guys abolish *kafala*, that's your job, and then leave the rest to us. We will do the comms to fix it.'

The PR agent let out a sigh.

'It sounds like it's one conversation but it's not. It's *years*.'

She thought that by the time she left, the government had begun to comprehend how an effective PR strategy works.

'They understood that it's not just about sugar-coating and spinning, it's about authentically changing the reputation of a country, which can only be done if it's matched by the policies.'

The supreme test for Qatar's new PR strategy was the blockade launched in June 2017 by Saudi Arabia, the UAE and their allies. Simmering tensions between Qatar and its neighbours over differing ideologies, and their support for opposing sides in the aftermath of the Arab Spring, exploded in the worst conflict the GCC had seen in its 36-year history. Almost overnight, Qatar found its borders shut. Basic imports of food and materials stopped. The country's commercial airliners were forced to take long detours to avoid Saudi airspace. At one point, Doha was gripped by the fear that Saudi Arabia was about to invade.

Once the military threats subsided and the problems of how to secure basic products were resolved, the conflict became a huge battle for global influence. Qatar dispatched its foreign minister to give a speech at Chatham House, the prestigious London think tank. The emir gave interviews with American TV. No realm was off limits. When a bootlegged version of Qatari channel beIN Sports was discovered, called 'beoutQ' and allegedly run out of Saudi Arabia, the lobbying stretched to sports organisations such as FIFA, Spain's La Liga and the English Premier League.

At work behind the scenes were an army of PR people tasked with winning over international opinion, including an Egyptian called Mohammed*. 'You needed governments like the UK and the US [on side],' Mohammed explained to me. 'But these are countries that rely heavily on Saudi money.' Because Gulf states had aggressively pursued sport as a key prong of building international influence, organisations from F1 to the Italian Serie A league found themselves in an awkward position. 'Getting someone like Formula 1 to make a public statement when they know that they're going to go and have a Formula 1 race in Saudi in a couple of years, or getting the Italian league to speak up when you know they're hosting the Super Cup in Saudi Arabia and that gets them a shit-tonne of money – it wasn't as easy as you think,' said Mohammed.

Qatar managed to turn the tide. It was helped in its efforts by the egregious behaviour of some of the blockading countries. In 2018, the state-backed murder of journalist Jamal Khashoggi in the Saudi consulate in Istanbul appalled the world. The sheer scale of the copyright infringement undertaken by beoutQ forced normally reticent football authorities to speak up. Mohammed watched with glee as headlines about Qatar supporting terrorists were replaced by wins. In 2019, the WTO ruled that Saudi had breached global intellectual property rights by failing to prosecute beoutQ. In 2020, the

International Court of Justice, the UN's highest court for disputes between countries, ruled in Qatar's favour in its challenge of the airspace restrictions imposed on the country. By 2021, it was becoming clear that the blockade had failed. In January of that year, Qatar's emir was invited to a GCC summit in Saudi Arabia, signalling the start of a détente that has subsequently gathered pace. Not only has Qatar refused to cede to the original demands laid down but, if anything, it has emerged from the dispute stronger.

Mohammed is still in awe of Qatar's soft power play. 'It's a case study what they've been able to do,' he said. 'Not just in sports but in art, in real estate, in influence when you are absolutely nothing on the map.' He compares Qatar to fellow Gulf states Bahrain and Oman. 'Have you ever seen a headline in any newspaper about either of those countries?' Mohammed had no qualms about the work he did. But just because Qatar is viewed more positively, he warned me, it doesn't mean it's necessarily acting better. He disagreed with the female PR consultant, who believed that spin is no good without substance. 'Having been in the kitchen, I know that it is not a result of reform or change. It's a result of a lot of money spent on people that can influence public opinion.'

Nowhere is the strategy more in evidence than football. Qatar has signed up a legion of the world's most famous footballers as 'ambassadors' for its World Cup, including Samuel Eto'o, Xavi Hernández and David Beckham. Their remit seems to involve being flown to Qatar to deliver a few bromides about

how great the place is while being photographed in a state-of-the-art football stadium. It is unclear to what extent these footballers know – or care – that they are the cutting edge of a massive PR campaign aimed at shifting the global conversation about Qatar away from corruption and exploitation.

With the US prosecution of former FIFA members ongoing, and reforms for low-paid workers stalling, stories linking Qatar to impropriety are likely to keep surfacing. Yet in all likelihood, any fallout will be forgotten when the tournament begins. 'It's disgusting to say something like this, but come tournament time no one cares about how the stadiums were built and any of that,' said Mohammed. 'Football fans will think about the football and nothing else.' This has long been in Qatar's mind, Mohammed told me. 'They've always known that we just need to get to the point where it can't be taken away from us.'

That point has been reached. In May 2019, FIFA abandoned plans to expand the number of teams from 32 to 48 for the 2022 World Cup – a logistical nightmare that would have required Qatar to share the tournament with its neighbours. The coronavirus pandemic erased any lingering fears of relocation. The 2022 World Cup will be played fully in Qatar or nowhere at all.

But I was drawn to something in Mohammed's words. His use of the first-person plural ('us') was telling. After seven years in the country, and despite professing indifference, perhaps even the guns for hire cannot separate themselves fully from Qatar.

'Challenges? Oh my gosh!'

Bernila* emits a nervous laugh, high-pitched and fast, like a *Looney Tunes* character.

'There are a lot of things that we cannot do here.'

She is speaking to me from the headquarters of a Filipino radio station in Qatar. It is housed in a small apartment in a non-descript building in central Doha. As she talks, four young members of staff – none out of their twenties – tap away at computers. Filipino soft rock is piped in from the booth next door, where the daytime DJ is at work.

The station takes its place in a large marketplace of migrant radio in Qatar. Flip between frequencies and you will find channels broadcasting in Malayalam, Hindi, Tagalog, English and Arabic serving Doha's many migrant communities. The same laws for print media apply to broadcasters: radio stations must have a Qatari partner and have to abide by strict regulations. And, just like print, radio staff are bound by restrictive rules about what they can and cannot do.

'One of our DJs said something about his experience in the Philippines,' recalls Bernila. She can't remember the precise details, something about his past work as an activist. Immediately the phone rang. It was someone from the Ministry of Culture, warning the station that talking about politics is unacceptable.

'They're really listening to us,' Bernila tells me.

'Even though he was talking about—'

'About an experience from the Philippines years ago?'

interrupts Bernila. 'No, you cannot talk about these kinds of things.'

She continues. 'You cannot say bad words about [Qatar]. Even if just a point – just an opinion of yours ... It's really more of us preaching [what] they [want].'

The jolly demeanour momentarily slips.

'It's just really sad if this is what news is.'

Most migrants in Qatar come from countries with more vibrant media environments. They are used to a broader scope of discussion and expression in public. Take for instance Malayalam speakers from Southern India. The anthropologist Irene Ann Promodh has studied Malayalam radio stations in Qatar and has noted that listeners generally crave 'politically charged content'. Most speakers of Malayalam come from the Indian region of Kerala, a state with a strong tradition of participatory democracy and debate (it was the first Indian state where the Communist Party was voted into power). And yet you'd be hard pushed to discover this via Malayalam radio in Qatar. As Promodh notes, Doha-based Malayalam stations remain stoically apolitical. The DJs are adept at self-censorship. The stations avoid live call-ins, preferring instead to pre-record any sections with listeners so that they can edit them if necessary.

But many – perhaps most – radio listeners are not interested in talking politics, whether in relation to Qatar or back home. Bernila told me that her audience mostly want to talk about matters of the heart. And yet even this seemingly innocuous subject is tricky to navigate.

'We can't go deep when it comes to love,' Bernila tells me.

I ask what going deep means. She pauses before responding. 'You know Filipinos are very loving persons.'

In the Philippines, no radio station is complete without the extended evening phone-in. From 9pm until midnight, listeners call up to share the problems they are experiencing with their husbands, wives or families. Other listeners ring in to offer consolation or advice.

'But here, you can't,' says Bernila. 'Even just general relationship [advice], we cannot talk about that.'

I try to establish what, exactly, draws the ire of the authorities. Bernila can't give a clear answer – a reminder that it isn't always apparent. She does know that any swearing or explicit mention of sex is a no-no. The staff have to keep a constant eye on the comments on the station's Facebook page. Anything that could get them in trouble is instantly deleted.

I ask Bernila about the listener profile. I assumed it would be solely Filipino, but she tells me a fascinating story. Two weeks after opening, the station was swamped with messages imploring them to stop speaking in Tagalog (the main language in the Philippines). There were other nationalities tuning in, they were told. Bernila and her colleagues were stunned. They had failed to anticipate non-Filipinos being interested in their station.

'We have African, we also have Indian. Nepali. Well, Qatari also and— British guys! Europeans.'

Bernila crinkles her brow into a puzzled expression.

'And it's funny 'cause what we play is original Filipino music.'

The diverse listener profile provides an important correction to my more pessimistic thoughts about Qatar. For all the stratification and segregation, experiences can overflow from the neat containers of 'nation' or 'ethnicity' that are proscribed for them. Bernila tells me that when she gets into taxis, Indian taxi drivers greet her with the words *po* or *opo* – Tagaolog epithets that they've learnt from the radio. Nepalis profess a new-found love for Filipino power ballads. Radio stands as a reminder of the unanticipated exchange that Qatar can generate.

The station adjusted. These days, the DJs speak in English with only the occasional foray into Tagalog. But now the complaints come from Filipinos wanting to hear more of their native tongue. Bernila adopts a matronly tone as she tells me how they respond. 'We always explain it to them that we need to cater also [for] our friends from other nationalities.'

Speaking to Bernila, I become keenly aware of the difficult balancing act faced by migrant radio stations: to cover events back home and also life in Qatar; to cater to a specific community but also be accessible to the wider public. Ultimately, she says, they have to remember where they're based. 'It's really more about your responsibility for Qatar,' she says. 'At the end of the day, yes, we [are] given a licence to cater to the Filipino, but at the same time it's more than bringing closer Filipinos not to be homesick for the Philippines. At the same time [it's] about being up-to-date with what's happening in Qatar.'

Bernila tells me how Filipinos in Qatar normally respond when she tells them what she does for a living. They exclaim that they no longer use their USB sticks full of Tagalog ballads. They let their Spotify subscriptions lapse. Now they have the station here in Qatar, there's no longer any need for them.

Bernila sits up in her chair proudly before delivering her sign-off.

'That's what success is for me.'

After a tour of the radio station and the opportunity to make a song request (I am disappointed to be told they don't have 'Radio Ga Ga' by Queen), I leave the station and hail a taxi.

The driver is already listening to the radio.

I am going to ask him to change the station so that I can hear my song request, but it's the top of the hour and the news is starting. After the classic news jingle, a female voice somewhere between plummy Brit and North American begins to speak:

> *Good evening! Under the wise leadership of his highness,*
> *the emir Sheikh Tamim bin Hamad Al Thani, the state of*
> *Qatar witnesses developments in all fields ...*

I settle back into the seat. A wry smile passes over my face. I think of Bernila and her team. They will have received the same email, the same exact wording, to be read out in its entirety:

> *Qatar has announced that with immediate effect the exit*
> *permits will be removed for expatriates who are not currently*

subject to Qatar's labour law. Qatar continues to strengthen its laws, ensuring policies are aligned with international labour standards. In this context, a number of agreements and memorandums of understanding have been signed with labour-exporting countries in order to achieve the highest standards and conditions of employment and fair recruitment. Also, the state of Qatar has exerted great efforts in establishing good practices in the recruitment process through a package of legislative reforms. Observers have praised the work and efforts exerted by Qatar in supporting the principles of human rights, congratulating Qatar for its achievements in this regard and the role played by the leadership as a model for examples in the field of human rights protection ...

12

'I was all alone. I had to do what I was told'

Armandhara village, Mangala Municipality, Myagdi District, Nepal

At first I can hear nothing but the crows of roosters.

Then I see a bright red wall. On it hangs a framed picture of a young man wearing glasses, his neat hair combed into a side parting. The pixels on my screen suddenly grow blotchy. When they again coalesce, a man in his forties is suddenly filling the frame.

Rekha Bahadur Sunar these days looks very different to the image of him in his youth. The round, jolly face is the same, but the glasses are now gone; the skin is altogether more stubbly and rough. On his head is what looks like a straw boater. And of course there are the scars.

'Our village is very beautiful,' Rekha tells me over the shaky video call we are using to talk. 'There are lots of mountains. But no jobs. Everyone has to leave for work.'

Nepal is a country of migration. Almost half of its households have a member working overseas or recently returned. Historically, people left for India or were recruited into foreign armies (some 200,000 Nepalis fought for Britain in the First and Second World Wars). In recent decades, the destinations have proliferated: Malaysia, Poland, Turkey, the Gulf. Every year, hundreds of thousands of Nepalis – mostly men, mostly untrained – leave the country to work abroad.

In 1987, an eighteen-year-old Rekha joined them. For the next two decades, he worked in a rice factory in India, journeying home when he could. But by 2009, the job was no longer enough. By then, Rekha had a wife, mother and five children to support. He decided he needed to migrate to where the real money was.

Qatar is currently the most popular destination on the planet for Nepalis (excluding India, which has an open border with Nepal). In 2018/19, it absorbed almost a third of all Nepali migrants. They joined millions of their compatriots already working in Saudi Arabia, the UAE and other states of the Gulf. Global inequality has created an easy quid pro quo: Qatar, thanks to its hydrocarbons, has huge wealth and citizens who don't need to wait tables or labour in the sun; Nepal has poverty, high unemployment and a government that has encouraged migration as a solution.

To fund the trip, Rekha borrowed 200,000 rupees – over $1,600 – from people in his village (most banks do not lend to people like him with no credit rating). Prior to his departure, Rekha was excited about the opportunity to make decent money. But when it was time to leave, he had a crisis of confidence. Even while journeying to the airport and checking in for his flight, Rekha had yet to make peace with his decision. He made his way through passport control, moved into the departure lounge and glimpsed the plane on the runway. 'Do I really have to go?' he thought one more time. And then something shifted. The other half of his brain, the rational side, spoke up. Rekha listened. He realised it wasn't really a choice at all.

'Yes, I must go.'

'It was the first time in my life I saw—' he doesn't know the word. Neither does Savitri Rajali, the Nepali producer who is translating our conversation. 'The beds on top of each other.'

'Bunkbeds?'

'Yes!'

Rekha was sleeping in a dormitory room with four other Nepalis. He discovered someone from his village working in the same company, but it didn't really help his mood.

'For two to three months, I was very sad that my family was so far away. I was missing them a lot,' he says. 'The surroundings, everything was totally different. You would not understand who is speaking what, who is going where. Very—' he pauses. 'I wouldn't say "confused", but not knowing much about the people, place, language.'

Unhappiness and bewilderment are common emotions among low-paid workers in Qatar. Before leaving home, individuals should receive pre-departure orientation to familiarise them with the laws and customs of their destination. In practice, it is only since 2018 that this has been done properly in Nepal. Once in the country, migrants are exposed to a cocktail of factors that can adversely affect their mental health. They are away from loved ones, working long hours in difficult conditions. They frequently live in unsanitary and overcrowded accommodation. They are subjected to financial stress, with the need to repay recruitment loans while facing tardy salary payments. Data released from the psychiatry unit of Qatar's main public health provider showed 36 per cent of patients admitted in the first two months of 2019 were male labourers. Of those, 15 per cent were suicidal cases.

Rekha had got a job with Peninsular Petrotech Engineering, a contractor in the engineering and construction sectors. He was officially recruited as a specialist scaffolder. He quickly understood, however, that he was expected to do whatever job needed doing. The company would transport him and his fellow workers to sites all over Doha. He worked at a bottling plant and a steel plant, hotels, restaurants and universities. For this he received 1,000 rials a month ($275), plus 200 rials for food ($55).

'Did he not want more?'

Rekha shrugs at my question. What he received was standard for low-paid labour.

A meagre salary in Qatar can be transformative back home. Nepali workers abroad earn, on average, more than twice what they could in Nepal. Money from overseas has transformed Nepali society. Boys drop out of school as soon as they turn eighteen and go abroad. Those with degrees or working in the civil service earn less than an untrained labourer in Saudi Arabia. The purchasing power in Nepal of a wage that is rock-bottom in Qatar serves as a stark reminder of the long tail of world poverty. Over 1.9 billion people, or 26.2 per cent of the global population, live on less than \$3.20 per day.

Rekha's life went on like this for years. He shares some photos of his time in Qatar. There is one of him in a high-vis jacket at work. Another shows him smiling with various men in a dormitory room. Camp. Bus. Worksite. Rinse. Repeat.

There are no images of Rekha in downtown Doha or on the beach.

An hour into our conversation, Rekha shifts position and I see his hands.

They come as a shock, scarred and black, his fingers all swollen. It's clear from the way he is moving them that he cannot close them properly.

He tells me about the accident.

It was 12 November 2018. Rekha was on a job erecting scaffolding in a petrochemical plant. Work had resumed for the afternoon when, at around 2.30pm, it started raining. Rain is incredibly unusual in Qatar. There are only around nine days of it a year. When it rains, it often does so heavily, flooding roads and dripping into houses that were never built for it.

On this day, the rain coincided with the afternoon prayer. The Muslim workers went and prayed while the others withdrew to a rest area to wait for the storm to pass. Were they not to have done this, the tragedy that was about to unfold would have been even more severe.

Once the rain began to lessen, Rekha and six others went back out to resume work. Rekha was standing on a 22-inch pipe when one of the team started up a generator.

Then, Rekha heard a noise unlike one he had ever heard. Before it had time to register, he was covered in flames. He remembers the heat, the panic. And then he blacked out.

Rekha came around fifteen days later in hospital. He was told that 28 per cent of his body had been burned and that, over the past fortnight, he had undergone a series of operations.

'For some time, I couldn't think how I ended up there,' he tells me. What had happened? Why was he in hospital? And then it came back to him.

Healthcare is free for all residents of Qatar. In 2000, the World Health Organization graded the country's health system 44th globally for overall efficiency. For acute care – such as the kind Rekha was receiving – there are few better places. 'The nurse from the hospital took care of me like my parents,' he says. 'Don't worry. You're alive,' she told him gently. From the nurse he learnt that six other people were involved in the accident. One returned to India for treatment. Two had minor wounds. Three workers died.

Where people like Rekha struggle is in access. Employers are responsible for applying for workers' health cards, but survey data shows somewhere between 50 and 90 per cent of them never receive one. Fearful of losing work, many feel unable to take time off to attend a doctor's appointment. Even if they want to, workers find it hard to travel to health facilities as the majority live far from public transport. Some contractors wait until they have sufficient numbers of ill workers and then send them together in bulk. Other employers deny treatment altogether.

Rekha was kept in hospital for almost three months. But there are always workers getting hurt in Qatar's construction industry and the bed was needed. He was discharged back into his old room in the camp. Every day he would journey to the hospital where the staff would bandage his wounds and check on him.

Back under his employer's care, Rekha says he was pulled into the fight for access. The vehicle the company was supplying to take him to appointments rarely arrived on time. Sometimes it wouldn't show at all. On those occasions, Rekha claims, he would be told that he didn't need to go to hospital today, tomorrow would be fine. But he was hearing the exact opposite from the doctors. When he was late, they would furrow their brows. When he missed a session, they would sound upset. They told him: 'If you don't come on a given appointment, your wounds won't get better.'

Rekha spent his days alone in the dormitory room. He was frequently dizzy. He couldn't see or hear properly. 'It was very hard to go to the toilet, even to stand.'

The burns made it hard to sit. He had to go to the toilet on all fours. To try to help, his friends took a plastic chair and cut a hole in it. But sometimes his feet would slip on the bathroom floor and he would fall off.

'I couldn't eat by myself,' he tells me. 'Both hands were stuck together.'

Rekha again lifts his hands into view. He demonstrates his limited range of motion, trying and failing to close his palms. He had difficulty grasping items – even drinking a glass of water by himself. The evenings brought relief, when his roommates returned from their shifts. Exhausted from the heat and work, they would nevertheless take the time to help him eat or guide him to the toilet.

'I was abroad, it was not my country,' Rekha continues, his voice somewhere between stoicism and helplessness. 'I was all alone. I had to do what I was told to do.'

Rekha had been receiving treatment for over a year when the company raised the prospect of a trip home. Normally, he would go back every two years. Even though he was overdue a journey home, however, he was unsure. The treatment was still ongoing. He talked with his doctor and was told it wasn't ideal. Yet Rekha had two months of holiday that would expire. He hadn't seen his wife and children for three years. His youngest son was unwell with suspected leukaemia. He didn't want to waste the opportunity. The doctors assented and in February 2020 Rekha flew home.

His wife met him at the airport. When they saw each other they burst into tears.

The eleven-hour drive back to the village was full of sorrow. When his children set eyes on his injuries, they all cried.

He had been home for barely a month when the coronavirus pandemic hit. Flights were halted and borders closed, stranding him in Nepal.

In the summer of 2020, Rekha received a call from one of his managers at Peninsular Petrotech in Qatar. He was told that the company was going to shut down and, unfortunately, it wouldn't be possible to bring him back to Qatar to finish his treatment. Most employers in Qatar pay their workers a lump sum when their contracts come to an end – usually a month's salary for every year worked. If Rekha wanted his end-of-service payment, he would have to sign the papers that the manager had just sent. Rekha had been with the company for nine years and so was entitled to $1,675.

At the same time, he was bitterly disappointed. He wanted to get back to Qatar and resume his treatment. His medicine supplies had long finished. The skin on his hands had started growing taut again. Rekha knew from previous experience that this was a precursor to being unable to clench them properly and that they needed to be recut by a doctor.

Rekha begged the manager to issue a visa to allow him to re-enter Qatar. But he says that the manager had only one sentence he would use: 'Company is going to shut down, you have to sign for your money.' He would call Rekha daily, pressuring him to sign the papers. For the first time in our conversation, Rekha's cheery demeanour slips.

'I was afraid I would lose that money,' he says glumly. 'I had no choice. I signed the paper.'

A few weeks later he chatted with the person from his village who worked for the same company. He told Rekha that it was still operating.

'I felt very terrible,' relates Rekha. 'I loved that company but now they betrayed me.' He believes he was tricked so that they could relinquish responsibility for his care. (Under Qatari labour law, the cost of treatment for occupational injuries must be met by the employer.)

Rekha forwards me a set of messages – a one-sided WhatsApp conversation with someone whose number is saved as 'Qatar PPE Ravi* sir'.

> *Sir, my operation was not good. Please send me an additional visa.*
>
> *hello sir give me visa.*
>
> *Answer me*
>
> *Hello sir*

'Now my situation is so bad,' Rekha continues. 'Look at it – my wounds are not properly cured.' He shows me his belly, which looks sore from where they've taken skin to graft it onto the wound on his neck. 'I took photos. I sent to them but no response.' He has trouble with ordinary daily activities. 'I couldn't hold a pickle jar in the supermarket,' he says. 'It slipped through my hands and smashed and I had to pay for it.'

A total of 446 'severe and moderate' injuries were recorded in Qatar in the year that Rekha was hurt. Nepalis, Bangladeshis and Indians suffer the overwhelming majority of workplace accidents in Qatar. They also make up the majority of deaths. Not because they are more accident prone, of course, but because they dominate the workforce on hazardous jobs. Almost certainly, the official statistics downplay the scale of injuries: the ILO noted that there is under-reporting, mostly because companies want to avoid paying compensation or damaging their reputation. It's not clear if Rekha's injury was among those recorded in 2018.

For workers who are hurt in these accidents, their lives are permanently altered. The consequences are not the same for the employers that try to cover them up. 'Despite the relatively severe penalties for failing to report occupational accidents,' wrote the ILO, 'employers are rarely sanctioned for non-compliance.'

I called Peninsular Petrotech, which is owned by a Qatari but run by Indian executives, to ask them about Rekha. I spoke with an HR official who insisted that Rekha was wrong to believe that he'd been tricked into ending his contract. Beginning in 2020, he told me, a lack of new projects had forced them to shut down all departments, including the mechanical and civil division where Rekha was working. All that was left was a small office team and a few dozen individuals employed as specialist painters. He said that Rekha was paid all the money he was owed by the company – a fact that Rekha does not dispute. 'I think the guy got a little upset because he was not able to come back,' I was told by the official. '[But] you should understand ... an employee cannot expect that he come back. The situation here should also be favourable to bring him back. If we don't have any new projects, how we can allow him to work?'

These days Rekha sits at home. He is reliant on his adult children, who go out to work in agriculture in the village. In the evenings they bring him food.

The Nepali economy is hugely dependent on money sent home from workers overseas. Remittance payments, as they are known, are estimated to be almost a quarter of Nepal's total annual GDP – one of the highest levels in the world. Payments from relatives overseas keep many families afloat. Deprived of Rekha's income, his family are struggling.

'Does he wish he never went to Qatar?'

'How can I say that I would not have gone to Qatar?' he replies, throwing his hands up in a gesture somewhere between amusement and admonishment.

'It was [because of] my family situation that Qatar became my destination. For work. To support my family. To help them.'

Rekha received around $22,600 through a combination of Nepali and Qatari private insurance schemes and the end-of-service payment from his company. The payments are not nothing: they total around seven years' earnings. But Rekha was planning to work in Qatar for twice that long, until he reached the company retirement age of 60. And no amount can compensate for his life-changing disability. 'I cannot touch hot things. I cannot cook. I cannot wash my clothes. And I cannot pick up stuff and put from one place to another place,' he says.

The Nepali government has begun to wake up to the malign aspects of the mass migration of its citizens. Since 2007, it has operated its own Foreign Employment Welfare Fund that compensates workers who are injured or the families of those who die. Rekha would be eligible for up to 700,000 Nepali Rupees ($5,870) from this fund. Despite applying to the fund within months of his arrival home, nearly two years later, they have yet to be in touch.

I ask Rekha what he would say to someone from his village contemplating following in his footsteps to the Gulf.

'If someone goes to Qatar to support their family, I would tell them first check the reputation of the company, how they take care of their workers,' Rekha says. 'And I would say use first safety.'

He adopts a schoolmaster's tone.

'If you have your life then the world is yours. If you don't have your life or health, then there is nothing in the world.'

He's not finished with this point.

'Use the safety!' he is almost scolding me in his fervency. It is only because he used full safety equipment – proper gloves, the fire-proof uniform, a helmet – that he is with us today. 'If I hadn't worn that, I would have been dead on the spot.'

Rekha suddenly gets up out of his seat. The phone moves around blurrily before the camera hovers over a certificate on the wall: 'Safe Man of the Month, November 2017.'

It's a template from Microsoft Word, printed out on an inkjet and laminated; one of those hollow corporate initiatives that companies come up with for their workers. But Rekha is beaming.

After nearly three hours, Rekha is almost done telling his story.

I surprise myself by being struck most of all by its sense of inevitability – not of the accident, perhaps, but of everything before and after. The inescapability of his being in Qatar; of having no choice but to sign the end of service papers; the inexorable fact that he would never get back to Qatar to resume his treatment. It all seems a consequence of the non-existent social and political capital Rekha has to influence proceedings. It's non-existent not because of anything he's done, of course, but by dint of where he's from.

Once we have finished talking, I ask Rekha if he can spin the camera around to show me his surroundings. I expect a cursory glimpse of the view – bucolic, probably, given the constant sounds of roosters. But Rekha really gets into it. He rises to his feet and takes me on a fifteen-minute tour.

'This is the water tank.'

'This is the electricity meter.'

'There are the bills.' He cheerfully flicks a few papers that are tied together and hanging next to the meter.

Inside, Rekha proudly shows off his TV and his collection of hand tools – spirit level, set square – that he brought back from Qatar. We head back outside where I am shown a chicken coop with sixteen chickens and a few goats that are grazing. The backdrop to all of it is the Nepali hills. Precipitous, beautiful. It is spring and everywhere is green and sunny. My mind's eye flicks to Qatar. In April, Doha is already too hot – the claggy Gulf air full of dust and exhaust fumes. I become unreasonably angry at the place. What right does it have to suck these men away from the most beautiful regions of the world? Why can't they stay?

13 'The lungs of Doha'

The foyer is like another world.

There is wall-to-wall marble. From the ceiling hangs a chandelier the size of a small car. The hotel manager, Faris*, is a large man with a big frame that makes his suit look uncomfortable. He shakes my hand with a smile and leads me through the lobby.

As we walk, Faris tells me about himself. He's from elsewhere in the Middle East, now in his ninth year in Doha. We pass the section with the grand piano playing itself and the large windows looking out on the private beach. We turn a corner and move into a side lounge, which is deserted apart from a man in a *thobe* making a phone call. We settle into armchairs facing one another.

'Hotels are like the lungs of Doha,' Faris tells me with a flourish. 'It's a place where all the expats are really living.'

In 2000, there were only nineteen hotels in all of Qatar. The scene was dominated by the ziggurat-shaped Sheraton, which stood on its own, surrounded by the as-yet undeveloped West Bay. By the time I arrived in 2019, there were close to 200. The construction has been driven in part by the World Cup. During the tournament there will be the need for hundreds of thousands of beds (the FIFA delegation alone requires 963 rooms). But hotels in Doha fulfil a different role to any other place I've lived – the people who use them the most are not visitors but those living in the city.

Hotels are the Switzerland of Qatar. Neutral territory. Behaviour that elsewhere would result in a fine, deportation or worse is not only allowed but often encouraged. Hotels assume this role as a consequence of two factors: censorious laws governing alcohol and sex and a need to keep well-remunerated foreigners happy. They are the only venues that can legally serve alcohol, and so all of Qatar's bars, pubs and clubs are in hotels. In a country where sex outside marriage is illegal, they also function as hook-up points. If public space in Doha is generally denuded of life, then hotels are where it is concentrated. They are pulsing centres of activity, portals to all that is deemed forbidden.

'Qataris, residents – all. People *love* to stay in hotels,' Faris continues. 'I really feel amazed,' he trills. '[You would assume] you're not gonna go and spend 200–300–400 dollars just to stay like 25 minutes away from your home. But I also do it!' he confesses excitedly. 'Just go, hang out at the pool, have a beer, relax and that's it.' Spend money. Treat yourself. Consumption and opulence are Qatar's calling cards. For the well-off, at least.

I ask about the staff.

'In our hotel is 60 to 70 nationality,' Faris tells me. There are many different mentalities, habits, ways of living. 'You learn from them and they learn from you,' he says proudly. 'Always we are very careful about we don't hurt each other because ... we're teammates.'

Faris paints a picture of multicultural harmony. But in the months after I meet him, as the World Cup draws closer, a less cheery picture emerges. With construction of the stadiums and roads almost complete, NGOs and media outlets have shifted their attention to the waiters, room attendants, cleaners, porters and chefs who will look after the expected 1.5 million guests. A report in July 2021 by the Business and Human Rights Resource Centre, a charity, revealed widespread exploitation of hotel workers in Qatar. In a different investigation that year, the *Guardian* reported that hotels listed on FIFA's hospitality website were employing staff who had suffered 'serious labour rights violations'. The abuses are the same wearily familiar ones: workers toiling for overly long hours, having their passports confiscated, being unable to change jobs. But they somehow seem all the more cruel, given the opulence and splendour that serves as the backdrop.

Not that many of the guests are likely to notice – or care. I ask Faris about the patrons.

'What I learnt, John, from beginning when you start hospitality, in one of the courses it said you do the job without expectation,' he tells me.

I try to get him to put down the corporate armour: 'You should still expect to be treated like a human, no?' I ask.

'Yeah but you cannot push people to do that.'

We've reached a poor state of affairs, I think to myself, when a person can't expect a customer to show them basic humanity.

'People are coming so stressed and they are coming here to relax. They look at it as escape,' says Faris. You could get a mouthful of abuse purely because you're the first person they interact with. 'By experience and putting the right people and proper trainings, you know how to absorb this stress of people.'

He outlines his tactics: with some people, you just know you can approach them straight off. Others are more frosty. You need to know how to break the ice and get closer to those ones. 'It's like enigma!' he exclaims loudly. Once you've cracked it, 'You start slowly, slowly taking all this anger, pure anger, you know, from each one.'

Pure anger? His choice of words shocks me.

I can tell I won't get the inside story here. Faris is too committed to his job, his company. He's too *nice*.

I move to wrap up our talk, but Faris interrupts me. Before we go, he wants to respond to those who accuse Doha of being boring.

'People say, "Oh, this is a very conservative country so you cannot have fun" – no!'

When you walk around Beirut or Athens you see people dancing and drinking, he acknowledges, but it's not so different in Doha.

'I will say if you choose not to look for something, it doesn't mean it's not there.'

The majority of the population of Qatar can't frequent hotels. Low-paid workers are stuck in their labour camps in the desert and, anyway, wouldn't spend the equivalent of a day's wage on a single drink. These establishments, then, despite their number, cater for the minority. But that still allows for astonishing stratification. The restaurants in the five-star places are some of the fanciest around, with celebrity chefs and pieces of artwork that convey no other vibe than: expensive. Then there are the mid-range establishments, the West Bay hotels which include Polynesian-themed outdoor bars, Irish pubs, jazz lounges and restaurants with views over the city.

And then there's Club Manila.

Club Manila is one of two venues in a non-descript hotel in the older part of town.

As I wait for my friend in the lobby, I survey the scene: yawning, jet-lagged travellers halt with their suitcases to let a hyped-up crowd in shirts and skimpy dresses go past. Concierges have to juggle smiling at the tourists with nightclub crowd control. In the battle for setting the scene, the revellers are winning – it's their raucous laughs and clouds of aftershave that follow us into the lift.

The club is housed in a rectangular space with a low ceiling. There are no outside windows and dim lighting means it takes a few minutes for my eyes to adjust. Scattered across the room are cocktail tables with worn-out bar stools arranged around them. The majority are occupied with men drinking beer and staring at a stage. My friend chooses this moment to reveal the motive behind his choice of venue. 'Oh, by the way there's live music.' We find a table close to the back. A Filipina waitress appears instantly and my friend orders a bucketful of beers. Literally. The cheapest way of buying alcohol in Club Manila is to order six bottles in a tin pail.

Onto the stage walks an all-female, all-Filipina seven-piece, to a scattering of applause. Without a word, the band strikes up a version of 'Killing Me Softly' and I'm pleasantly surprised. After 90 seconds of Roberta Flack/The Fugees, they switch to another song. And then another. I groan inwardly. The entire 30-minute set proceeds as a medley. Taylor Swift becomes Aerosmith becomes – I don't know any more. I look around at the crowd and they seem unbothered. It's dominated by morose-looking men drinking and staring at girls half their age.

Despite the setting, my friend is in the mood to confide. He's a 'local' – born in Qatar to Indian parents – and so familiar with Doha that it bores him.

'The dating scene here, it's such that you normally hold on to people for longer,' he tells me. 'I've lived in London. If you don't like someone, people just stop and you can find someone else the next day. But here it's not so easy to find someone else, so you stick with it a bit longer.'

He tells me about a girl he was seeing until two months ago.

'I tried to keep it going but ...' he trails off wearily.

He revives when telling me the story of a friend of his, an Indian who recently hit it off at work with a Qatari woman.

They wanted to sleep together and so hatched an elaborate plan. He rented a hotel room. She had a personal driver but took an Uber. In the taxi and hotel she wore a full veil so no one could see her face on the security cameras. (An aside from my friend: 'Don't think women in full veils in hotels are pious. It's the opposite – they're about to meet their lovers.') 'They go to the room, they do their business. Then she dresses and leaves, he leaves fifteen minutes afterwards.' The way he describes the tryst makes it sound like a veterinary appointment. 'It's so risky!' he says, finally letting some emotion flood into his story.

Life in the bar seems quite normal. The band eventually address the audience, saying they can do song requests. People hand them suggestions written on napkins, none of which they actually play. A few guys come in and one starts singing along, flailing his arms around. Next thing I know, the huge bouncer at the bar has stepped in, manhandling the exuberant singer to the door. I can't shake a sense of sleaze. Perhaps it's the dynamic of all-female band and all-male audience, or maybe the dead-behind-the-eyes stares of the singers.

I wonder in how many bars across Doha this scene, or a version of it, is being replicated. A multinational mix of people trying to forget where they are. Peel away any razzmatazz, shake off the drunken haze and a general sadness seems to permeate the room, as it often does when I go out in Doha.

How many people truly want to be here?

'If you don't have a drinking problem when you first arrive in Qatar, don't worry, you'll soon develop one,' writes Mikolai Napieralski in *God Willing*, his guide to the country, published in 2017. 'The key to surviving life in Qatar is to keep yourself just drunk enough to ignore the fact you're actually in Qatar.' In this laddy-laddy 'wahey!' tone, the book proceeds to evaluate the beach parties, clubs and general escapades that many Westerners indulge in.

To someone who has never visited, such debauchery might sound incongruous. Most outsiders know that Qatar has some of the world's strictest alcohol laws and that beer is prohibitively expensive. It is an offence to drink alcohol in public – or be drunk. To enter any bar you need to show either a passport or a residence permit, which are scanned at the door. It's illegal to import booze, as I found out at the airport when two bottles of ginger cordial I had in my suitcase were mistaken for wine (and the chef Gordon Ramsay discovered when he once had a bottle of Dom Pérignon taken off him).

The entire country has only one shop which sells alcohol, the euphemistic 'Qatar Distribution Company' (QDC), a large warehouse-type complex on the outskirts of Doha. When I visited on a regular weekday afternoon, its car park was so busy that staff in high-vis jackets were having to divert the traffic to the overflow next door. The taxi driver who brought me shrugged and said that it looked quiet to him. 'If you come Thursday evening – *khalas*.' Finished, he told me. 'You need two hours just to get in!'

Streams of people were exiting with trolleys piled high with

booze and sausages (the shop is also the only place in Doha where you can buy pork products). I waited for a gap and entered, only to find a security man directing me upstairs, past the framed adverts for Famous Grouse whisky, onto a landing that resembled a doctor's waiting room. I took a number from the machine and sat in the functional furniture to wait my turn.

You need a permit before you can purchase alcohol from the shop. I read the large board affixed to one of the walls outlining everything required to get one: you must be over 21, possess a Qatari ID, be willing to pay 150 rials for the licence and hold a letter from your employer outlining your position, basic salary (minimum 3,000 rials a month) and marital status. I had a residence permit as a visiting academic but was receiving no salary. I considered asking my sponsor for a letter regardless, but I have to admit that the 'social-shaming' aspect of the system weighed on me. What would my manager or the friendly assistants in the office think? And to reveal myself at work only to be denied by some jobsworth here in the QDC office ... I put the queue number in the bin and headed out, deciding to limit my drinking to bars, where no permit is required.

Numerous patrons of QDC told me that it is common to see middle-aged South Asian drivers loading crates of gin and whisky that cost more than their annual salaries into shiny Land Cruisers. The rumour is that they are buying alcohol for their Qatari sponsors. Locals who want to get their hands on alcohol without attracting opprobrium assign liquor licences to low-level employees, inflate their salaries on the paperwork and send them to the store. One commentator on the Doha News website claims to have seen a man in a *thobe* dispense with the subterfuge – he just sat in his vehicle in the car park while his driver loaded the alcohol in the back.

Despite the social unacceptability of Qataris drinking, almost everyone I met in Doha had a story involving locals and alcohol. My favourite was told to me by a primary school teacher. During a beach clean-up in environmental awareness week, his class came across a cache of empty bottles and cans. One of his Qatari kids picked up a wine bottle, turned to him and said, 'This is the drink that mum has at home!'

In a place with such strict interdiction on alcohol, recreational drugs are obviously even more of a no-no. But it is equally obvious that you can find them if you want. Napieralski begins his book with the tale of one of his first nights out in Doha, which involved being offered bumps of coke in the VIP section of a club by the Qatari boss of a friend. Someone I know claims to get his weed from a member of the Al Thani ruling family.

You might be thinking that having only one alcohol shop, punitive sanctions and the most expensive drink prices in the world is perhaps not the best infrastructure for hosting a month-long party for 1.5 million football fans. The authorities are aware of this. 'Alcohol is not part of our culture,' Nasser Al-Khater, chief executive of the 2022 World Cup, has said. 'However, hospitality is.' During the 2019 FIFA Club World Cup, held in Doha in part to help the country prepare, a 'fan zone' was created where the beers were a bargain-basement 30 rials ($8) a pint – roughly half what a middle-of-the-road bar would charge. Before the final match between Liverpool FC and Brazilian side Flamengo, I conducted a highly unscientific straw poll in the fan zone. I found that a good half were fans of neither team. They had no interest in the football but were keen to capitalise on the (comparatively) cheap alcohol.

Qatar's proposed solution for the World Cup, having a number of these zones where fans will be able to drink, seems eminently sensible to me. Just because football in the UK is indexed strongly to drunken revelry doesn't mean it is – or has to be – everywhere. Having lived in Muslim-majority countries for much of the past decade, I've grown to enjoy the possibility of watching sport in alcohol-free places. The outraged tone of some Brits writing about alcohol at the World Cup seems to me to contain a thinly veiled sense of cultural superiority – that other places should endeavour to be as similar as possible to them.

And if you're poor and you want to drink in Qatar? Well, there's always bootleg alcohol. In the mid-2010s, increasing numbers of low-income workers were purchasing colognes with high-alcohol content in order to drink them, until the government tightened their importation and sale. Another choice is *sadeeqi* – Arabic for 'my friend' – a bootleg liquor distilled by amateurs that is sold out of the back of cars. A 2014 investigation by Doha News found the *sadeeqi* sold in the Industrial Area contained butanol and pentanol, two alcohols that cause brain and eye damage when consumed. 'Now, even the texts from my wife, I cannot see,' one worker who drunk the substance for two years told the news site. As well as impaired vision, he attributed his frequent stomach pain, bleeding during defecation and short-term memory loss to drinking *sadeeqi*.

Qatari police crack down heavily on bootleggers. While it is obviously right to protect peoples' health, the aggressive enforcement of sobriety at the lower end reveals the double standards of life in Qatar. Westerners in a five-star hotel can be three sheets to the wind but those toiling long hours for rock-bottom pay are not allowed anywhere near alcohol. The extent of the policing was brought home to me on a visit to a labour camp. The security staff at the gate made me open my bottle of water so that they could sniff it and confirm it wasn't spirits.

The impediments of permits, high cost and harsh punishments don't stop low-income workers from drinking – it just pushes their drinking underground, making it more dangerous. 'The consumption of alcohol runs rife in camps,' the researcher Tristan Bruslé wrote. 'It is a way of passing the time.' Using alcohol as a form of escape, social lubricant or temporary cure for homesickness is not limited to any class, nationality or ethnicity. Better than prohibition would be to recognise that drinking will happen and ensure that it can be done safely by all.

Another activity forced to be clandestine is sex.

In October 2020, a newborn baby was found abandoned in a toilet at Doha's Hamad International Airport. Eighteen Australians, along with women from other nations, were removed from ten different flights – including a Qatar Airways plane to Sydney – and subjected to forced vaginal examinations in an apparent bid to determine if one of them had just given birth. There was, rightfully, an uproar at the women's treatment. But missing in a lot of the news coverage was the question of what circumstances could have led a woman to feel her only option was to abandon her baby in an airport bathroom.

The Qatari penal code criminalises consensual sex between adults outside of marriage. Gay sex is also illegal. That of course doesn't stop unmarried heterosexuals – or LGBT people – from having sex. Tinder operates in Qatar. People hook up in night-clubs and go home together. And one of Qatar's incongruities is that, in a country where extra-marital sex is illegal, prostitution is highly visible. Many bars and clubs – including those at the high-end – tacitly allow sex workers to operate. That includes sports bars, as I found out when going to watch the 2019 Champions League quarter-final and ending up sharing a table with a woman I didn't know. She was completely uninterested in the match, but not to the men who kept approaching our table, one of whom she disappeared with before Son Heung-min gave Tottenham the advantage over Manchester City.

If you're male, well-paid and show a modicum of common sense you won't fall foul of the law on sex. It's a different matter for the sex workers, however. They can find themselves rounded up by police, detained and deported. It's also very different if you are a low-income worker.

Qatar's prisons and deportation centres contain many

pregnant women detained on charges of *zina*, 'illicit relations' outside of marriage. One prison official, speaking to Amnesty International, estimated that they made up as much as half the total number of women in detention.

The majority of these women are domestic workers. While they are clearly not the only people having extra-marital sex in Qatar, they are overwhelmingly the ones jailed and deported for it. I learnt about the difficulties of having relationships from two unmarried Filipina domestic workers, Jasmine* and Dolores*, who chatted with me over coffee one Friday afternoon.

'There is a lot of experience here in Qatar!' Jasmine told me before descending into a fit of laughter.

'What do you mean?'

'Experience,' she repeats, as if it's obvious. Seeing my incomprehension, she begins to explain.

'Finding someone and then you're just cheating each other. Playing. Nobody will go with you until the end of your life.'

'They just want fun?'

'Yessssssss.'

But having fun as a domestic worker is rife with hazard. The combination of the *kafala* system and laws on unmarried sex enforces a de facto celibacy. Sponsors are held responsible for workers' behaviour, turning them into morality police. One foreigner used her anonymous blog about life in Qatar to describe her experience of policing her live-in domestic worker. 'Many months ago when she asked to meet someone outside, we asked to meet and speak to the guy first,' she wrote. 'It made us feel

sick and feudal. But we had to do it because ... as her employers/
sponsors, we would be held responsible if we knowingly allowed
[her] to place herself at any risk.'

'It's just human. We're just human,' Dolores tells me quietly.
There's a pause.

'For me, yeah, before I have here.'

It takes a few seconds before I realise that this is her roundabout way of telling me that she's had partners in Qatar. Then
a change in tone, deflated and low.

'He's married.'

She talks about rendezvous in hotels. 'Just for one hour, two
hours – like that.'

'They say there is no "forever" in this country,' says Dolores.

Jasmine finishes the second half of the joke: 'But there is
together!'

The journalist Ana Santos has spoken to a host of victims of Qatar's morality laws. Women like Wazilfa, who met a
Bangladeshi man online while employed as a domestic worker.
They had a relationship for a year, but he disappeared when
she told him she was pregnant. When she began to show, her
employer turned her over to the authorities. In 2018, she was in
jail, awaiting trial for unmarried illicit sex and pregnancy outside
of wedlock. The prosecutor had been unable to track down the
man to prosecute him.

Even if a woman is the victim of rape, she can be prosecuted
if the authorities don't believe that the sex was non-consensual.
Abortion is illegal in most circumstances. Women frequently

give birth while incarcerated. There are wings of prisons that more closely resemble labour wards, full of women about to give birth or with small babies. 'When a woman is pregnant, the last place she should be is in detention,' Vani Saraswathi of Migrant-Rights.org told Santos. 'What danger can a pregnant woman possibly pose to society?'

The 'standard' sentence for unmarried illicit sex is a year's prison followed by deportation. But it's not uncommon for women to be detained for longer. Santos spoke to a Filipina woman called Joanne who had to spend a total of two years and ten months in jail, her sentence extended because of unpaid loans. 'I was carrying a newborn baby in my arms when I went into jail,' she told Santos. '[And] I was walking out with a toddler holding my hand.'

Pardis Mahdavi, a researcher who has spent years talking to victims of *zina* crimes in the Gulf, captures the absurd paradox: the women who are imported to perform the most intimate of tasks for others – looking after peoples' families, caring for the elderly – are deemed 'immoral' if they search for some intimacy themselves and are deemed 'unfit to parent' if that intimacy results in a child.

I had the opportunity to view Qatari hotel culture first-hand when I visited the country during the Covid-19 pandemic. I had given up my previous flat at the start of the pandemic and wasn't planning to stay long enough to need a new one. The country's borders were closed to anyone not a citizen or resident so I knew there would be no tourists. Every guest I encountered would be someone working in Qatar.

I chose a hotel towards the lower end of the spectrum. A small establishment, 60-odd rooms across five floors, advertising itself as 'boutique'. It had the usual *mise en scène* – chintzy decor, non-smoking rooms that smell of smoke, air con permanently set on 'arctic', a Quran and prayer rug in the wardrobe and a sticker on the ceiling to show which way to face to point towards Mecca. The religious accoutrements seemed wildly optimistic, a clash between what the state might want the guests to be doing and the reality. As if knowing this, the sticker in my room had shrivelled up.

After a few days, I began to understand the hotel's rhythm. In the mornings, the pace was slow. The lift disgorged the occasional guest who hurried out without a look around. The lobby was deserted aside from the odd business meeting. As the afternoon headed into evening, the pace cranked up. Various couples checked in, often Filipina or South Asian women with Arab men. Was it love? Was it a one-night stand? Was it any of my business?

But it was on weekend nights that the hotel exploded into life.

One Thursday night, the end of the working week in Qatar, I took a seat in the lobby and watched the comings and goings.

Two guys in business attire entered the hotel speaking Arabic and headed up in the lift. A Filipina woman exited, or at least attempted to, yanking at the door with the 'Please use other door' label on it. 'Aiii!' she exclaimed as a buzzer sounded. A middle-aged man in a *thobe* came in and chatted in Arabic to the bouncer on the door before disappearing. Was that the owner? On reception, the harried Tunisian attendant was printing off room agreements and dishing out keys. The phone rang constantly but she was too busy to answer. There was a queue of people building up. A guy with a blazer and greying Hugh Grant haircut was visibly impatient.

Not long into the evening, the member of staff on the door gave up checking everyone's temperature, as per Covid-19 requirements.

'Have room?' He would ask people. If they said yes, he just let them wander in.

Food deliveries came continuously. South Asian men who looked barely old enough to ride a scooter carried packages into the lobby. Security grilled them aggressively. 'Which room number?' They shrugged and stood waiting – sometimes for up to ten minutes – at which point someone shuffled up, handed over some bank notes, grabbed the food and turned and disappeared back towards the lifts.

By the second hour, the Nepali bouncer seemed a bit freaked out by my presence. My excuse that I was waiting for someone seemed to be wearing thin.

'Your visitor is lady?' He asked me. 'If she says your name, I will send her up.'

'No! No! Just a friend!'

I tried to dispel the image that I was there for sex. But I then wondered if, in my response, I planted an even more confusing idea in his head.

Going back to my room, there was all kinds of bustle and noise in the corridor. A towel trolley had emerged with some poor cleaning guy having to make up a room. African music came from behind one door, the cackle of laughter from behind another.

Truth be told, I was a bit disappointed by how well everyone behaved. Perhaps it's my British upbringing, but I presume that nights out require a mandatory amount of lairiness – if not from you then from someone you encounter at least. But in Qatar maybe everyone is a bit more cautious. Or just better mannered.

In the morning, I was woken up at 5.30am by the giggling and singing of women in the room next door. Once my annoyance subsided, I resolved to go for a run. In September in Qatar, six in the morning is the only time of day that a run won't give you heatstroke.

The staff in the lobby had yet to change. It was still the Nepali bouncer on the door.

'How's it going? Good night or bad night?' I asked.

'Good night,' he said with a weary grin.

'Why was it a good night?'

Before he could speak the Tunisian woman on reception replied for him.

'Still breathing!'

14 'It's getting hotter and hotter every year'

I wonder if there will be crowds.

The race doesn't begin until midnight but, given how Doha's malls and coffee shops are always busy through to the early hours, that shouldn't be a discouragement. I walk the final 500 metres to the Corniche. When I arrive, I'm disappointed to find only small gaggles of people, including two men in *thobes*, a group of twenty or so Sri Lankans and three African men musing on the weather.

It is September, a year before my hotel stay, and the start of the IAAF World Athletics Championships – the biggest global occasion for track and field after the Olympics. Qatar is the host, the contest meant to serve as yet another opportunity to burnish the county's sporting credentials. Today's other events took place in the air-conditioned Khalifa International Stadium. I was sat in there earlier, watching the heats of the steeplechase, 5,000 metres and high jump. Climate-controlled, open-air arenas are one of Qatar's innovations, developed in part to counter the fact that summer temperatures would be unbearable for World Cup footballers (and then FIFA moved the World Cup to the winter anyway). It was around 23 degrees in the stadium – not exactly an icebox but cool enough to forget the mean, relentless humidity of a September in Doha.

With its 26.2 miles of racing, however, the marathon race can't take place in a stadium. And so I am here, gone midnight, watching it on a specially devised course on the Corniche – a large 4.37 mile loop from the harbour to the Sheraton hotel and back that the athletes must complete six times. Organisers moved the marathon to night-time to try to capitalise on Doha at its coolest. But the heat is still oppressive – it is 30-something degrees and so humid that my short walk has covered me in sweat.

I have arrived just in time to see the first runners pour past in what to me looks more like a sprint than long-distance pace.

'Go on Charlotte!' shouts an unmistakably British voice.

I spin around to spot a woman in Great Britain kit stood with what I assume are her parents. It turns out she is a runner herself and the roommate of Charlotte Purdue, Great Britain's entrant in the marathon.

We get chatting while waiting for the athletes to come back round. They tell me about the family's previous life in Dubai and the lack of money in athletics. I have just started to explain what there is to do in Doha when we are interrupted by a golf buggy zipping past with a stretcher on it.

'Oh dear,' says the mum.

I thought it was empty. 'Was someone on there?'

'Yes,' she says glumly.

We stop talking to cheer as the athletes come down the stretch on the far side of us. There is the group of three or four at the front. The athlete and her parents start to mull over where Charlotte is.

'She was about fourteenth I think ...'

'After that woman ...'

They wait and scan the road.

After twenty minutes the field is already strung out. There's a huge gap between the first runner and the last. The lead athletes pass directly in front of us again. The ones at the front look languid and relaxed·in their movements. But quickly, once you get to tenth position and lower, you can see just how much they are all struggling.

The crowd adopts an air of camaraderie.

'Go on Japan!'

'Go on Hetsworth!' shouts one person, reading the name off the bib.

'Come on girls!'

But heads are lolling, running gaits are tightened.

A gulf buggy zips past again. In it sit three runners.

'This is ridiculous,' says the mum, getting angry now.

'These are prime athletes. They shouldn't be forced to—' her words fail her. 'To be ground into the ground like this.' The tiredness and the outrage perhaps contribute to the bungling of the metaphor.

Charlotte never turns up.

With the clock past 1am, and no longer able to cheer for their friend, the athlete and her parents decide to call it a night. I catch a yawn and decide to watch the finish from the comfort of my flat.

On television the course looks more deserted than it did

when I was trackside – moon-like in its abandonment and weirdness. The shouts of the crowd and the purr of the TV bike filming the runners echo off the asphalt.

The camera focuses on a Bulgarian athlete who is walking.

'You often say take a breather if you're struggling,' says one of the commentators.

'Well, even while she's walking, she's still in eighteenth position!' replies the other.

It turns out that of the 68 runners who started, 28 have had to withdraw – a 40 per cent dropout rate.

Ruth Chepng'etich of Kenya ended up winning the race, but her victory was never going to be the story. 'The Doha World Championships descended into carnage in the early hours of Saturday morning,' wrote the next day's *Daily Telegraph*. 'Close to half the women's marathon field failing to finish as sweltering conditions caused shocking scenes of multiple athletes collapsing in distress,' the article stated. Purdue, who dropped out after less than an hour, called the event a 'shitshow'.

In the end, what stole the show was not feats of human excellence but the weather.

Qatar is heating faster than anywhere else on the planet, the consequence of being a peninsula surrounded by overheating seas in one of the hottest corners of the world. Average temperatures have already risen more than 2°C above pre-industrial levels (the Paris Climate Accords are trying to limit rises to 1.5°C globally, after which the processes set in motion by climate change are deemed unstoppable). Qatar is one of the driest countries on the planet. Rainfall in some years can be as little as two centimetres. The country has no lakes or rivers. It has to desalinate most of its drinking water, which in turn requires an enormous amount of energy.

'We started hearing stories that it's getting hotter and hotter every year,' one Qatari studying energy and the environment told me, a worried look on his face. 'I remember when we were kids we'd go fishing. And now we'd have to drive out [in our boats] another twenty extra minutes to get the fish we used to get on the coast.'

Recent scientific research predicts that, by 2070, the Gulf will experience heatwaves beyond the limits of human tolerance. It is not the pure heat as much as its combination with extreme humidity that has people worried. 'When there is abundant humidity in the air, our body's ability to regulate our temperature and cool down through sweating is impeded,' I was told by Dr George Zittis, an expert on climate change in the Middle East at the Cyprus Institute, a research centre. 'We breathe more rapidly as we get increasingly hotter. Our heart pumps more blood to our extremities, and less to our internal organs and brain. If not hydrated, our body overheats and cannot maintain temperature. In such cases, heat exhaustion or heat stroke may be fatal.' The marathon runners at the World Championships had frequent refreshment options and doctors on hand. Most workers toiling in the heat in Qatar do not.

In May 2021, the Qatar government trumpeted its extension of a moratorium on working hours during summer. Along with other mitigation measures, the new law stated that, from 1 June to 15 September, no one would be able to work outside between 10am and 3.30pm. But the IAAF marathon race, which took place on 27 September 2019, showed that even outside of that window, and in the middle of the night, conditions are detrimental to human exertion. 'The humidity kills you,' said one of the competitors who did manage to finish. She perhaps didn't realise that this has literally been happening in Qatar.

Qatar is not just vulnerable to temperature increases. Its topography, a flat peninsula with huge developments on reclaimed land, make it one of the Arab countries most at risk from sea level rises. According to the academic Mari Luomi, the physical damage and economic disruption caused by a one- to three-metre rise would knock up to 5 per cent off GDP. If the increase is more than five metres above pre-industrial levels, over 18 per cent of Qatar's land would be permanently reclaimed by the ocean. Air quality, too, is a problem. The Gulf is already a dusty place, courtesy of the sand. Add to that the growing traffic and industry fumes, increasing soil erosion and the detritus kicked up by non-stop construction and the result is increasingly poor air quality. One Qatari told me anecdotally that there was a period when there was no antihistamine medication in Doha – there had been a run on chemists as people suffered respiratory issues caused by the pollution.

Qatar has been slow to mitigate the effects of climate change, despite being on course to be threatened more than most. Sitting on one of the world's biggest reservoirs of gas, Doha has little incentive for promoting renewable energy, given that the world's gas dependency keeps its economy afloat. One young Qatari working in the sustainability sector recalled a testy exchange he had with a government energy official in the 2000s. 'Why are you shedding light on renewables?' he was asked by the representative. 'You're accelerating our demise.' In 2018, the World Bank labelled Qatar the largest per-capita emitter of CO_2 on the planet. Many in Qatar take umbrage with this distinction, pointing out that included in the sums are the vast quantities of liquefied natural gas (LNG) exported to countries around the world. Would it not, they ask, make more sense to pin the emissions on the nations using it?

Yet withdraw those emissions and Qatar still produces plenty of greenhouse gases. According to consumption-based calculators, in 2020 the country came 38th globally. Part of the problem is that Qatar doesn't charge locals for electricity or water – one of the perks it offers citizens (migrants have to pay). As a result, the consumption of both utilities is at enormous levels. Gulf households make those in the US look like Scandinavians in terms of energy use. A shocking 70 per cent of total electricity use in the Gulf goes on air conditioning (compared to around 15 per cent in the US and 10 per cent in China and India). Government building regulations are weak, resulting in many houses and offices that are energy inefficient. West Bay is littered with skyscrapers sheathed in glass facing the sun all day – impossible to make habitable without prodigious amounts of air conditioning. To maintain the semblance of ordinary life through the summer months, many businesses air condition the outdoors. Cafés and restaurants deploy industrial-sized units to keep al fresco diners cool. Top-end shops have air-conditioned grilles in front of them blowing out cold air to make window shopping tolerable.

Qatar's current approach to climate change fits an all-too-familiar pattern. Doha talks a good talk: it hosted the COP18 climate talks, it claims to be organising the first carbon-neutral FIFA World Cup, and at the 2019 UN Climate Action Summit the emir pledged $100 million to support small island states and 'the least developed states' to mitigate climate change. The nation also does a good line in expensive, flashy technological solutions. World Cup stadiums have huge buildings next to them to allow the storage of cool water at night as part of a high-tech air conditioning system. The new inner-city neighbourhood of Msheireb has been designed to be more energy efficient, with solar panels, sun-blocking canopies and streets pointing north to capitalise on the prevailing wind.

The substance is more worrying. In its 2015 submission to the Paris Accords, Qatar not only avoided setting any quantitative targets, it also described gas as 'a clean energy' and presented its biggest export – a fossil fuel – as 'contributing indirectly to the global efforts to mitigate climate change' (it has since submitted a target of 25 per cent reduction of emissions by 2030). In 2021, the Al-Kharsaah solar plant was scheduled to come online, providing 10 per cent of the country's energy needs. But in the same year, Qatar Petroleum signed a contract to boost LNG output by 40 per cent a year up to 2026. The World Cup's pledge of carbon neutrality relies heavily on offsetting and doesn't take into account many infrastructure projects, like roads and the metro, because they are considered part of the country's pre-existing development plan. Nor does it engage with the incontrovertible truth that spending billions on hosting a four-week tournament in a place with no existing infrastructure is the very definition of unsustainable. Qatar has been accused of 'greenwashing', making a song and dance about small environmental achievements while not addressing the wider issue. But I wonder if the better framework is to view the behaviour as consistent with the nation's near-obsessive policy of hedging: build solar capacity but pump out more gas; talk about the environment but don't alienate the oil companies. Be all things to all people and hope that it allows you to squeeze through.

Among citizens of Qatar, there has been rising unease about quality of life in the country. 'People started complaining about air quality and started linking that to development, started linking that to the way we're living – is it sustainable?' one Qatari working in government told me. 'It wasn't just about climate change, it was just how we're living, how the country was developing so fast, how it's getting more expensive.' It reached a point where some people decided to do something about it.

I am on a stretch of coastline in north-western Qatar. It is not so much a beach – more where the desert scrub ends and the shallow waters begin. To my left and right the horizon stretches away flat and uninterrupted. The only sounds are the squawks of birds and the whip of the wind as the afternoon sun slowly begins to slip into evening.

But the illusion of peace falls away when I turn around, for stood behind me are some 40 men, women and children looking pumped and ready to go.

Dressed in a sun hat, polo shirt and cargo pants, José Saucedo steps forward and delivers his pep talk:

'Today we're gonna be doing beach clean-up *one hundred and seventy eiiiiight*, so let's give each other a round of applause!'

There are some whoops and claps from the group.

'I think we have a *lot* of first-time volunteers,' continues José. 'Raise your hand if this is your first clean-up with us.'

I put up my hand gingerly, along with half of the volunteers.

'All right! Let's give these guys a round of applause!'

With the shout-outs and can-do demeanour, José's Americanness is really shining through.

'Thank you for joining us. We are the Doha Environmental Actions Project – DEAP,' he continues. 'We do this every Friday, with the help of a lot of people like you guys, who have decided to take your time to try to make a difference and help raise awareness of the problem of plastic pollution in Qatar.'

José then dives into the particulars. We'll be cleaning for an hour. Each of us is handed a sack and divided into two groups, team Green and team White, soon to be sent in opposite directions. Once we fill up a bag, we leave it where it is and continue – he'll collect them in his pick-up truck. Be careful for broken glass, wood with nails, that type of thing. The wind is so strong it grabs his next words and flings them out of my hearing. All I catch is:

'... And leave the dead animals alone!'

Then another round of applause and a whoop.

'All right, well let's go!'

When José moved to Qatar in 2017 because of his wife's job, he was shocked by the amount of rubbish he encountered on beaches.

'I lived in Miami, right? So I'm used to being on the beach and I *never* saw *anything* like this,' he tells me in an expressive voice that emphasises every other word. Looking for some way in which he could help, José came across DEAP, at that time a small group of friends led by a Canadian woman. Not long afterwards, she left Qatar and José took the reins.

'It's a full-time endeavour for me,' José tells me when I set up a chat with him a few weeks after the clean-up. He works with groups of schoolchildren and with companies as part of their corporate social responsibility mandates. José is a regular panellist and speaker at environmental events in Qatar, and is omnipresent as head of the weekly Friday clean-up. 'In the past two years, I don't think I skipped a single Friday,' he tells me with a smile. 'I love it. I'm all in.'

We volunteers have fanned out and set to work. Closest to me is a family speaking what sounds like an Eastern European language. The dad, barrel-chested and gruff, is coordinating three blonde children of varying ages who scrabble around with speed, plucking things from the sand and putting them in his sack.

Given the remote setting and the healthy turnout, I wasn't sure whether there would be enough litter to keep us occupied. But five minutes training my eyes on the ground reveals my naivety. Tangled around scrub and washed up in mounds is the most astonishing diversity of products. I come across shotgun cartridges, a plastic fork, a piece of electrical wire, a toilet brush, a tea strainer, lots of plastic bottles, pieces of Styrofoam, plastic tubing, floats from fishing weights and lines upon lines of plastic rope. I'm shocked by the amount of plastic roping. 'I believe 65 per cent of the plastic waste in the ocean is fishing gear,' José muses gravely. Dubious that the proportion could be that much, I later look it up. Many studies think it's even higher.

I pause for a minute to see how everyone else is doing. A woman in an *abaya* is directing a small four-year-old to something on the floor. I catch the clipped, northern English vowels of a man in his late middle age, talking to José with the familiarity that marks him as a regular. A bit further away is a young Filipina woman wearing a T-shirt bearing a picture of Qatar's emir, collecting alongside a woman wearing one with a picture of a beer. There's even someone dressed in what looks like a summer party dress with a straw hat that keeps falling off. 'We are a representation, a microcosm of what Qatar is,' José tells me later. 'People from all over the world. Any background you can imagine – from professors, to workers, to bankers, to engineers.'

'Also Qataris?' I ask.

José tells me that, for the first 100 or so clean-ups, there weren't any locals involved at all – something he knew had to change. 'Because it's *them* who's gonna be able to help us fix this problem ... ultimately it's their country, they're the ones who have the means to say, "Hey, we should do something about this."'

So José gave a subtle tweak in his pitch: out went talking about the masses of rubbish they were finding; in came an emphasis on the hundreds of people that love Qatar and want to keep it clean. The rationale was that celebrating, rather than criticising Qatar would disarm locals more readily. At the same time, he found his phone blowing up with requests from schools to give presentations and take their pupils on beach clean-ups. 'It didn't take very long until I was going to schools where the majority of students were Qataris,' he says. 'So all of a sudden you have 100–200 Qatari kids with me on a beach clean-up. Well, guess what's going to happen after we do a beach clean-up? They're going to go back to their house and they're going to tell their parents what they did, and how much fun they had, and how much trash they found. Some of these kids, their parents are very influential people.'

Soon, José was welcoming Qataris on clean-ups. He had some very high-profile volunteers, including the Minister of Environment Abdulla Al-Subaie and Sheikha Al-Mayassa Al Thani, chairwoman of the Qatar Museums Authority and sister of the emir. 'We've had clean-ups where 25 per cent of the participants are Qataris,' he enthuses. 'And I'm not talking about school clean-ups. I'm talking about clean-ups on Fridays that are open to the public. Man, *that's*—' he breaks off in excitement. 'I have this smile for a reason. Like, that's *awesome!*' he grins. 'That tells me we're onto something.'

The hour is almost up. I have made it perhaps only a kilometre from our starting point but I'm already on my third bag. When I get back, I'm shocked at the number of sacks: more than 50. Someone is going down the line with baggage scales, measuring it all. We have collected a combined weight of 700 kilograms of rubbish, we are told.

Beach cleaning seems the very definition of a Sisyphean task. Sometimes DEAP clean a beach and go back two months later and it's filthy again. 'You get this feeling, I get it from time to time, that no one cares,' concedes José. He says that when he goes to collect the sacks from the Ministry of Environment they look bemused that he's still plugging away. 'But then, to me, it's like, well, if I don't care, then I become part of this vicious cycle.'

I ask him if picking up plastic is focusing on the symptom rather than the cause. Wouldn't his time be better spent convincing businesses to give up single-use plastics?

'The green movement here is in diapers. It's just starting,' says José. Campaigning to remove plastics from supply chains would be the logical next step, but it's too early. 'We're still on step number one, you know? We're still talking to people about why it's important to put trash in the bin, or why it's important to perhaps recycle.'

The more he describes the activities of the group, the more I understand that José sees DEAP as a vehicle for instilling some much-needed individual agency into the climate movement. 'I advocate for people to focus on the things they have control over,' says José. So much of what the climate movement has to battle against is the sense of having no influence on events. In the face of ice flows melting and forests going up in smoke it's easy to feel completely powerless. 'This is something that people can actually *do*,' José explains. 'What I tell people is, well, I cannot fix plastic pollution in the world. But *I* personally feel that we can fix plastic pollution in Qatar – a country of 3 million people, that is this big,' he presses finger and thumb together to indicate smallness, 'with incredible leadership at the top of the house, with the resources to do it. Oh man! Why not?'

With the bags collected and weighed, all that is left is the post-clean-up photo. We volunteers gather together in a group behind the sacks of waste.

'One, two, three!' shouts José.

'KEEP QATAR CLEAN!' scream the volunteers.

'Beach clean-up *one-hundred-and-seventy-eiiiiiiight*!' screams José.

'Wooo!' reply the crowd.

'Thank you everyone. Good job everybody.'

After the clean-up, the volunteers head to their cars and return with folding chairs, cans of juice and bags full of treats. They set themselves up on the shoreline, sip and watch the sun go down. The many children – and a few adults – roll up their trouser legs and go for a paddle in the sea. I get chatting to an Indian couple who, like me, don't have a chair and so just sit on the beach. They introduce themselves as environmental architects and tell me it is also their first time on a clean-up. They heard about it through friends and decided to give it a go. They say they'll be back again.

I have to confess to being sceptical of how much one group can actually accomplish by picking up litter. But José's enthusiasm is infectious. I'm bowled over by the depth of care he shows for a country where he arrived barely three years previously, a place where he will never be a citizen and will, eventually, have to leave. To have ridden out the confused looks, the mockery and indifference and to have fashioned an active environmental community is impressive and admirable. Qatar is lucky to attract such energetic, humane people. If only it did more to empower them.

Like everyone in this transient place, José can't say what his or DEAP's long-term future will look like.

'I don't know what I'll be doing in ten years,' he admits. 'But I know what I'll be doing tomorrow. And this Friday and the coming Friday and the coming Friday.'

Neeshad Shafi talks in a forthright tone.

'Frankly speaking, my team is very critical of the beach cleaning thing.'

He talks like a whirling dervish, thoughts tripping out one after the other.

'It gets credibility like this,' he clicks his fingers. 'Because it's easy stuff to do, and it's a fast PR ... [But] you're not talking the bigger picture ... You're actually putting the box in their mind that environmentalism is a beach-cleaning ... you're not building a movement. Because after going to two beach clean-ups, they're like, "OK, I'm done!"'

He fixes me with a firm look.

'I'm not being critical, but you're taking the climate and environmental conversation in Qatar in a wrong direction.'

Shafi is the co-founder of Arab Youth Climate Movement (AYCM) another environmental group in Doha. Established in 2015, AYCM have taken a different tack to José Saucedo. A key focus is lobbying entities in Qatar for solutions and change. 'There is a big *vacuum* of having a real environmental organisation,' says Shafi. 'In Europe, we will say, "OK, I can join 350[. org], I can join Greenpeace International, I can join—" I don't know how many number [of organisations] you have in your country. Here we have zero.'

There are academic think tanks, university departments and student groups in Doha devoted to the environment, but it is a world almost entirely contained within the ivory tower. AYCM wants broader impact. 'We want to make it so [climate change] is not a government thing any more, it's a public thing – your safety, your health,' Shafi tells me. 'When the government understand the public perspective is changing, they are automatically changing. So we need to build a dialogue, and that has to be done through an institution.'

There was, however, a large stumbling block as the founders sought to get AYCM off the ground: Qatar doesn't particularly want organisations like this.

There isn't really a charity or NGO sector in Qatar. Organisations frequently referred to as charities – the Qatar Foundation, Education Above All – are usually government-funded and often headed by the immediate family of the emir. Bottom-up or citizen-led activities and groupings, if not actively discouraged, often wither from lack of support. The right to freedom of assembly is constrained for Qataris and doesn't apply to non-citizens. Organisers of public events have to apply for a permit from the Interior Ministry. 'AYCM is not like – what do you call? – Greta Thunberg doing a march to the parliament,' says Shafi, drawing a contrast with the young Swedish environmentalist who has galvanised the global climate movement.

To formally register as a non-profit association, AYCM was told it would need the infrastructure of a profit-making business: a certain number of employees, a certain annual turnover, a registered address that couldn't be a residential property. 'These things will break you from day one,' Shafi exclaims. 'No wonder any Tom, Dick or Harry didn't survive because if you want to be a legit organisation, you have to be registered by the government of Qatar. If not, *yalla'* – off you go. 'You can do beach clean-ups, that's it.'

Shafi and AYCM weren't to be discouraged. They submitted applications to the Qatar Financial Centre. For almost a year they were stuck in a Kafkaesque cycle of delays followed by rejections. It looked as if they would never become registered when, through personal contacts, one member of AYCM managed to pull some strings and make the organisation official. But it is obviously not a route other climate or civil society organisations can easily follow.

This is a shame, because such groupings reflect the best of Qatar – its dynamic cosmopolitanism and the creative, intelligent people that it draws. Shafi is an Indian citizen. AYCM events are attended by people of all stripes. Their activities touch many of Qatar's communities, whether through generating carbon calculators for school children or hosting a series of public talks on air toxicity at the Qatar National Library. 'People say there is a lot of discrimination [in Qatar]. Of course there is,' Shafi says to me. 'But I never felt that I am leading an organisation which is very Arab as a non-Arab guy.' Shafi tells me that it is actually at international climate summits that he has suffered the most. 'For me I face a lot of racism not because I was brown and from India but because I was from Qatar,' he tells me with a laugh. 'They used to say, "Oh Neeshad, you're from Qatar, you have the worst carbon footprint in the world!" Back then I was ashamed to even speak up.' Now he points to their achievements: AYCM represented Qatar at the first UN Youth

Climate Summit; the Qatari government recently invited them to take part in discussions about Qatar's nationally determined contributions in line with the Paris accords. 'There are people fighting to have youth voices in Europe [while] we are already sitting with the government,' he says proudly.

With its diminutive size and vast wealth, Qatar could accomplish much more on climate change. But Shafi argues that goes for many nations. 'I will not just go, "Oh Qatar is doing bad" – every country is doing bad. But I'm not sitting in a country like India and talking about what we can do about plastic – man, you're in Qatar, one of the richest countries in the world! You can test *anything*. If you fail you're OK'.

One thing's for sure, Shafi wants to ensure that AYCM is part of the mix.

'The organisation is now *l*egal and *l*egit,' says Shafi, trilling the 'L' sounds. His hope is that it becomes Qatar's leading NGO. Perhaps even a rich benefactor will decide to take it under their wing. 'It may not be today, but someday they will say, "I will take this organisation from you,"' he tells me.

Shafi's eyes sparkle and the sense of opportunity in his voice is palpable.

'That is Qatar. One person can change everything.'

Khalid* admits to not having been very interested in climate change until recently. The twenty-something Qatari who works for the government talks to me on his lunch break in the shadow of the skyscrapers of West Bay. He tells me what it was like growing up.

'If you look back ten years ago ... Schools wasn't teaching it, the government weren't promoting for it.'

He's softly spoken and low key. When compared to the exuberance of José and Neeshad, his demeanour could be taken for disinterest. But as we chat, a quiet determination reveals itself, allied with a self-criticism that I rarely found when speaking to Qataris.

'People don't look into how much they consume,' he tells me of his fellow countryfolk. 'They look into why isn't someone treating it for us so that it doesn't have an impact on the nature.'

Khalid got into environmentalism through his job, when they asked him to research sustainability. But he also volunteers from time to time with AYCM. He has helped AYCM work on some of their policies, particularly liaising with government departments. 'They suffer because when they go they can't speak Arabic,' he tells me of his non-Qatari fellow activists. 'If you work with governments here ... you kinda need to have a [Qatari] national to help you expedite things.'

For Khalid, the lack of engagement with environmental issues is due in a large part to Qatar's youth as a country. 'We kinda had to be very—' he pauses while thinking of the right word. 'Generic, initially, to build up the nation.'

Qataris first had to be educated in key industries, such as engineering and construction. 'But I think that people now have an opportunity to study things that are more specific, that includes sustainability of course.'

Key to convincing more Qataris of the importance of the environment, says Khalid, is challenging the idea that sustainability and environmentalism are alien Western concepts. As an example, he cites AYCM's Eco-Literacy for Imams programme. The scheme trains imams to talk to their congregations about environmental awareness and conservation. The hope is that casting climate activism in religious terms will help to make the message more compelling for Qataris. 'People here are very religious ... very patriotic,' says Khalid. 'So you kind of just have to frame it with the people's beliefs – tell them that this is for the good of your country... religion is saying you have to preserve this, you have to maintain that. This also means climate change.'

For Qataris who want to battle climate change, a bigger impediment than mistrust of the West is a society that has grown used to unconstrained consumption. 'If I go to anyone that's in the general public and I ask them, "What do you think about the plastic issue?" They'll be like, "Why isn't there recycling?"' Khalid tells me. There seems little awareness in Qatar of the need to change individual behaviour and rein in consumption. People leave their air-conditioning units on when they go away on holiday. Qatari supermarkets don't charge for plastic bags. Petrol prices are rock-bottom. I once got a lift back from an event outside Doha with a Qatari guy. He filled up his car – a hulking Land Cruiser – with 123 litres of petrol. I looked at the pump: it came to 213 rials, less than $59.

'I'm guilty of that. I drive a four-wheel [drive] car when I'm most of the time alone,' confesses Khalid.

I ask if he has a Land Cruiser.

'I have a Lexus!' he laughs sheepishly. 'I try to drive it as eco as possible but the consumption is really high.'

Speaking to Qataris about the environment offers a reminder that the battle against climate change takes on a different hue when viewed from the developing world. 'It's easy to look at the UK or very environmentally progressive countries and say, "Well they're doing such a great job" – net zero and so on,' another Qatari activist in the climate movement reminded me. 'But actually those countries, their revenues do not depend on fossil fuels.' There is an understandable irritation with the hectoring tone of industrialised countries – a feeling that it is a bit rich coming from those who have used up a disproportionate amount of the world's carbon budget. 'I think Qatar is doing more than what other countries potentially would have done if they were in the same boat,' the Qatari activist countered. 'We're doing everything you're supposed to do, right? Diversify the economy, move into other sectors.'

Many Qataris, not just those in the green movement, are becoming aware that the way the country has got rich – through sales of hydrocarbons, construction and consumption – cannot be the model that will sustain that wealth into the future. They had a glimpse of Qatar's precarity with the 2017 Gulf crisis. 'You had the blockade happening and it really affected us financially,' recalls Khalid. 'More things will happen ... you will get into problems ... so we will need to have a resilient economy.'

He surprises me by suggesting the government should resort to more dramatic measures.

'To be honest, I'm pro the idea of having taxes,' he says. 'Some people reach a point where they have ten to twenty cars. So, then, why don't they have to pay for that?'

Paying tax would build a sense of social responsibility, says Khalid. It would remind people that they have responsibilities to their government rather than just being recipients of its largesse. He points to the introduction of military service for men, begun in 2014, as a precedent for such a move. 'I think partly is to let people be aware of what they have and be thankful for what they have and preserve it better.' Perhaps the key is to overlap environmentalism with the increasing cost savings the Qatari government needs to make. 'I am aware of how much people are getting here, how much extra they're getting. But it's time for them to kind of give back, so that the country can reach a level where they kinda can *keep* giving back to you,' says Khalid. Even Qatar's emir has publicly hinted at the need for some kind of shift, suggesting in a 2015 speech that high oil prices had led to 'dependency on the State to provide for everything' and reduced the motivation for individuals to be 'sophisticated and proactive'.

Khalid concedes that Qatar is currently far away from introducing the kind of bold measures he suggests, but he nevertheless thinks that the country will eventually reach that level of understanding.

'I feel it will, definitely, but it will take time'.

Yet climate change is *the* issue on which the world doesn't have time.

Driving around Doha, I watch the steep towers being built on reclaimed land and imagine the place submerging, Atlantis-like, into the sea.

In my mind's eye, fish dart in and out of the wooden pillars of the shops of Souq Waqif. The canals of Porto Arabia overflow. The walls of long-abandoned buildings are caked in seaweed and mud.

15 'I've met lots of happier people than us in Qatar'

In both appearance and manners, Khalid Al-Jaber is not your stereotypical biker. A big man with a friendly face, glasses perched on the nose, he tells me in a soft voice the origin of his passion.

'It started when I was seven years old. I was going to the zoo with my mother and there was some traffic. And in the middle of the traffic there was a policeman who was on a motorcycle.'

Khalid saluted the policeman. The policeman saluted him back, and in that moment he had a jolt of realisation. He turned to his mum and told her that he wanted to be a police officer when he grew up. Looking at him, she asked why.

'Because', I told her, 'officers have motorcycles – look at his bike.'

Khalid and his bike have ventured to all corners of the globe. He unfurled the Qatar flag at Everest base camp and was invited to join a police motorcade in Buenos Aires. He was accused of being a terrorist in Turkmenistan and had to enter Panama under a different nationality when the border guard couldn't find Qatar in his system. In the process, he made a film, quit his job, moved to Germany and opened a motorcycle showroom and restaurant – the centrepiece of which is his bike, which sits resplendent, covered in photos from his trips.

But it almost didn't happen. Like many young Qataris, Khalid fell into a high-level government job. It paid absurdly well and was his for life.

What would you do with your life if you had all the money you needed? Most of us have asked ourselves the question at some point. But for many young Qataris today it is a reality, courtesy of the huge windfalls the country has received from gas and oil. There are those who spend their cash on flash cars, designer handbags and stays in five-star hotels in London. The stereotype of the lavish Gulfi throwing money around is perhaps the main lens through which citizens of the region are viewed. But neither work nor leisure felt particularly reward-ing to Khalid. In fact, it oppressed him. As he puts it, 'I felt like a butterfly that you trapped in a cookie box. If I don't fly, I'll die.'

If falconry is seen as a traditional Qatari pastime, then riding bikes around the world sits at the opposite end of the spectrum. 'I got lots of bullying, to be honest,' explains Khalid. 'Not many Qataris would leave their comfort zone.' He told me of the incomprehension he would face trying to drum up potential sponsors. 'I keep explaining to them that this is an adventure, there'll be lots of knowledge, I can be an influencer, I can be a changer, I can show the Qataris how the real travelling is.' But to no avail. 'They don't understand the concept of adventure travelling. It doesn't exist to them.'

What kind of place does Qatar want to be? It feels that this question is being answered differently on a daily basis: a petrochemical boom town; a pioneer of education, technology and sports; a corral for the exploited and unhappy; a global actor strutting the international stage; a place where tradition and family are respected; a tourist destination; a place where the sky's the limit; another Dubai; another Riyadh. Every country faces internal battles over how it should look and act. But in few places are those battles turbo-charged by the wealth that can make any ambition a reality.

It is the youth of Qatar who feel most keenly the force of change. They are inheritors of a set of cultural traditions forged in circumstances of poverty, but they live in a world of fast cars, international travel and government handouts. At home they are taught the primacy of the tribe and at school instructed in Western curricula that emphasise individual fulfilment. They have unrivalled opportunity courtesy of fossil fuel income. But those same fossil fuels are contributing to climate change that is making their country more uninhabitable by the day.

Qatar's youth are tasked with picking their way through the contradictions to fashion a coherent country (and self) out of wildly contrasting parts. Will we see, in the future, a cadre of educated Qataris shaping global agendas? Or a nation of spoilt rich kids, left to clear up the mess when the gas runs out, the sea levels rise and the migrants move on?

I ask Khalid what has been the most formative takeaway from his travels.

'Well,' he says and pauses for a second.

'I've met lots of happier people than us in Qatar.'

Much of my time in Doha was spent struggling to become friends with Qataris, young or old. It wasn't the case that locals were hard to find. I shared in many of the same privileges and perks as them, frequenting the same coffee shops, supermarkets and malls. It also wasn't because people were aloof or rude: nearly everyone was unfailingly polite and gracious. I had plenty of pleasant conversations with those sat next to me at football matches, with students at the university where I spent a year as a visiting fellow and with government officials and businessmen. Their voices have appeared throughout this book.

But that was ... *it*. My day with Nasser and his falcons turned out to be the only time we met. I was rarely privy to the personal views of Qataris on anything other than the incidental. With some, my lack of Arabic was a significant handicap. That is my own failing, of course. But it felt that the barrier wasn't purely linguistic. Throughout my interactions I couldn't shake the feeling that something was being held back.

Chatting with other foreigners in Doha made me realise this was not an uncommon experience. 'They are a bit of an enigma here,' one Antipodean told me. 'A lot of people don't know any Qataris, other than maybe at work [where] they know the guy who's the boss. You don't really socialise with them at all.' A Doha-born Indian described Qataris as 'insanely private'. He cited his interactions at work as an example: 'You will *never* hear them talk about their home life. If I'm having a crappy day, I want to tell my work colleagues, because they're a bit like my friends. "My son failed in his exams and

I'm so angry ... blah blah." But Qataris never say anything. If they're late to work because of a family issue, they'll just say, "Something came up.'"

Among the foreigners, everyone has their pet theory for the origins of this stand-offishness. Maybe, because migrants are so transient, many Qataris feel there's no point making friends with them because they'll have left in a year or two. Perhaps it's general conservatism. Possibly it's the result of a state-backed campaign of ethnic nationalism that breeds xenophobia. In any case, as a social anthropologist – someone whose occupation is to go around trying to befriend people different to myself – it proved a struggle.

It was with low expectations, then, that I accepted an invitation one evening to an event championing Qatari adventurers. Held on the outside terrace of a gym in Lusail, it brought together four young Qataris – two male, two female – to speak about their experiences. I got a hint that it might stray from the familiar pattern when the MC began by gently lampooning his home. 'I am Qatari, hailing from Qatar,' he began. 'A relatively new country, where everything is a, "Why do you do this?" or a, "Why would you want to do that?"'

The next two hours proved revelatory. I listened as the film director Hamida Issa spoke of becoming the first Qatari woman to set foot in Antarctica and Mohammed 'Moe' Al Thani related tales from his successful attempt to climb the highest peaks on the world's seven continents. The speakers talked of the challenges they had faced, in particular having to overcome the scepticism of friends and family, and spoke articulately about their dreams, fears and what drives them. 'Sometimes people ask you, "Tell us why do you do it?"' Sheikha Asma Al Thani said, who in 2018 ventured to the North Pole. 'But you become the true self that you want to be on those mountains.'

It needs mentioning that the Qataris climbing mountains and speaking at events in perfect English very much represent an elite. These people are usually Western-educated and have often spent significant amounts of time marinading in multicultural environments. They speak as effortlessly as natives in the patois of the clichéd Western adventurer-cum-life-coach ('You will get challenges, you will get barriers, you will find 100 people telling you you can't do it. You just have to find it in you to fight, to say, "No, I can."'). Two of the speakers at the event were from the Al Thani tribe that rules Qatar. It was also no coincidence that the other two, Hamida the film director and Khalid the motorcyclist, had spent significant chunks of their lives abroad.

While the adventurers are bold, give the kaleidoscope a twist and it's possible to make the argument that Qatar's young are more conservative than their forbears. Surveys of university students in 2010 showed that many considered tribal identity important when choosing a life partner and would not want their own children to marry into a 'lower' tribe. Young Qataris are some of the strictest adherents to national dress. In the 1960s and 1970s, people would often wear Western clothes in public. Today in Doha, the black *abaya* for women and the white *thobe* for men are so omnipresent they have come to be dubbed 'the national uniform' by nationals and foreigners alike.

Young Qataris continue to marry their biological relatives in high numbers. Government statistics from 2019 showed that 43 per cent of Qatari marriages were to a relative, most often a first cousin. The high proportion of marriage within families leads to above-average instance of genetic disease. The academic miriam cooke has written about being taken on a tour of Shafallah Medical Genetics Centre in Doha, where the director acknowledged the hereditary problems this practice causes. But, he added, 'it is also proof of the purity of Qatari bloodlines'. The comment underlines how marriage has become entwined with growing Qatari nationalism. The past decade has also seen the number of Qataris marrying foreigners decrease sharply. Today, only around 13 per cent of Qataris marry foreigners. The majority of those marriages are with other Gulf Arabs, who are often seen as part of the larger Gulf family.

In all of this, young Qataris are taking their cues from the state. Sheikh Tamim (born in 1980) is widely considered to be a more conservative ruler than his father, Sheikh Hamad (born in 1952). Tamim was the driving force behind recent populist decisions, including changing the language of instruction at Qatar University from English to Arabic and introducing military service for all males. Alongside the deluge of modernisation, it's possible to glimpse a parallel track in government policy fixated on preserving tradition, as rulers try to keep Qatar's conservative factions onside.

Reactionary comments and incidents persistently intruded around the edges of my time in Doha. In a chat with a Qatari media executive, the delight I expressed in Qatar's diversity prompted a sniffy, 'I don't like it,' followed by a rant about how Qataris are strangers in their own country (all in front of a Sudanese member of staff). Another time, in the changing rooms at Hamad Aquatic Centre, I witnessed a man complain to security that another patron was naked in the changing room. Stern security guards waded in and hoicked out the man in question, an incredulous-looking foreigner. It turned out he wasn't naked, but the smallness of his underwear had nevertheless irritated the Qatari plaintiff. As I got changed, I locked eyes with another swimmer. 'Man, this country. It can be a bit crazy,' he said.

The simultaneous emphasis on tradition and modernity leaves many scratching their heads. But it's only mysterious if you subscribe to a simplistic idea of the course of history: from a benighted past, the arrow tracks ever upwards, with each generation becoming more educated, more progressive. There are plenty of examples from around the globe to show that view to be misguided. Recourse to small-c conservatism is a very common response among those who feel as if things are careering out of control. Turning to tradition – resurrecting falconry, zealously enforcing a dress code – at least offers something to *do*. It provides a branch to cling to, the promise of retaining a sense of familiarity amid all the flux.

Midway through the Arab adventurer event, a young man in a *thobe* stands up and asks a question.

'Do you think that you've accomplished a cultural shift today ... or are we five, ten, fifteen years away from diversifying what the identity of a Qatari is?'

I sit up straight. That's a great question.

'Us just *being* here today is a cultural shift,' answers Moe Al Thani. 'If I did this ten years ago, I would just be by myself.' But with his next sentence, Al Thani muddies the waters: 'All of us here, we're not trying to change the culture. We're just saying that if you live up to your dreams and you dream high up to the stars, there's no reason you cannot.'

This comment puzzles me. He is ruling out wider cultural change, despite speaking at an event which seemed designed precisely to achieve that goal. The same inconsistency emerged in my conversation with Khalid. 'I did say that I'm a changer and I want to be a changer, but what I'm doing with travelling, and motorcycling, I'm just doing it for myself,' he told me when we sat down for a one-on-one chat after the adventurer event. 'When I decided to leave my job and move to Germany, I just did it in peace. I did it quietly. I didn't wanna announce it, I didn't want to talk about it in public.' Whenever conversation veers into talk of their impact on Qatari society, the adventurers would yank it back onto the terrain of self-discovery and individual fulfilment.

The move seems in part a defence mechanism. I grew up in the UK and as an adult have lived in the US, Germany and Turkey, but I had never come across such intense social conformity as I witnessed in Qatar – perhaps explaining why so many who spoke to me only did so on condition of anonymity.

'There's nothing wrong with being an outlier,' another Qatari told me defensively when I raised the topic. 'And there's nothing wrong with being not an outlier ... I just want to be clear that there's nothing wrong with being either. And I'm not pushing to be one or the other, I'm just saying that there are people who are outliers, and there are people who are not outliers.' There seems to be a general wariness about being seen as a negative role model, a desire to avoid becoming a poster person for any movement that challenges traditional values.

Qatar's adventurers can be forgiven for striking a cautious tone. In 2012, a Qatari poet, Mohammed Ibn Al-Dheeb Al-Ajami, was jailed for life for a verse that was claimed to encourage the overthrow of the Qatari regime (he was released in 2016). When speaking of the need to forge ahead in building a 'modern state', Sheikh Tamim is careful to stress in the same breath that this must be done 'without abandoning our authentic Qatari Arab belonging and our most tolerant Islamic faith'. Sheikha Moza, the former 'first lady' of Qatar, has fought for girls' education and women's rights while also declaring: 'To be frank with you, I'm not a feminist.' In my encounters with progressive Qataris I can feel them straining at the leash, desperate to throw their weight behind the more open vision of Qatar's future. '[When] you see people with all these privileges and they're doing nothing with it, that's what really bothers me,' said the same Qatari in a rare moment of letting down his guard. But given the mixed messages, it would be rash to voice too strong a criticism in public.

The French philosopher Henri Lefebvre famously wrote on the enduring power of transgression: 'State-imposed normality makes permanent transgression inevitable.' Regardless of authoritarian gestures or the iron-clad will of states, he suggested, defiance and disobedience will find a way to emerge. Doha seems no exception.

In my time in Doha, I heard tales of – and sometimes witnessed – Qataris partaking in the city's club and bar scene. I once stepped out onto a bar's terrace to see a couple of men in *thobes* who had squirrelled themselves away in the corner and were nursing beers. Stories abound of consumption of harder substances. I was sadly never invited to any Qatari parties, but those who have been report that they can be wild. 'As closed up as they pretend or as they claim they are, these motherfuckers don't kid around,' said Mohammed, the Egyptian PR, who has Qatari friends. 'They party.'

At night, especially on the weekends, Doha echoes to the sound of high-performance engines. Across the Gulf, there is an active subculture of joyriding, racing and 'drifting', which involves performing stunts at high speed. The practice is typically portrayed as a symptom of malaise, a pursuit for rich nihilistic thrill seekers. But in his brilliant book *Joyriding in Riyadh*, Pascal Ménoret makes the case for viewing drifting as a form of resistance. In countries where the media is regulated, trade unions banned and civil society discouraged, joyriding and racing is a form of expression, a way of coping with the pressure and of making oneself heard. That may also be the case in

Doha, yet it is mostly seen as a menace and a blight. 'I got no sleep last night,' a glum Brazilian waiter with sunken eyes once told me. He lived in the new city of Lusail – at that point still only partially completed. The roads around his place were so new they had yet to have speed cameras installed, meaning that drifters and racers had taken to speeding right past his apartment all night.

And of course, like people the world over, there are Qataris who date and have relationships with those that they 'shouldn't'. A conservative view of sex, combined with strict gender segregation, means that behaviours considered harmless in the West obtain an illicit quality. The artist Sophia Al-Maria, the daughter of an American mother and Qatari father, has written vividly of flirting, Qatari-style, in her memoir, *The Girl Who Fell to Earth*. 'As we walked through the mall, boys slowed down and muttered their numbers at women ... Men slipped notes with their phone numbers into the open purses of girls drifting past. There was an intense energy of longing and desire that hung over the long strips of mall corridors, and it had nothing to do with what was displayed in the windows of the shops.' While at high school in Doha, Al-Maria was in a relationship that entailed snatched phone calls, forbidden rendezvous in empty compounds and lying spreadeagled on the floor in the back of her boyfriend's car to avoid detection. Innocent as it may seem, to be caught would have wrecked not just her own standing but the honour of her family. And yet she couldn't resist.

Al-Maria's telling of the romance is playful, her experience and outlook no doubt shaped by being half-American and spending part of her childhood in Seattle. The majority of Qatari women are constrained by deeply patriarchal structures and traditions, as well as by a penal code that sets out a sentence of up to fifteen years in jail for extramarital sex. Research suggests that, along with their male counterparts, many female Qataris also hold deeply conservative values. Only 61 per cent of married Qatari women under the age of 49 were in favour of contraception, according to a 2011 study.

A rather ironic quirk of strict gender segregation is that those in same-sex relationships often find it easier to spend time together. Homosexuality is illegal in Qatar and is pathologised by the state. In 2009, a social rehabilitation centre opened in Doha offering to treat 'deviant and unusual sexual behaviours'. But of course gay Qataris exist. There is a great deal of sexual and gender fluidity in Qatari society but it is mostly under the surface.

Straight or gay, the need to keep relationships hidden doesn't make for particularly happy people. 'It hurts me that we have to be like this for the rest of our lives and raise children with women that we feel no desire towards,' one gay man told the sociologist Geoff Harkness as he prepared for his upcoming arranged marriage with his second cousin. 'We have to do what our family thinks is right because we love them. I don't want to make them unhappy or bring shame to their name.' An Arab from another Middle East country who managed to forge a circle of close Qatari friends witnessed first-hand their Jekyll and

Hyde existence. 'I saw ... [them] struggle with having to be a completely different character when they're around their local friends and not liking that, but knowing that's the only way to ever be accepted,' he told me.

A lot of energy is channelled into one activity that is permitted: consumption. Qatar topped a 2015 survey of luxury spending in the Middle East with an average spend of $4,000 a month per person. The Qatar Investment Authority (QIA), the main state sovereign wealth fund, purchased the British luxury store Harrods and owns stakes in high-end brands Valentino and Tiffany. In the parts of Doha designed for Qataris, ostentation is everywhere. Villaggio Mall contains an ice hockey rink and replica Venice canals, complete with gondolas. The metro has a VIP section. When I attended one falcon competition, twenty brand-new Land Cruisers were parked in the shape of a fan outside the entrance – the prize for the winners.

The consumption also has a darker side. Three-quarters of all Qatari families are in debt, and often not by small amounts. The majority of debtors have loans totalling at least 250,000 rials, close to $70,000. A 2018 government report put this level of indebtedness down to 'an excessive consumerism culture and poor financial management'. Spending beyond one's means has become so bad that it has been described by some Qatari commentators as a 'social curse' and likened to a 'fever spreading from house to house'.

Motorcyclist Khalid is all too aware that lusting after new possessions rarely brings satisfaction. 'During my trips, it's just appreciation of life,' he told the audience at the adventurer event. 'You see people who have got nothing but happiness. And then I come back to Qatar, sitting with my friends, having a coffee and one of them is depressed because he didn't get the car he ordered, he got another colour.' In their rejection of the consumerist life, progressive types find themselves echoing the views of Qatar's conservatives. 'I want to inspire people to reconnect with nature and reconnect with the nature of our souls,' says the filmmaker Hamida. 'Because with modern concrete existence it's very easy for us to become blocked.' It is a sentiment that could easily have come from Nasser the falconer with his nostalgic love of the desert.

Some worry that the wealth and opulence is robbing the next generation of the drive to compete on the global stage. 'I think the government's in a tough spot, because they want to give everything to their people,' mused one young Qatari I spoke to over Zoom. 'They want to make sure that people are taken care of but also want people to be resilient in making the future.' He felt that Qatar has been listing too far towards pampering and indulgence. 'It's one of the reasons why I wanted to move,' he told me from his new home in London. He was worried his two young children had become accustomed to the gilded nature of life in Doha. 'Here we don't have a car. We recycle. They have to walk to school. We live in a *very* nice neighbourhood,' he says, naming one of London's premier destinations, 'but for them, it's like, "Why do people live like this here?"'

A smile plays across his face at the recollection of his children's naivety.

'I tell them the world is not like Doha. And it's not gonna be like this forever.'

What will the Qatar of the future look like?

For its entire existence as an independent nation, hydrocarbons have been at its heart – firstly in the form of oil and then, as the 20th century drew to a close, liquefied natural gas. Without these substances there would have been none of the migration, the construction, the sport. But on a heating planet, fossil fuels cannot be sucked out of the ground forever. Gas won't be phased out as quickly as coal, but it still counts as carbon in a world that is trying to wean itself off it. The climate crisis presents profound existential questions for an energy exporter: how will the country adapt? Will it retain its vast wealth? What will its identity be?

The Qatari government's answer is its National Vision 2030, a 39-page roadmap for transforming the nation and putting it on a path to lasting prosperity. 'Future economic success will increasingly depend on the ability of the Qatari people to deal with a new international order that is knowledge-based and extremely competitive,' it warns. Contained within the document are an array of development targets, but there are questions about the viability of many of its hugely ambitious goals.

Central to the plan is the need to turn Qatar into a 'regional hub for knowledge and for high-value industrial service activities'. It is unclear precisely what this means in practice. For all the resources pumped into Al-Jazeera and beIN Sports, it's debatable that Qatar's future will be as a media behemoth, given the illiberal environment, the self-censorship and persecution of critics. These characteristics also undermine its desire to become an education powerhouse. 'Qatar aims to build a modern world-class educational system that provides students with a first-rate education, comparable to that offered anywhere in the world,' coos the National Vision. But in 2020, University College London closed its Doha branch over worries about the viability of the overseas campus model. The remaining universities of Education City have been asked to deliver budget cuts of 20 per cent amid pandemic-induced belt tightening and disquiet from locals at the amount of government money going to institutions promoting liberal Western values.

There are also doubts over whether, despite the billions spent on stadiums and training facilities, Qatar's niche can ever be as a global sports hub. 'With the World Cup approaching it'll grow,' a consultant to the Qatari government told me in the lead-up to the contest. 'Companies will come and invest here and it will look like a sports industry is growing. But what happens after?' He said that Qatar can't build an industry around major global sporting events because they're too infrequent. They can't build it around the production of sporting intellectual property because there are two few indigenous companies doing innovative work. And it can't be constructed around consumption (be that match tickets or merchandise) because there aren't enough people in the country. Taking on board what he told me, I tried to summarise his argument: 'So your job was to investigate how sport can help diversify the economy and you've researched and decided that basically it can't?'

'Yes,' he said, a bit uncomfortably.

So what is left? Tourism? Dubai seems to have the market for Gulf tourists sewn up and, anyway, Qatar has publicly stated that it doesn't want to attract people who 'lie on the beach all day and walk around with a backpack and shorts'. Finance? The Qatar Financial Center is seeking to lure international businesses to set up regional offices in Qatar but again it faces stiff competition from Dubai which is already a well-established hub. Science and technology? Possibly, but Doha's innovation parks and start-up 'accelerators' have yet to produce anything of note. It looks as if Qatar's best bet for the future may be as a landlord. The Qatar Investment Authority and its subsidiaries have been snapping up overseas real estate, from studio flats in East London to the Empire State Building. The *Daily Telegraph* has suggested that Qatar owns more of London than the Queen. Doha has also poured money into buying stakes in private and publicly listed companies. The Qatari state's investment vehicles have at various times owned parts of the German car makers Volkswagen and Porsche, the British supermarket Sainsbury's and a string of French companies including Lagardere, Total and Louis Vuitton. But the highly secretive QIA discloses few details about its asset allocations or its performance.

Maybe it's OK to have fingers in many different pies. All through Qatar's precipitous rise in wealth and influence, the

country's rulers have been commensurate hedgers. In foreign policy they balance adroitly the competing interests of the West and Asia. Prior to the collapse of the Afghan government in August 2021, they carved out a role as a mediator, hosting talks between the US and the Taliban. The balancing is also visible domestically in the attempt to countervail conservative tradition and modern change. For all Doha's museums, art galleries, hotel bars and universities, it remains the case that most Qataris are very conservative. And so every perceived policy of modernisation is followed with a sop to tradition: new labour laws make it easier for workers to leave their jobs, but the government looks the other way if sponsors prohibit the movement of employees by accusing them of 'absconding'. A church is opened for foreigners and so the main mosque in Doha is named after Muhammad Ibn Abd Al-Wahhab, the Saudi founder of the ultra-conservative Islamic doctrine of Wahhabism.

To date, Qatar has shown an ability to prosper via this balancing act. It upended the global gas industry and positioned itself as one of the world's biggest suppliers. It managed to see off the almost four-year blockade by its neighbours, emerging stronger. The leadership seems secure and its citizens remain some of the richest in the world. Given this track record, it would be foolhardy to dismiss the idea that Qatar can come up with effective new methods of ensuring the country's prosperity in the years ahead.

But for the young Qataris caught in the crosswinds, it can be a confusing and challenging time. How can they personally shape the future of Qatar? They can't vote for a political party with a different vision for the country because parties are not allowed. Civil society activities are also discouraged, making it hard to generate pressure from the grassroots. For all the high numbers of women in education, Qatari women are rarely the heads of businesses or government departments. At the first partial elections for the Shura Council, Qatar's legislature, in October 2021, not a single woman was chosen.

It is probably unfashionable to feel sorry for young Qataris. But at the end of my stay, that was the point I had reached – for the most progressive and outward-looking ones, anyway. 'Last week I was sitting with a friend of mine ... and she was telling me that it's very difficult to just live here and do nothing,' one told me. To have the necessity of hard work removed is many people's dream. But if the reality is a context in which you are boxed in by social expectations and the smallness of your country, then it can be a poisoned chalice. I left Qatar feeling grateful. Grateful that I'm not compelled to bridge Grand Canyon-sized generational gaps between me and my grandparents or be forced into an elaborate juggling act to balance the competing pressures of conservatism and modernisation.

But I also left Qatar feeling ultimately a little disappointed. My flat was located in a neighbourhood of mostly Qatari households. On the nights when I was home, I would go for a walk, enjoying the blessed relief that came with the setting sun. On these strolls I got to know the South Asian caretaker of the opposite villa who I would wave at as he watered his vegetables.

I became friends with the Turkish guys working in the hole-in-the-wall kebab shop. I even got to know some of the families waiting to pick their children up from the crèche round the corner. Yet I never met any Qataris. I interacted with their material presence – the Land Cruisers in the drive and their flags fluttering from the carports – but never with *them*.

My evening walks seemed to embody a bigger truth about my stay. I came to understand excellently the lives of Westerners in the Gulf, given that I was living basically the same existence myself. I became familiar with South Asians in Qatar through cricket. I even got to know a bit about those whose existence in the country was the polar opposite of mine, courtesy of frank conversations with domestic workers, labourers and taxi drivers. But I'm saddened that, after a year of trying, I didn't know any Qatari well enough to truly hear how they are grappling with the big questions that their country is confronting.

I ask Khalid the motorcyclist how he reconciles life in Qatar – with its opulence and privileges, its ultra-conservative zealots, its constant reforms – with the world he encounters on his motorcycle trips.

'You will have lots of mixed feelings,' he tells me with a sigh.

'You don't know which one is reality and which one was a dream.'

Epilogue

It is a December evening, and I am in the Doha fan zone talking to Amandeep*, a Liverpool fan from Singapore.

'This is ... rubbish,' says Amandeep. He trills the 'r', luxuriating in the sound of his assessment.

'I've been to numerous World Cups, I've been to numerous Champions League finals, OK? This is rrrrrubbish.'

I try to elicit what, exactly, he dislikes so much.

'Look at it! This is probably the emptiest fan zone I've been to pre-game.'

I look around. It was busy earlier but the crowd in front of the stage has dwindled to a few hundred. The rain drips slowly off the wooden huts. The whole place has the feel of a party where you've stayed too long.

'So they've not got your seal of approval?' I quip.

'Not at all!'

Amandeep is in Doha for the 2019 FIFA Club World Cup, a mini-tournament of teams from every continent. The biggest fish in this year's contest is Liverpool FC. Fans have flown to Doha from all over the world to see the side in action. It's hard to predict what Qatar will look, sound and feel like during those four weeks when the biggest sporting event in the world rolls into town, but this is perhaps the closest we can get.

Amandeep, for one, is not impressed. 'They only released the tickets a month before. Then they changed stadiums two weeks before. There's almost next to nothing in alcohol. And the stuff there is, it's damned expensive,' he thunders.

Another announcement comes over the tannoy, telling us to head towards the buses. I say goodbye to Amandeep, down the remainder of my beer and get on one of the free buses parked outside.

The vehicle is half-full. I get talking to a middle-aged Jordanian man who works as a pilot with Qatar Airways, when we're interrupted by the singing of four Liverpool fans at the back. Everyone turns to watch with a look somewhere between fear and awe.

One of the four breaks off to chat to the Arab teenagers in Liverpool shirts sat in front of him.

'Is it your first game? I still remember me first game,' he says in a strong Scouse accent. 'It was against Leeds in '92. We were shit. But it don't matter. You never forget your first game.'

He claps a friendly arm on the shoulder of the skinny teenager, who is too frightened to speak.

'Have fun tonight,' the scouser continues. 'And don't worry about the singing, none of us can sing!' He then launches into a semi-tuneful chant as if to prove his point.

It is at moments like this that I love Qatar the most. The incessant events. The hyper-diverse crowds and the incongruent juxtapositions they allow. I have come to feel quite fond of the possibilities.

The bus is being given a police escort. Blue and red flashes reflect in the windows and puddles as we stream down the highway. Past the fake cultural village at Katara, past the skyscrapers of West Bay over to our left. Our little capsule of football – containing Scousers, Arab teenagers, an airline pilot and an anthropologist – shoots through the futuristic landscape of Doha. By chance or design, the Liverpool semi-final match coincides with Qatar National Day, a public holiday, and the roads are busy. Out of the right window, cars are backed up. In every third vehicle someone (usually a child) is poking their upper body out of the sunroof and waving a Qatar flag.

Twenty minutes later we pull up in the shadow of Khalifa International Stadium.

'Did you notice that we didn't stop once on the journey?' the pilot remarks to me.

'You live in Doha – when is the last time you drove across the city and didn't stop once?' He is giddy at the VIP treatment.

'I feel like a Sheikh!'

Inside the stadium, the theme of multicultural babel continues. It is like someone has designed the most representative sports crowd imaginable. To my right, an older guy in his sixties is speaking Arabic. In front, a man and his small kids are in *thobes*. Behind us, a mum, dad and teenage child are speaking what sounds like a South Asian language.

On the surface, Qatar plays to this diversity. It makes cultural investments in museums and arts. It has opened its national day celebration to Qatar's migrants. It speaks in its National Vision about providing a high standard of living for 'all its people'. But it rings hollow. The museums are mostly empty. The majority of the population, men earning tiny amounts, have neither the means nor encouragement to enjoy its national celebrations and showcase sports events (unless it looks like the stadium will be embarrassingly empty, in which case they are hastily bussed in to generate the semblance of a crowd). The country's laws, geography and culture all seem to say to non-Qataris, the 89 per cent: it is for us to decide when, how and where we want you.

At the game, the vast majority of the crowd are Liverpool supporters. Or rather, not Liverpool supporters but fans of Mohamed Salah, the team's top striker and football's most famous Muslim. Across the Arab world, Salah is clung to the breast with pride. Whenever the Egyptian forward gets the ball, there's an audible intake of breath. I see behind me a small boy, around ten years old in a Liverpool top. He is holding a home-made sign: 'M Salah We Want Your Shirt PLEASE!!!'

At half-time, an MC comes on the big screen, an annoying man in a blue suit who seems to have one volume setting: an ear-piercing SHOUT.

'OK EVERYBODY LET'S HAVE YOU READY. GET YOUR PHONES OUT AND YOUR LIGHTS ON. WE'RE GOING TO DANCE TO COLDPLAY, "SKY FULL OF STARS". OK? NOW. HERE. WE. GOOOOOOOOOOO!'

I physically recoil. But around me people seem to be complying. Phones are out, lights are on and people enjoy having a wave and a dance.

It can be tempting to use the word 'multicultural' to describe Qatar. But the more time I spent in the country, the more I grew to think that the term's not quite right. Multiculturalism isn't simply an objective description of diversity. The concept contains within it a humanistic ethics. It implies mixing, a sense of learning from difference and growing as a result. The structure of Qatar is deliberately designed to prevent such learning and growth. The law denies citizenship to foreigners born in Doha and forbids the naturalisation of those who live there for decades. Low-income male workers are prevented from entering parks and shops. It is illegal to house certain types of workers (read: poor ones) in residential neighbourhoods. Many Qatari nationals have separated themselves off legally, racially and culturally from everyone else, leaving a small elite espousing a growing sense of ethnonationalism and an underclass stripped of all rights, able to be jailed or deported at the mere word of a local.

Qatar does provide opportunities – for some. I think of Ali and his flourishing cricket business, the Spanish coaches with Aspire Academy, Abu Yusuf and his health and safety certificates pulling him up through the strata of workers like a balloon inflated under water. But for all the stories of enterprise, resilience and success that I discovered, I couldn't help but feel they were in spite of, rather than with, the support of Qatar.

The country has become extremely adept at knowing what to say and show to outsiders. The soundbite and the flashy gesture are perfectly crafted to draw the sting out of any criticism. 'There is not a single nation in the world today that can claim they have the perfect labour system ... and we are no different,' said head of the World Cup preparations, Hassan Al-Thawadi disarmingly. 'More work needs to be done.' The smooth presentation can be extremely effective in setting the mood music. It is for this reason that, with his deeply negative stance, Amandeep's was in the minority among those I spoke to at the Club World Cup. Qatar pulled out the stops and most visitors were pleasantly surprised. The same will probably be true for the World Cup.

But the litmus test of a humane society is not how you treat visitors or your middle classes. It is how you look after your most vulnerable. And by this yardstick Qatar absolutely fails. It allows its poorest to be exploited by their sponsors. It doesn't uphold their rights to be paid, housed properly or to leave their jobs. It fails to effectively shield them from abuse and, if they are unfortunate enough to suffer, neglects to support them in getting sufficient recourse. If the worst occurs, it doesn't even properly investigate their deaths.

When I told people back home that I was writing a book about Qatar, their first query would nearly always be about the death of labourers. It's a valid question, of course. But the bigger question I wish they would ask is why, in light of all this, do so many still want to come?

The answer is often because people have no other choice. Like Rekha, the scaffolder, who couldn't earn enough in Nepal to feed his growing family. Or Maggie, the Kenyan domestic worker, who lost her breadwinner and had to adapt. Another answer is that everything functions in Qatar. There are no rolling electricity cuts, no disruptive public unrest, next to no petty crime. Further up the ladder, the calculation is different: Qatar offers higher wages, a mortgage paid off quickly, a great professional opportunity. If I'm honest, the final one is also what brought me to the country.

In many ways, the issues I encountered in Qatar are no different from those in the wider world. 'This happens to Mexican workers in Canada. It happens to Thai workers in agriculture in Israel. It happens to Filipino electronics workers in Taiwan,' Nicholas McGeehan, human rights researcher and director at FairSquare consultancy told me. The country doesn't have a monopoly on labour exploitation, pollution and growing inequality. It is perhaps just a point on earth where the threads of these larger maladies reveal themselves more readily.

But McGeehan thinks that there are particular elements that set the Gulf apart: the *kafala* system, passport confiscation, lack of civil society and trade unions, the imbalance of citizens to migrants. 'It's a particularly nasty model of this type of migration,' he concluded.

What McGeehan didn't say, but what I experienced, was how coming face to face with the model up close forces you to examine who you are and what you believe. At the start of my adventure, I felt apart from what I was witnessing. It wasn't *me* forcing individuals to work in unsafe temperatures, directly withholding their wages or denying them trips home. The lack of direct involvement was a salve for my discomfort.

But there came a point where that defence began to look thin. As time went on, I felt I slipped into a no-man's land: no longer able to deny my complicity in what was going on around me, but unsure how to alter it. Should I be doing more? If so, what? In the face of what I discovered, writing a book feels an insufficient act.

Yet what lingers with me most is not the extreme inequality or my role in upholding it. It is, rather, the fear that seems to stem from the inequity; a fear among labourers of their bosses, that they could be beaten or their visa terminated overnight; but also the Qatari citizen's fear of the migrant. That they might overflow the strict system of control designed to keep everyone in their place. The big buildings, the futuristic stadiums, the flash cars – for me, all of it seemed suffused with terror and agitation that it might be taken away. Maybe fear is an emotion that always accompanies inequality. Perhaps it is entirely my projection. Yet to be prosperous but ever-fearful seems a particularly Faustian bargain.

Writing these words at home, far from Doha, I find myself frequently returning to an experience early on in my stay.

I am in a taxi to yet another conference in another five-star hotel.

The Sri Lankan driver, a cheery man who introduces himself as Sudeera*, approaches a junction. 'Shit,' he says as he prevaricates before electing at the last minute to turn right.

Suddenly there is a huge honk from that direction. My taxi has just cut up a big Land Cruiser. We're not close to having an accident but Sudeera holds his hand up to the car and apologises to me. I assume that the incident is over but as we carry on down the road we discover an unfortunate fact.

The Land Cruiser has been waiting for us.

As our taxi gathers speed on the dual carriageway, the driver of the Land Cruiser overtakes.

He speeds up, moves in front and then after 500 metres or so, rams on the brake. There is a screech as Sudeera is forced to stop centimetres before going into the back of the car.

Having got our attention, the Land Cruiser then pulls over. The taxi driver pulls up alongside and they lower their windows, letting the heat and dust of Doha billow in.

He is wearing a *thobe* and in his early twenties. A mate sits on the passenger seat. Ignoring me completely, he starts speaking in Arabic to my driver.

The taxi driver responds, his accent heavy and his words basic. But fair play to him – replying in Arabic is more than I or most other foreigners could manage.

The Qatari answers in an aggressive tone. The taxi driver is clearly nervous and emits a laugh – the strangled chuckle of the nervous.

The laugh seems to infuriate the driver of the Land Cruiser. He mocks Sudeera, adopting a gormless grin and drawing attention to it. He does this a couple of times. I find it borderline racist. Sudeera repeatedly stutters that he is sorry.

The driver sneers. It is an ugly sneer, one that contorts his face into a snarl.

It drips aggression and entitlement.

Then he winds up the window, accelerates and is gone.

Notes

CHAPTER 1

8   **From my interactions:** 'Population', Qatar Monthly Statistics, December 2021, Qatar Planning and Statistics Authority, p. 79, https://www.psa.gov.qa/en/statistics/Statistical%20Releases/General/QMS/QMS_PSA_96_Jan_2022.pdf. There have been roughly three males to every female in Qatar for most of the 21st century.

8   **many get by on earnings of around:** 'Qatar's New Minimum Wage: Infographic', 30 August 2020, International Labour Organisation, https://www.ilo.org/beirut/projects/qatar-office/WCMS_754395/lang--en/index.htm.

9   **'a quasi-caste system based on national origin':** E. Tendayi Achiume, 'Visit to Qatar: Report of the Special Rapporteur on contemporary forms of racism, racial discrimination, xenophobia and related intolerance', United Nations, 27 April 2020, p. 5.

CHAPTER 2

15   **Helen Macdonald, author of:** Helen Macdonald, *H is for Hawk*. London: Vintage, 2014.

15   **fn. From 2002 to 2014:** 'GDP per capita, current prices (Purchasing power parity; international dollars per capita)', International Monetary Fund, https://www.imf.org/external/datamapper/PPPPC@WEO/ADVEC/WEOWORLD/MAE/OAE/EUQ/ARE/USA/CHE/SGP/QAT/NOR/IRL/LUX.

16   **With a climate unsuited to:** Allen J. Fromherz, *Qatar: Rise to Power and Influence*. London and New York: I.B. Tauris, 2017, pp. 118–19.

16   **By 1940, the population:** Jill Crystal, *Oil and Politics in the Gulf: Rulers and Merchants in Kuwait and Qatar*. Cambridge: Cambridge University Press, 1990, p. 117.

16   **The situation was so parlous:** Ibid.

16   **In 1949, oil exports began:** Valentina Mirabella, 'The Qatar Oil Concession Ushers in a New Era for British Relations with Doha',

Qatar Digital Library, https://www.qdl.qa/en/qatar-oil-concession-ushers-new-era-british-relations-doha.

17 **Despite the superficial resemblance:** Helen Macdonald, *Falcon*. London: Reaktion, 2006, p. 19.

18 **Its sperm is taken up:** Ibid., pp. 136–9.

18 **The rise of falconry:** Ibid., p. 96.

18 **'what you have taught your hunting birds and beasts to catch':** Surah 5 (Al-Maida), Ayah 4, Malik Quran translation, https://www.alim.org/quran/compare/surah/5/4/.

18 **In the 9th century:** Birgit Krawietz, 'Falconry as a Cultural Icon of the Arab Gulf Region', in *Under Construction: Logics of Urbanism in the Gulf Region*, edited by Steffen Wippel et al., pp. 131–47. London: Routledge, 2016, p. 132.

18 **Falcon imagery has been incorporated:** 'Standard: 17th Century (made)', Victoria and Albert Museum, 26 June 2008, https://collections.vam.ac.uk/item/O157561/standard/.

19 **the bird's toes have:** Macdonald, *Falcon*, pp. 23–4.

20 **Politically, the wealth has:** Mehran Kamrava, *Qatar: Small State, Big Politics*. Ithaca, NY: Cornell University Press, 2015, pp. 125–7.

20 **political parties are banned:** 'Qatar: Government', CIA World Factbook.

20 **In November 2021 it stood:** 'Monthly Figures on Total Population', Qatar Planning and Statistics Authority, November 2021, https://www.psa.gov.qa/en/statistics1/StatisticsSite/Pages/Population.aspx. The exact number of Qataris is absent from the Qatari government's otherwise detailed population statistics. This is presumably due to sensitivity caused by citizens being massively outnumbered by foreign residents. The figure of approximately 300,000 is widely accepted and features in many publications, arrived at by the triangulation of various sources of public data. See 'Have Qataris always been a minority in their own country?', Priya DSouza Communications, 7 January 2017, https://priyadsouza.com/have-qataris-always-been-a-minority-in-their-own-country/.

22 **The feathers on the *tilwah*:** BirdLife International, 'Asian Houbara: *Chlamydotis macqueenii*', The IUCN Red List of Threatened Species, 18 August 2021, https://dx.doi.org/10.2305/IUCN.UK.2021-3.RLTS.T22733562A205364424.en.

23	**During a 2014 hunt:** Declan Walsh, 'For Saudis and Pakistan, a Bird of Contention', *The New York Times*, 7 February 2015.

23	**To get the hostages released:** Robert F. Worth, 'Kidnapped Royalty Become Pawns in Iran's Deadly Plot', *The New York Times*, 14 March 2018.

23	**When they dive:** Macdonald, *Falcon*, p. 37

23	**a kestrel can see:** Ibid., p. 31.

23	**when a falcon pulls:** Ibid., p. 38.

24	**they migrate so far:** Ibid., p. 40.

25	**'to assuage the anxiety':** Natalie Koch, 'Gulf Nationalism and the Geopolitics of Constructing Falconry as a "Heritage Sport"', *Studies in Ethnicity and Nationalism*, 15, no. 3 (2015), pp. 522–39, p. 529.

26	**Close to two-thirds:** Macdonald, *Falcon*, p. 35.

27	**There is an easy omission:** For the history of fixed populations in Qatar a good placed to start are the following: *Qatar, India and the Gulf: History, Culture and Society*. Exhibition Catalogue. Doha, Qatar: Qatar National Library, 2019, Crystal, *Oil and Politics in the Gulf*, p. 113 and Fahad Ahmad Bishara, 'Mapping the Indian Ocean World of Gulf Merchants, c. 1870–1960', in *The Indian Ocean: Oceanic Connections and the Creation of New Societies*, edited by Abdul Sheriff and Engseng Ho, pp. 69–93. London: Hurst & Company, 2014.

29	**On weekend afternoons:** Quentin Müller and Sebastian Castelier, 'High-Risk Dune Bashing Helps Qataris Forget the Gulf Crisis', Middle East Eye, 30 October 2017.

30	**Women have been:** '"Everything I Have to Do Is Tied to a Man": Women and Qatar's Male Guardianship Rules', Human Rights Watch, 29 March 2021, p. 70.

30	**Three times as many:** 'Chapter 4: Education Statistics 2020', Qatar Planning and Statistics Authority, 2020. https://www.psa.gov.qa/en/statistics1/pages/topicslisting.aspx?parent=Social&child=Education, Table 78.

30	**a 'purer' form of Islam:** James M. Dorsey, 'Qatari Wahhabism vs. Saudi Wahhabism and the Perils of Top-down Change', HuffPost, 4 December 2017.

30	**Women require the approval:** '"Everything I Have to Do Is Tied to a Man"'.

31   **twenty-something daughters chafe:** Ibid., p. 6.

34   **fn. The Al Thani tribe are so important:** See https://priyadsouza.com/the-al-thani-family-tree/.

34   **The rest are ranked:** A. Hadi Alshawi and Andrew Gardner, 'Tribalism, Identity and Citizenship in Contemporary Qatar', *Anthropology of the Middle East*, 8, no. 2 (December 2013), pp. 46–59, p. 56, Fromherz, *Qatar*, p. 138–41.

34   **a Quaker from Lancashire:** Hugh Trevor-Roper, 'The Invention of Tradition: The Highland Tradition of Scotland', in *The Invention of Tradition*, edited by Eric Hobsbawm and Terence Ranger, pp. 15–41. Cambridge: Cambridge University Press, 1992.

34   **'clan tartan':** Ibid., pp. 30–31.

35   **'invention of tradition':** Eric Hobsbawm and Terence Ranger (eds), *The Invention of Tradition*. Cambridge: Cambridge University Press, 1992.

35   **Crucially, they suggest**: Ibid., pp. 4-5.

CHAPTER 3

38   **These mid-sized wooden ships:** Dionisius A. Agius, *Seafaring in the Arabian Gulf and Oman: The People of the Dhow*. London and New York: Routledge, 2005.

CHAPTER 4

58   **Private individuals:** Mohammed Dito, 'Kafala: Foundations of Migrant Exclusion in GCC Labour Markets', in *Transit States: Labour, Migration and Citizenship in the Gulf*, edited by Abdulhadi Khalaf et al., pp. 79–100. London: Pluto, 2015, p. 79.

58   *Kafala* **was designed:** Ray Jureidini and Said Fares Hassan, 'The Islamic Principle of Kafala as Applied to Migrant Workers: Traditional Continuity and Reform', in *Migration and Islamic Ethics: Issues of Residence, Naturalisation and Citizenship*, edited by Ray Jureidini and Said Fares Hassan, pp. 92–109. Leiden and Boston: Brill, 2019, p. 94.

59   **An essential element:** Ibid., p. 95

59   **When Britain started:** Omar Hesham AlShehabi, 'Policing Labour in Empire: The Modern Origins of the Kafala Sponsorship System in the Gulf Arab States', *British Journal of Middle Eastern Studies*, 48, no. 2, 2021, pp. 291–310, p. 8.

59   **Beginning in the 1920s:** Ibid., pp. 5–8.

59   **Small colonial bureaucracies:** Ibid., p. 14, pp. 17–18.

60   **'on the cheap':** Ibid., p. 3.

60   **The academics:** Jureidini and Hassan, 'The Islamic Principle', p. 105.

60   **These fees:** Ray Jureidini, 'Migrant Labour Recruitment to Qatar: Report for Qatar Foundation Migrant Worker Welfare Initiative', Doha, Qatar: Bloomsbury Qatar Foundation Publishing, 2014, pp. 39–43.

61   **'taste':** Ibid., pp. 44–50.

61   **When workers arrive:** 'Reality Check 2020: Countdown to the 2022 World Cup – Migrant Workers' Rights in Qatar', Amnesty International, 18 November 2020, p. 15.

61   **Many workers:** Jureidini, 'Migrant Labour Recruitment to Qatar', pp. 87–9.

61   **'Each bedroom was crowded':** Geoff Harkness, *Changing Qatar: Culture, Citizenship, and Rapid Modernization*. New York: New York University Press, 2020, p. 215.

61   **Other similar accounts:** Leana Hosea, 'Inside Qatar's Squalid Labour Camps', BBC News, 7 March 2014, 'Investigating conditions in Qatar migrant camps', Amnesty International, YouTube, 2016, https://www.youtube.com/watch?v=a6SacfV9ZCU, and Benjamin Best Productions GmbH, 'Migrant Workers in Qatar – Trapped in Slave-like Conditions as they work for World Cup 2022', YouTube, 2019, https://www.youtube.com/watch?v=BjgYVHdU0Zo (see from 5:50 to 7:40).

61   **2018 audit on World Cup sites:** 'Annual External Compliance Report of the Supreme Committee for Delivery & Legacy's Workers' Welfare Standards: Changing the Game, Towards Real Impacts for Workers', Impactt, February 2018, https://impacttlimited.com/wp-content/uploads/2018/03/SC-Annual-Report-2018-Issue-6.2-digital.pdf.

61   **One poor soul:** Ibid., p. 37.

62   **Some had backlogs:** 'Reality Check 2020: Countdown to the 2022 World Cup', p. 28.

62   **In 2020 alone:** 'Progress report on the technical cooperation pro-gramme agreed between the government of Qatar and the ILO'.

International Labour Organisation, 9 October 2020. https://www. ilo.org/wcmsp5/groups/public/---ed_norm/---relconf/documents/ meetingdocument/wcms_757599.pdf, p. 8.

62 **'rampant in Qatar':** 'Reality Check 2021: A Year to the 2022 World Cup – The State of Migrant Workers' Rights in Qatar', Amnesty International, 16 November 2021, p. 27.

62 **In February 2021:** Pete Pattisson et al., 'Revealed: 6,500 migrant workers have died in Qatar since World Cup awarded', *Guardian*, 23 February 2021.

63 **For a third of the year:** Andreas D. Flouris et al., 'Assessment of occupational heat strain and mitigation strategies in Qatar', FAME Laboratory: University of Thessaly, 2019, p. 2.

63 **One in three:** Ibid., p. 5.

63 **A 2019 article:** Bandana Pradhan et al., 'Heat Stress Impacts on Cardiac Mortality in Nepali Migrant Workers in Qatar', *Cardiology*, 143, no. 1 (2019), pp. 37–48.

63 **'My conclusion as a cardiologist':** '"In the Prime of Their Lives": Qatar's Failure to Investigate, Remedy and Prevent Migrant Workers' Deaths', Amnesty International, 26 August 2021, p. 21.

63 **In Qatar:** See for instance Menatalla Ibrahim, 'Misleading: Critics slam "deceptive" *Guardian* report on migrant worker deaths'. Doha News, 24 February 2021.

63 **As the ILO has reported:** Francesca Re and Max Tunon, 'One is too many: The collection and analysis of data on occupational injuries in Qatar', International Labour Organization, 18 November 2021, https://www.ilo.org/beirut/projects/qatar-office/WCMS_828395/ lang--en/index.htm, p. iv.

64 **Statistics from the Bangladeshi:** '"In the Prime of Their Lives"', p. 8.

64 **'Everyone dies of':** Ibid., p. 9.

64 **Qatar prohibits post-mortems:** Article 2, Law No. 2 of 2012 on Autopsy of Human Bodies, Al-Meezan – Qatar Legal Portal (2012), https://almeezan.qa/LawPage.aspx?id=4568&language=en.

64 **'in most cases':** Asmahan Qarjouli, 'Qatar slams Amnesty's "sensationalist" claims over migrant worker deaths', Doha News, 26 August 2021.

64 **But in six deaths:** '"In the Prime of Their Lives"', p. 37.

66   **'We have the know-how':** Ibid., p. 33.

66   **With the help of:** Re and Tunon, 'One is too Many', pp. 5–6.

66   **the National Trauma Registry:** Ibid., p. 9.

66   **deaths are not disaggregated:** Ibid., p. 11.

66   **Qatar's 'list of occupational diseases':** '"In the Prime of Their Lives"', p. 10.

67   **a complaint against Qatar at the ILO:** Articles 348–351, 'Minutes of the 322nd Session of the Governing Body of the International Labour Office', International Labour Office, 2014, https://www.ilo.org/gb/GBSessions/previous-sessions/GB322/ins/WCMS_341702/lang--en/index.htm, p. 77.

67   **Top of its demands:** 'Leaflet on the ILO Project Office for the State of Qatar', International Labour Office, 26 October 2018, https://www.ilo.org/beirut/projects/qatar-office/WCMS_648005/lang--en/index.htm.

67   **Stung by the international criticism:** 'Supreme Committee for Delivery and Legacy's Workers' Welfare Standards', Second Edition, https://www.qatar2022.qa/sites/default/files/documents/Workers-Welfare-Standards-Qatar-2022-EN.pdf.

71   **'Eighty-four per cent of workers':** Supreme Committee for Delivery and Legacy's Annual Knowledge Sharing Conference, 1 March 2020, Sheraton hotel, Doha.

71   **They have carried out:** Ibid.

71   **Almost 104 million rials:** Menatalla Ibrahim, '"Ground-Breaking" Supreme Committee Initiative Forces Contractors to Reimburse Millions to Migrant Workers', Doha News, 23 December 2021. For average recruitment fee cost see Jureidini, 'Migrant Labour Recruitment to Qatar', pp. 39–43.

72   **(by law only Qatari):** 'Reality Check 2021', p. 32.

72   **Employees were owed:** Ibid., p. 28.

72   **In 2019, only around 35,000 people:** 'Qatar: Take Urgent Action to Protect Construction Workers', Human Rights Watch, 27 September 2017, 'Annual labour force bulletin 2019', Qatar Planning and Statistics Authority, https://www.psa.gov.qa/en/statistics1/pages/topicslisting.aspx?parent=Social&child=Labor Force.

72   **In 2015, the government introduced:** Decree No. 4 of 2015 with employees' WPS controls subject to the Labour Law, Qatar Ministry of Administrative Development, Labour and Social Affairs, https://adlsa. gov.qa/en/Pages/wpsMinisterialDecree.aspx.

72   **It has increased:** Fahad Al-Mana, 'LTE to *The Guardian* by the Media Attaché of the State of Qatar to the United Kingdom'. Qatar Government Communications Office, 23 November 2021, https://www.gco.gov.qa/ en/2021/11/23/improving-migrant-workers-lives-the-guardian/.

72   **To improve worker safety:** Yousef bin Mohamed Al-Othman Fakhroo, Decision of the Minister of Administrative Development, Labour and Social Affairs No. (17) for the year 2021 specifying measure to protect workers from heat stress, 24 May 2021, International Labour Organization, https://www.ilo.org/wcmsp5/groups/public/--- arabstates/---ro-beirut/documents/legaldocument/wcms_794551.pdf.

72   **Companies still get away:** Ray Jureidini, 'Assessment of the Wage Protection System in Qatar', Doha: ILO Project Office for the State of Qatar, International Labour Organization, June 2019, https://www. ilo.org/wcmsp5/groups/public/---arabstates/---ro-beirut/documents/ publication/wcms_726174.pdf.

73   **even at midnight:** See Twitter thread by FairSquare, https://twitter. com/fairsqprojects/status/1397885070837436416.

74   **'forced labour [and] servitude':** '2022 World Cup in Qatar: Sherpa Files Complaint against Vinci Construction and the Management of Its Qatar Branch QDVC', Sherpa, 24 March 2015, https://www. asso-sherpa.org/2022-world-cup-qatar-sherpa-files-complaint-vinci- construction-management-qatar-branch-qdvc.

76   **But in 2019 Sherpa opened:** 'Vinci lawsuit (re forced labour in Qatar)', Business and Human Rights Resource Centre, https:// www.business-humanrights.org/en/latest-news/vinci-lawsuits- re-forced-labour-in-qatar/.

78   **Qatar has been ruled:** miriam cooke, *Tribal Modern: Branding New Nations in the Arab Gulf*. Berkeley: University of California Press, 2014, pp. 56–7.

78   **Prominent relatives would bargain:** Fromherz, *Qatar*, pp. 131–3.

78   **In the past 70 years:** Michael Herb, *All in the Family: Absolutism, Revolution, and Democracy in the Middle Eastern Monarchies*. Albany, NY: State University of New York Press, 1999, p. 110, pp. 114–19.

78   **It's only since the 1990s:** Fromherz, *Qatar*, p. 86, p. 132.

79   **Qatari society is still shaped:** Ibid., p. 37.

79   **During the coronavirus pandemic:** 'Progress report', ILO, p. 4.

80   **The government says:** Fahad Al-Mana, 'LTE to The Guardian'.

80   **Some have invented:** Vani Saraswathi, 'The Kafala is alive and kicking... migrants where it hurts most', Migrant-Rights.org, 29 October 2020.

80   **The icing on the cake:** 'Qatar Shura Council recommendations threaten to undo reforms', Migrant-Rights.org, 23 February 2021.

80   **As Amnesty concluded:** 'Reality Check 2021', p. 4.

80   **'Discussing potential changes':** Andrew Gardner, 'Reflections on the Role of Law in the Gulf Migration System', *The Journal of Legal Studies*, 47, no. S1 (2 January 2018), pp. 124–47, p. 10.

81   **the Minister of Labour is on record:** 'Qatar Shura Council recommendations threaten to undo reforms'.

81   **'The problems that migrants encounter':** Gardner, 'Reflections on the Role of Law in the Gulf Migration System', p. 8.

82   **None of which translates to "misinformation":** 'Joint Public Statement: Kenyan Labour Rights Activist Leaves Qatar after Paying Hefty Fine for Publishing "False News"', Migrant-Rights. org, 19 August 2021, https://www.migrant-rights.org/wp-content/uploads/2021/08/Malcolm-Bidali-Statement-8-19.pdf.

83   **It said that he and his team:** '2021 Trafficking in Persons Report', United States Department of State, June 2021, p. 65.

84   **The Qatari company:** 'Essex Lorry Deaths: Men Jailed for Killing 39 Migrants in Trailer', BBC News, 22 January 2021.

CHAPTER 5

87   **In 2019, 883,000 people in Qatar:** 'Labour Force Sample Survey 2019', Qatar Planning and Statistics Authority, July 2020, https://www.psa.gov.qa/en/statistics/Statistical%20Releases/Social/LaborForce/2019/Annual_Bulletin_Labour_force_2019_AE.pdf, Table 22, p. 83.

88   **Because of this fact:** By my count there are close to half a million (462,600) Africans in Qatar. I arrive at this figure by adding up the totals for all African nations recorded on Jure Snoj, 'Population of

Qatar by nationality – 2019 report', Priya Dsouza Communications, 15 August 2019, http://priyadsouza.com/population-of-qatar-by-nationality-in-2017/.

89   **The sea north of Qatar:** Daniel Yergin, *The Quest: Energy, Security and the Remaking of the Modern World*. London: Penguin, 2012, p. 322.

89   **From Ras Laffan:** Ibid., p. 315.

89   **In mid-2021:** 'Energy Trends: UK, April to June 2021', United Kingdom Department for Business, Energy and Industrial Strategy, 30 September 2021, https://assets.publishing.service.gov.uk/government/uploads/system/uploads/attachment_data/file/1021989/Energy_Trends_September_2021.pdf, p. 10.

93   **Then it's fluid in the lungs:** 'Hydrogen Sulfide – Hazards', Occupational Safety and Health Administration – United States Department of Labor, https://www.osha.gov/hydrogen-sulfide/hazards.

CHAPTER 6

106   **Britain's trade with Qatar:** 'Trade and Investment Factsheets: Qatar', UK Department for International Trade, 24 November 2021.

107   **along with an estimated 22,000:** Snoj, 'Population of Qatar by nationality'.

108   **There are many professionals:** Zahra Babar, (ed.), *Arab Migrant Communities in the GCC*. London: Hurst & Company, 2017.

108   **They comprise around 5 per cent:** The percentage figure is arrived at by adding up the numbers from individual countries listed on Snoj, 'Population of Qatar by nationality'. I define 'Western' as citizens from the UK, US, Canada, Australia, New Zealand, the Balkans and countries of the EU, which make up 5.34 per cent of the given population.

108   **In the vocabulary of Qatar:** The word 'expat' implies the racial category of whiteness, see Neha Vora *Teach for Arabia: American Universities, Liberalism, and Transnational Qatar*. Stanford: Stanford University Press, 2019, pp. 132–3. Westerners from ethnic minorities would largely avoid the term, while non-Western migrants wanting to use the appellation would have to qualify it (for example, 'I'm an Arab or Indian expat').

109   **fn. Of course:** See AlShehabi, 'Policing', pp. 305–6.

110 **Ronald Cochrane was:** Crystal, *Oil and Politics*, pp. 123–4, and Ishaan Tharoor, 'A History of Middle East Mercenaries', *TIME*, 23 February 2011.

110 **The stress of his role:** Crystal, *Oil and Politics*, p. 125.

110 **He went on to spend:** Ibid., p. 128.

110 **'Within this general flow of arms':** Fred Halliday, *Mercenaries: 'Counter-Insurgency' in the Gulf*. Nottingham: Spokesman, 1977, p. 15.

110 **It is a significant purchaser:** Pieter D. Wezeman et al., 'Trends in International Arms Transfers, 2020', Stockholm International Peace Research Institute (SIPRI), March 2021, https://www.sipri.org/sites/default/files/2021-03/fs_2103_at_2020_v2.pdf, Table 2, p. 6. For the UK see 'Country Profiles: Qatar', Campaign Against Arms Trade, 4 June 2021, https://caat.org.uk/data/countries/qatar/.

111 **It hosts the largest:** 'Qatar and US plan "expansion" of al-Udeid airbase', Middle East Eye, 24 July 2018.

111 **For Britain in particular:** 'UK Defence and Security Export Statistics: 2020', UK Defence and Security Exports, 26 October 2021, https://www.gov.uk/government/statistics/uk-defence-and-security-exports-for-2020/uk-defence-and-security-export-statistics-for-2020, Charts 5–7.

111 **As the academic David Wearing:** David Wearing, *AngloArabia: Why Gulf Wealth Matters to Britain*. Cambridge: Polity, 2018, pp. 184–5.

111 **The current emir:** 'Profile: Qatar Emir, Sheikh Tamim bin Hamad Al Thani', BBC News, 25 June 2013.

111 **Lagging behind the US:** Wearing, *AngloArabia*, pp. 183-4.

111 **There have been foreign oil workers:** Crystal, *Oil and Politics*, p. 116.

111 **As the UK's North Sea:** 'North Sea Oil: Facts and Figures', BBC News, 24 February 2014.

113 **By 2008, the figure:** 'First Section Population and Social Statistics', Qatar Planning and Statistics Authority, 2012, https://www.psa.gov.qa/en/statistics/Statistical%20Releases/Population/Population/2012/Pop_Population_Chapter_AnAb_AE_2012.pdf, Table 1, and 'First Section Population and Social Statistics', Qatar Planning and Statistics Authority, 2014, https://www.psa.gov.qa/en/statistics/Statistical%20Releases/Population/Population/2014/Pop_Population_Chapter_AnAb_AE_2014.pdf, Table 5. For the population numbers in 2013

there is a typo in the English year. The Arabic confirms the data relates to 2013.

114 **The Pearl is Qatar's most exclusive district:** Ashraf Salama and Florian Wiedmann, *Demystifying Doha: On Architecture and Urbanism in an Emerging City*, Surrey: Ashgate, 2013.

114 **Rents are London-level:** 'Real Insights Qatar H2 2019: Affordability, a prime theme across Qatar real estate market', KPMG, April 2020, https://assets.kpmg/content/dam/kpmg/qa/pdf/2020/4/kpmg-real-insights-qatar-h2-2019.pdf, p. 11.

116 **The average price:** James Arney, 'World Beer Index 2021: The Cost and Consumption of Beer Around the World', Expensivity, 23 August 2021, https://www.expensivity.com/beer-around-the-world/.

116 **The cost is inflated:** Palko Karasz, 'A 6-Pack of Beer for $26? Qatar Doubles the Price of Alcohol', *New York Times*, 1 January 2019.

116 **'Come on guys …':** Sherbetcane, 'Easter and Recent Services' on 'Friday Brunch at the St Regis Doha', TripAdvisor, 27 March 2016, https://www.tripadvisor.com.au/ShowUserReviews-g294009-d3203250-r359467827-Vine-Doha.html.

116 **Investigations revealed years:** Ben Hubbard, et al., 'How a Massive Bomb Came Together in Beirut's Port', *The New York Times*, 9 September 2020.

117 **In recent decades:** Vora, *Teach for Arabia*, p. 31, and Maryam Al-Subaiey, 'Qatarization Policy – Implementation Challenges,' Brookings Center Doha, 2011, www.brookings.edu/wp-content/uploads/2016/07/06_bdc_essay_winner.pdf. For Qatarization in the energy sector, see Strategic Qatarization Plan, 2020, https://qatarization.com.qa/en/Pages/default.aspx.

118 **Government statistics, however:** 'Labor Force Sample Survey: The First Quarter (January–March) 2021', Qatar Planning and Statistics Authority, 2021, Table 2, p. 13, https://www.psa.gov.qa/en/statistics/Statistical%20Releases/Social/LaborForce/2021/LF_Q1_2021_AE.pdf.

121 **Most are oblivious:** Katie Walsh, 'Emotion and Migration: British Transnationals in Dubai', *Environment and Planning D: Society and Space*, 30, no. 1 (February 2012), pp. 43–59, p. 53.

126 **Other examples include:** Tom Finn, '"Bachelor Ban" in Qatar Tests Relations with Migrant Workers'. *Reuters*, 17 May 2016.

126 **Look at the response:** Carlos Vargas-Silva and Cinzia Rienzo, 'Migrants in the UK: An Overview', *Migration Observatory*, 6 November 2020, https://migrationobservatory.ox.ac.uk/resources/briefings/migrants-in-the-uk-an-overview/ and Abby Budiman et al., 'Facts on U.S. Immigrants, 2018'. *Pew Research Center*, 20 August 2020, https://www.pewresearch.org/hispanic/2020/08/20/facts-on-u-s-immigrants/.

127 **Qatar does allow foreigners:** 'The Areas of Non-Qataris' Real Estate Ownership,' Qatar Ministry of Justice, https://www.moj.gov.qa/en/Moj_committy_laws/table1.pdf.

128 **Each caused significant belt:** Kristian Coates Ulrichsen, *Qatar and the Gulf Crisis*. London: Hurst & Company, 2020, pp. 154–5, p. 136, and Simone Foxman, 'Qatar Cuts Pay for Foreign Employees Working for Government', Bloomberg, 10 June 2020.

128 **Commercial properties stood empty:** Real Insights Qatar H2 2019: 'Affordability, a prime theme across Qatar real estate market', p. 4.

CHAPTER 7

131 **Qatar has fewer than:** The figure was given by a senior figure at Aspire during a conversation with the author.

132 **Football talk shows:** James Montague, 'Qatar Has a World Cup Date. It Still Needs a World-Class Team.' *New York Times*, 9 October 2017.

132 **One of the Qatari government's investment funds:** Adam Reed, 'Paris Saint-Germain's Qatari owners have spent $1.17 billion on players, but the Champions League is still out of reach', CNBC, 18 September 2018, https://www.cnbc.com/2018/09/18/paris-saint-germains-qatari-owners-on-players-and-champions-league.html.

132 **The first club in the country:** 'Football', Supreme Committee for Delivery and Legacy, captured by the Wayback Machine, 6 February 2015, https://web.archive.org/web/20150206084225/http://sc.qa/en/qatar/football.

133 **They include former Barcelona player:** Adwaidh Rajan, 'From Batistuta and Desailly to Xavi and Sneijder: Qatari football's highest-profile signings ever', ESPN, 29 July 2021.

134 **In 1999, the Qatari weightlifting team:** 'PLUS: ARAB GAMES – WEIGHT LIFTING; Qatar Disqualified', *The New York Times*, 19 August 1999.

134 **In 2003, Kenyan runner Stephen Cherono:** 'Kenyan Anger at Qatar 'Defector'', BBC News, 27 August 2003.

135 **In 2004 he ran:** 'All time Top lists: 3000 Steeplechase Men', World Athletics, https://www.worldathletics.org/records/all-time-toplists/middlelong/3000-metres-steeplechase/outdoor/men/senior.

135 **The move so infuriated:** 'Fifa Rules on Eligibility', BBC Sport, 18 March 2004.

135 **It is so large:** Sebastian Abbot, *The Away Game: The Epic Search for Soccer's Next Superstars*. New York and London: W. W. Norton & Company, 2018, p. 65.

135 **When the academy was established:** Law No. 16 of 2004 Establishing the Aspire Academy for Sports Excellence (2004), Al-Meezan – Qatar Legal Portal, https://www.almeezan.qa/LawPage.aspx?id=4063&language=en.

136 **He supposedly has:** Abbot, *The Away Game*, p. 72.

139 **Named 'Football Dreams':** Abbot, *The Away Game*, pp. 255–6.

139 **Between 2007 and 2014:** 'Football Dreams', Aspire Academy, https://aspire.qa/football/football-dreams.

139 **In total, just eighteen:** Ibid.

140 **As late as December 2017:** 'Men's Ranking', FIFA, 21 December 2017, https://www.fifa.com/fifa-world-ranking/men?dateId=id12042.

142 **A ban on direct flights:** David Harding, 'Qatar football team arrives in political rival UAE for Asian Cup', AFP/Yahoo Sports, 5 January 2019.

142 **Saoud Al-Mohannadi, vice-president:** David Harding, 'Qatar FA official in UAE after being denied entry', AFP/Yahoo Sports, 4 January 2019.

142 **A British man claimed:** Diane Taylor, 'UK football fan launches legal action after alleged torture in UAE', *Guardian*, 27 May 2021.

142 **They went on to win:** James Montague, 'Dare to Aspire', *The Blizzard*, Issue 33, 7 June 2019.

143 **The players became household names:** David Harding, 'Huge crowds greet Asian Cup winners Qatar as they fly home', AFP/Yahoo News, 2 February 2019.

144 **They include the top goal scorer:** Thomas Ross Griffin, 'Homeland:

National Identity Performance in the Qatar National Team', in *Football in the Middle East: State, Society, and the Beautiful Game*, edited by Abdullah Al-Arian. London: Hurst & Company, 2022, Table 1, p. 7. Draft shared with author prior to publication.

144 **The academic Ross Griffin:** Griffin, Ibid., p. 3.

144 **Fifteen members of the France side:** Tom Williams, 'Why France Are Carrying Africa's Hopes in the World Cup Final', Bleacher Report, 13 July 2018, https://bleacherreport.com/articles/2785862-why-france-are-carrying-africas-hopes-in-the-world-cup-final.

144 **Thirteen of England's 26-man squad:** Jonathan Liew, 'The England squad is built on immigration – yet our xenophobic government dares to cheer it on', *New Statesman*, 7 July 2021.

144 **fn. For the emir to bestow citizenship:** See Articles 2, 6 and 17, Law No. 38 of 2005 on the acquisition of Qatari nationality (2005), Al-Meezan – Qatar Legal Portal, https://www.almeezan.qa/LawArticles.aspx?LawArticleID=39324&LawId=2591&language=en. Also see Achiume, 'Visit to Qatar', pp. 14–15.

146 **There is no discernible difference:** Griffin, 'Homeland: National Identity Performance in the Qatar National Team', pp. 15–31.

146 **(difficult, given the number):** Achiume, 'Visit to Qatar', p. 15.

151 **With success rates:** For a good insight into football academies in the UK, see Chris Green, *Every Boy's Dream: England's Football Future on the Line*. London: A & C Black Publishers Ltd, 2009, and Michael Calvin, *No Hunger in Paradise: The Players: The Journey: The Dream*. London: Arrow, 2018. The statistic is from Calvin (p. iv).

151 **A whopping 81 per cent:** 'Labour Force Sample Survey 2019', Table No. 23, p. 85.

152 **The Gulf is:** Ankush Chibber, 'Middle East Sales Drive Rolls-Royce's Record Year', *Gulf Business*, 6 January 2015.

153 **'Could it be that hosting':** Abbot, *The Away Game*, p. 123.

154 **They pumped money into:** 'Qatar handball team coach faces questions over foreign players', BBC News, 29 January 2015.

CHAPTER 8

158 **The country has passed:** Article 50, The Permanent Constitution of the State of Qatar, Al-Meezan – Qatar Legal Portal, https://www.

almeezan.qa/LawArticles.aspx?LawArticleID=25803&LawID=2284
&language=en.

158 **limited forbearance:** Hilal Khashan, 'Religious Intolerance in the
Gulf State', *Middle East Quarterly*, 23, no. 3 (2016), p. 4.

159 **Two weeks after opening:** John Fahy, 'Out of sight, out of mind:
managing religious diversity in Qatar', *British Journal of Middle
Eastern Studies*, 46, no. 4 (2019), pp. 640–62, p. 17.

159 **fn. There are of course:** Nick Cumming-Bruce and Steven Erlanger,
'Swiss Ban Building of Minarets on Mosques', *New York Times*,
29 November 2009, Demetrios Ioannou, 'Athens's First Mosque
since the 19th Century Is "a Dream Come True"', Middle East Eye,
8 November 2020.

160 **It is forbidden to:** '2020 Report on International Religious Freedom:
Qatar', Office of International Religious Freedom, 2020, https://www.
state.gov/reports/2020-report-on-international-religious-freedom/
qatar/, p. 4, p. 10.

160 **What little presence:** Emma Loosley, 'A Historical Overview of
the Arabian Gulf in the Late Pre-Islamic Period: The Evidence for
Christianity in the Gulf', Abu Dhabi Islands Archaeological Survey,
16 April 2002.

160 **There have been small groups:** Fahy, 'Out of sight, out of mind',
p. 12.

160 **But it is only:** The government of Qatar do not publish statistics on
the religious affiliations of its residents. The figures I use come from
'Table: Religious Diversity Index Scores by Country', Pew Research
Center, 4 April 2014, https://www.pewforum.org/2014/04/04/
religious-diversity-index-scores-by-country/. Now over a decade old,
they are at best a rough approximation of the number of Christians in
Qatar.

161 **the Anglican community:** Fahy, 'Out of sight, out of mind', p. 13.

161 **In 1988, an Indian Pentecostal:** Ibid., p. 13.

161 **The US ambassador to Qatar:** Joseph Ghougassian, *The Knight and
the Falcon: The Coming of Christianity in Qatar a Muslim Nation*,
Escondido, California: Lukas & Sons, 2008, pp. 1–2.

161 **Under Sheikh Hamad:** 'Diplomatic Relations Of The Holy See',
Permanent Observer Mission of the Holy See to the United Nations,
https://holyseemission.org/contents/mission/diplomatic-relations-of

-the-holy-see.php, and 'Qatar inter-faith conference begins', Al-Jazeera, 29 June 2005.

161 **The deputy prime minister:** 'Christians gather in first church ever built in Qatar', France 24, 15 March 2008, https://www.france24.com/en/20080315-christians-gather-first-church-ever-built-qatar-qatar-christianity.

169 **'Non-integration ...':** Anh Nga Longva, *Walls Built on Sand: Migration, Exclusion and Society in Kuwait*. Boulder, Colorado: Westview, 1997, p. 44.

169 **Some religiously conservative figures:** Khashan, 'Religious Intolerance', p. 5, and Fahy, 'Out of sight, out of mind', p. 12.

170 **In 2015 in neighbouring Kuwait:** 'Kuwait Shia mosque attack: Bomber "was Saudi"', BBC News, 28 June 2015.

170 **The academic John Fahy:** Fahy, 'Out of sight, out of mind', p. 21.

CHAPTER 9

178 **The country supplied:** *Qatar, India and the Gulf*, p. 77, p. 84, pp. 88–95.

178 **Indian money lenders:** Ibid., p. 60.

178 **Merchants from the subcontinent:** Ibid., pp. 59–60 and Andrew Gardner, *City of Strangers: Gulf Migration and the Indian Community in Bahrain*. Ithaca: ILR Press, 2010, p. 35.

178 **British representatives in the region:** Matthew Teller, 'Tales from the India Office', BBC News, 22 October 2014.

178 **Low-level Indian bureaucrats:** Gardner, *City of Strangers*, p. 27.

178 **As late as the 1960s:** *Qatar, India and the Gulf*, p. 104.

178 **Indians would still come:** Gardner, *City of Strangers*, pp. 27–28, *Qatar, India and the Gulf*, pp. 140–43.

178 **most noticeably in Gulf cuisine:** *Qatar, India and the Gulf*, p. 122, pp. 124–7.

179 **South Asians in the Gulf:** Neha Vora, *Impossible Citizens: Dubai's Indian Diaspora*. London: Duke University Press, 2013.

181 **'Every quarter ...':** Peter Oborne, *Wounded Tiger: A History of Cricket in Pakistan*. London: Simon & Schuster, 2014, p. 65.

183 **Qatar is spending:** Zahraa Alkhalisi, 'Qatar slashes budget for 2022 World Cup by at least 40%', CNN Money, 5 April 2017.

183 **Since buying Paris Saint-Germain:** John Sinnott, 'Qatari takeover heralds new dawn for Paris Saint-Germain', BBC Sport, 3 August 2011, and Reed, 'Paris Saint-Germain'.

188 **Despite the unfavourable conditions:** 'Men's T20I Team Rankings', International Cricket Council, https://www.icc-cricket.com/rankings/mens/team-rankings/t20i.

189 **In Pakistan, people cover:** Oborne, *Wounded Tiger*, p. 367.

CHAPTER 10

201 **A 2020 report:** '"Why Do You Want to Rest?" Ongoing Abuse of Domestic Workers in Qatar', Amnesty International, 20 October 2020, p. 6.

202 **There are approximately 176,000 officially registered:** 'Labour Force Sample Survey 2019', p. 85.

203 **As with construction work:** Jureidini, 'Migrant Labour Recruitment to Qatar', pp. 87–9.

204 **Ethiopian Lensa Lelisa:** 'Lebanon: Migrant Worker's Abuse Account', Human Rights Watch, 6 April 2018.

204 **Joanna Demafelis, 29, whose body:** 'Joanna Demafelis: Employers of Filipina maid found dead in freezer arrested', BBC News, 24 February 2018.

204 **Tuti Tursilawati, 34, executed for:** Areeb Ullah, 'Saudi Arabia Executes Indonesian Maid Who Killed Man She Says Assaulted Her', Middle East Eye, 2 November 2018.

207 **In August of that year:** 'Labour Law Promulgated by Law No. (14) of 2004 and Domestic Workers Law Promulgated by Law No. (15) of 2017 and its English Translations', Qatar Ministry of Administrative Development, Labour and Social Affairs, 2018 Fourth Edition, https://adlsa.gov.qa/en/Laws/LABOUR%20LAW.pdf, pp. 92–100.

207 **Three years after the passage of the law:** '"Why Do You Want to Rest?"', p. 6.

211 **Such trade in work permits:** Jureidini, 'Migrant Labour Recruitment to Qatar', pp. 92–3.

212 **'It also recalls the historical reliance':** Achiume, 'Visit to Qatar', p. 7.

212 **From August 2020:** 'Labour market mobility in Qatar', ILO, 8 September 2020, https://www.ilo.org/beirut/projects/qatar-office/WCMS_753585/lang--en/index.htm.

217 **'The Qatari people ...':** 'Migrant Workers in the Gulf Region: The Changing Economic and Legal Status', Gulf International Forum, 16 September 2020.

218 **It was the Qatari government:** '"Why Do You Want to Rest?"', pp. 22–4.

218 **Qatar has sought to emphasise:** Rima Kalush et al., 'Lived Experience of Migrant Women: Qatar, Bahrain, and Kuwait', Migrant-Rights.org, 2019, https://www.migrant-rights.org/wp-content/uploads/2019/11/Lived-Experiences-of-Migrant-Women.pdf, and '"Why Do You Want to Rest?"', pp. 22–7.

CHAPTER 11

222 **Doha has created and hosted:** Doha Debates first ran from 2005 to 2012, funded by the Qatar Foundation and broadcast by BBC World News, see 'About the Debates', Doha Debates, https://archive.dohadebates.com/pages/indexfb91.html?p=3259. In 2019, the debates were relaunched under the sole aegis of the Qatar foundation, see Amjad Atallah, 'It's time for a new kind of debate', Doha Debates, https://dohadebates.com/letter-from-managing-director-amjad-atallah/its-time-for-a-new-kind-of-debate/.

222 **'We want freedom of speech':** Charlie Rose, 'Qatar's emir stands defiant in face of blockade', CBS News, 29 October 2017.

222 **Freedom of assembly:** 'Freedom in the World 2021: Qatar', Freedom House, https://freedomhouse.org/country/qatar/freedom-world/2021.

223 **It is fully funded:** 'Board of Directors', Qatar Foundation, https://www.qf.org.qa/about#section-5.

224 **In return for their outposts:** Vora, *Teach for Arabia*, p. 5.

224 **The one independent news organisation:** 'Freedom in the World 2021: Qatar', and Harkness, *Changing Qatar*, pp. 228–9.

224 **Qatar's law governing the media:** Article 46, Law No. 8 of 1979 on Publications and Publishing, Al-Meezan – Qatar Legal Portal, https://www.almeezan.qa/LawView.aspx?opt&LawID=414&language=en.

224 **The law gives the government:** Ibid., Article 58.

224 **Penalties for violation:** Ibid., Articles 66–70, 74–7, 81–2, 86–7, 90.

224 **Qatar ranks 128 out of 180:** '2021 World Press Freedom Index,' Reporters Without Borders, https://rsf.org/en/ranking.

225 **Students have also been detained:** Told to author by senior administrators at the university.

225 **In January 2020:** Alexander Cornwell, 'US university in Qatar cancels Lebanese band talk after anti-gay backlash', Reuters, 3 February 2020.

226 **fierce debates over decolonising curricula:** James Muldoon, 'Academics: it's time to get behind decolonising the curriculum', *Guardian*, 20 March 2019.

226 **the questionable origin:** Mick Brown, 'Questionable donors and hypocrisy: where our universities really get their money from', *Telegraph*, 9 November 2021.

226 **and a history of surveillance:** Frances Stonor Saunders, 'Stuck on the Flypaper', *London Review of Books*, 8 April 2015.

226 **The scholar Neha Vora:** Vora, *Teach for Arabia*, p. 9.

226 **'And only if you subscribe':** 'Can Academic Freedom Survive Repressive Governance in the Gulf?', Gulf International Forum, 27 August 2020.

227 **Launched in 1996:** Hugh Miles, *Al-Jazeera: How Arab TV News Challenged the World*. London: Abacus, 2005, p. 28.

227 **Al-Jazeera English:** David B. Roberts, *Qatar: Securing the Global Ambitions of a City-State*. London: Hurst & Company, 2017, p. 95.

227 **Al-Jazeera reported:** Miles, *Al-Jazeera*, pp. 241–279.

227 **It supported the 2011:** Roberts, *Qatar*, pp. 124–8.

227 **And it has run shows:** Ibid., p. 95.

227 **When its editorial lines:** Patrick Wintour, 'Qatar given 10 days to meet 13 sweeping demands by Saudi Arabia', *Guardian*, 23 June 2017.

227 **The channel reported widely:** David Chater, 'Delegates at free speech conference condemn Qatar blockade', Al-Jazeera, 26 July 2017.

228 **While Al-Jazeera loudly supported:** Ulrichsen, *Qatar and the Gulf Crisis*, p. 47.

228 **But after a year:** 'Robert Ménard and staff leave Doha Centre

for Media Freedom', Reporters without Borders, 23 June 2009, https://rsf.org/en/news/robert-menard-and-staff-leave-doha-centre-media-freedom.

228 **(it limped on in):** 'Freedom in the World 2020: Qatar', Freedom House, https://freedomhouse.org/country/qatar/freedom-world/2020.

229 **They garner no support:** Roberts, *Qatar*, pp. 96–7.

229 **The Qatari foreign minister:** 'Speech by His Excellency Deputy Prime Minister and Minister of Foreign Affairs at Chatham House – The Crisis in the Gulf: Qatar Responds', Qatar Ministry of Foreign Affairs, 5 July 2017, https://mofa.gov.qa/en/speeches/speeches-of-deputy-prime-minister-and-minister-of-foreign-affairs/speeches/45-chatham-house---the-crisis-in-the-gulf-qatar-responds.

229 **The fledgling reporter:** Harkness, *Changing Qatar*, p. 228.

231 **How could the tiny nation:** 'Qatar 2022 Bid Hopes Suffer Blow', BBC News, 17 November 2010, and '2022 FIFA World Cup Bid Evaluation Report: Qatar', FIFA, 2010, https://digitalhub.fifa.com/m/3041e390c9c0afea/original/fd4w8qgexnrxmquwsb7h-pdf.pdf, p. 5, p. 34

231 **Suspicions were deepened:** 'Justice Department Approves Remission of Over \$32 Million in Forfeited Funds to Victims in the FIFA Corruption Case', United States Department of Justice, 24 August 2021, https://www.justice.gov/opa/pr/justice-department-approves-remission-over-32-million-forfeited-funds-victims-fifa-corruption.

231 **journalists had also reported:** Jonathan Calvert, and Heidi Blake, 'Plot to buy the World Cup', *The Sunday Times*, 1 June 2014, Andrew Jennings, *The Dirty Game: Uncovering the Scandal at FIFA*. London: Arrow, 2015, p. 130, p. 234.

231 **Their claims were bolstered:** Tariq Panja and Kevin Draper, 'US Says FIFA Officials Were Bribed to Award World Cups to Russia and Qatar', *The New York Times*, 6 April 2020.

231 **Qatar continues to deny:** 'Qatar denies allegations of corruption in World Cup 2022 bid', Al-Jazeera, 7 April 2020.

233 **Qatar was one of the few:** Coates Ulrichsen, *Qatar and the Gulf Crisis*, p. 49.

233 **The country was already:** Sudarsan Raghavan and Joby Warrick, 'How a 91-Year-Old Imam Came to Symbolize Feud between Qatar and Its Neighbours', *The Washington Post*, 28 June 2017.

233 **an Islamist group that had:** David D. Kirkpatrick, 'Is the Muslim Brotherhood a Terrorist Group?' *The New York Times*, 30 April 2019.

233 **In the years after:** Elizabeth Dickinson, 'The Case Against Qatar'. *Foreign Policy*, 30 September 2014.

233 **Members of the Egyptian Muslim Brotherhood:** Ibid.

233 **There were also accusations:** 'Treasury Designates Financial Supporters of Al-Qaida and Al-Nusrah Front', US Department of the Treasury, 5 August 2015, https://www.treasury.gov/press-center/press-releases/Pages/jl0143.aspx.

233 **Qatar, which denies:** See for instance Declan Walsh, 'WikiLeaks Cables Portray Saudi Arabia as a Cash Machine for Terrorists'. *The Guardian*, 5 December 2010.

234 **David Cohen, a senior US Treasury official:** 'Remarks of Under Secretary for Terrorism and Financial Intelligence David Cohen before the Center for a New American Security on "Confronting New Threats in Terrorist Financing"', US Department of the Treasury, 4 March 2014, https://www.treasury.gov/press-center/press-releases/Pages/jl2308.aspx.

234 **like the time:** Mark Lobel, 'Arrested for Reporting on Qatar's World Cup Labourers', BBC News, 18 May 2015.

235 **Qatar dispatched its foreign minister:** 'The Crisis in the Gulf: Qatar Responds', Chatham House, YouTube, 5 July 2017, https://www.youtube.com/watch?v=8ksR1C8B2HA.

235 **The emir gave interviews:** Rose, 'Qatar's emir stands defiant'.

235 **When a bootlegged version:** Tariq Panja, 'FIFA and Premier League Document Saudi Link in BeIN Piracy Fight'. *The New York Times*, 16 September 2019.

236 **In 2018, the state-backed murder:** 'Inquiry into the killing of Mr Jamal Kashoggi', Office of the UN High Commissioner for Human Rights, https://www.ohchr.org/EN/Issues/Executions/Pages/Inquiry.aspx.

236 **In 2019, the WTO ruled:** Emma Farge and Philip Blenkinsop, 'WTO says Saudi broke global rules in Qatar broadcast dispute', Reuters, 16 June 2020.

236 **In 2020, the International Court of Justice:** 'Appeal Relating to the Jurisdiction of the ICAO Council under Article 84 of the Convention

on International Civil Aviation', International Court of Justice, 14 July 2020, https://www.icj-cij.org/public/files/case-related/173/173-20200714-SUM-01-00-EN.pdf.

237 **Qatar has signed up:** 'Ambassadors', Qatar 2022, https://www.qatar2022.qa/en/about/ambassadors, and Nick Miller and Matt Slater, 'Explained: David Beckham, ambassador for Qatar', The Athletic, 25 November 2021.

239 **In May 2019, FIFA abandoned:** 'World Cup: Fifa drops plan to expand Qatar 2022 to 48 teams', BBC Sport, 22 May 2019.

241 **The anthropologist Irene Ann Promodh:** Irene Ann Promodh, 'FM radio and the Malayali diaspora in Qatar: at home overseas', *Journal of Ethnic and Migration Studies*, 47, no. 9 (4 July 2021), pp. 1957–75, p. 1966.

241 **Most speakers of Malayalam:** Greg Jaffe and Vidhi Doshi, 'One of the Few Places Where a Communist Can Still Dream', *The Washington Post*, 27 October 2017.

241 **As Promodh notes:** Promodh, 'FM radio and the Malayali diaspora in Qatar', p. 1967.

241 **The stations avoid live call-ins:** Ibid., p. 1971.

CHAPTER 12

246 **Almost half of its households:** 'Migration in Nepal: A Country Profile 2019', International Organization for Migration, 18 December 2019, p. 2, p. 39.

246 **Historically, people left:** Sanjay Sharma and Deepak Thapa, 'Taken for Granted: Nepali Migration to India', Centre for the Study of Labour and Mobility, 2013, https://www.ceslam.org/our-publications/taken-for-granted, and 'Who are the Gurkhas?' BBC News, 27 July 2010.

247 **Every year, hundreds of thousands:** 'Nepal Labour Migration Report 2020', Ministry of Labour, Employment and Social Security, Government of Nepal, 2020, https://moless.gov.np/wp-content/uploads/2020/03/Migration-Report-2020-English.pdf, Figure 1, p. 3, p. 12, p. 33.

247 **Qatar is currently:** See Sharma and Thapa, 'Taken for Granted'.

247 **In 2018/19, it absorbed:** 'Nepal Labour Migration Report 2020', Figure 4, p. 13.

247 **(most banks):** Bandita Sijapati, et al., 'Labour Migration and the Remittance Economy: The Socio-Political Impact', Centre for the Study of Labour and Mobility, March 2017, https://www.ceslam.org/our-publications/the-socio-political-impact, p. 10.

248 **In practice, it is only:** 'Nepal Labour Migration Report 2020', p. 54.

249 **Data released:** 'Improving Single Male Laborers' Health in Qatar', Center for International and Regional Studies, Georgetown University Qatar and World Innovation Summit for Health, November 2019, https://cirs.qatar.georgetown.edu/publications/improving-single-male-laborers-health-qatar/, p. 11.

249 **Nepali workers abroad earn:** Sijapati et al. 'Labour Migration and the Remittance Economy', p. 37.

249 **Those with degrees:** Ibid., pp. 37–8.

250 **Over 1.9 billion people:** 'Nearly Half the World Lives on Less than $5.50 a Day', World Bank, 17 October 2018, https://www.worldbank.org/en/news/press-release/2018/10/17/nearly-half-the-world-lives-on-less-than-550-a-day.

250 **There are only around:** 'Average monthly rainy days in Doha', Weather and Climate, https://weather-and-climate.com/average-monthly-Rainy-days,doha,Qatar.

251 **In 2000, the World Health Organization:** Ajay Tandon et al., 'Measuring Overall Health System Performance for 191 Countries', GPE Discussion Paper Series: No. 30, World Health Organization, 2000, https://www.academia.edu/21021930/MEASURING_OVERALL_HEALTH_SYSTEM_PERFORMANCE_FOR_191_COUNTRIES, p. 18.

251 **Employers are responsible:** Andrew Gardner et al., 'A Portrait of Low-Income Migrants in Contemporary Qatar', *Journal of Arabian Studies*, 3, no. 1 (June 2013), pp. 1–17, p. 9, and Abdulbari Bener, 'Health Status and Working Condition of Migrant Workers: Major Public Health Problems', *International Journal of Preventive Medicine*, 8, no. 1 (2017), 68, Table 2, p. 3.

252 **Some contractors wait:** 'Improving Single Male Laborers' Health in Qatar', p. 14.

255 **(Under Qatari labour law):** Article 109, Law No. 14 of 2004 on the promulgation of Labour Law, Al-Meezan – Qatar Legal Portal, https://www.almeezan.qa/LawPage.aspx?id=3961&language=en.

256 **A total of 446:** 'Qatar Voluntary National Review 2021', Qatar Planning and Statistics Authority, 2021, https://sustainabledevelopment. un.org/content/documents/280362021_VNR_Report_Qatar_ English.pdf, p. 77.

256 **Nepalis, Bangladeshis and Indians:** Re and Tunon, 'One is Too Many', p. 19.

256 **They also make up:** '"In the Prime of Their Lives"', p. 46.

256 **the ILO noted:** Re and Tunon, 'One is Too Many', p. 7.

256 **'Despite the relatively severe':** Ibid., p. 7.

257 **Remittance payments:** 'Annual Remittances Data: Inflows (updated as of May 2021)', World Bank, https://www.worldbank.org/en/topic/ migrationremittancesdiasporaissues/brief/migration-remittances-data.

258 **Rekha would be eligible:** 'Nepal Labour', p. 79.

CHAPTER 13

261 **In 2000, there were:** 'Accommodation Capacity and Occupancy Rate', United Nations World Tourism Organization (UNWTO), https:// www.unwto.org/accommodation%E2%80%93demand-and-capacity.

261 **By the time I arrived:** Farah AlSharif, 'Checking in? Qatar unveils over 100 hotels ahead of FIFA 2022 World Cup', Doha News, 13 July 2021.

262 **(the FIFA delegation alone):** '2022 FIFA World Cup Bid Evaluation Report: Qatar', p. 19.

263 **A report in July:** Isobel Archer and Danielle McMullan, 'Checked Out: Migrant Worker Abuse in Qatar's World Cup Luxury Hotels', Business and Human Rights Resource Centre, July 2021.

263 **In a different investigation:** Pete Pattisson, '"We have fallen into a trap": Qatar's World Cup dream is a nightmare for hotel staff', *Guardian*, 18 November 2021.

268 **'The key to surviving':** Mikolai Napieralski, *God Willing: How to Survive Expat Life in Qatar*. American 80s, 2017, pp. 87–8.

268 **It is an offence:** Article 270 Law No. 11 of 2004 Issuing the Penal Code, Al-Meezan – Qatar Legal Portal, https://www.almeezan.qa/ LawArticles.aspx?LawTreeSectionID=253&lawId=26&language=en.

268 **It's illegal to import booze:** Tina Nguyen, 'Gordon Ramsay Gets Champagne Confiscated in Qatar, Hates Islamic Nation's Alcohol

Ban', Mediaite, 14 January 2014, https://www.mediaite.com/food/gordon-ramsay-champagne-doha/.

271 **One commentator on the Doha News:** Wayne H., comment on Peter Kovessy, 'WHO: Black-market booze makes up 40% of alcohol consumed in Qatar', Doha News, 18 May 2014, https://www.dohanews.co/black-market-booze-makes-40-alcohol-consumed-qatar/.

271 **Napieralski begins his book:** Napieralski, *God Willing*, p. 4.

271 **'However, hospitality is':** Brian Homewood, 'Qatar promises accessible alcohol for World Cup visitors', Reuters, 26 September 2019.

272 **The outraged tone:** For instance Nick Parker, 'Fears as WC Host Runs out of Booze', *The Sun*, 6 July 2019 and Charlie Wyett, 'Qatarstrophe', *The Sun*, 23 December 2019.

272 **In the mid-2010s:** 'Cologne sales at certain Qatar shops in spotlight before new rules take effect', Doha News, 2 February 2013.

272 **A 2014 investigation:** 'Qatar's workers vulnerable to charms of bootleg liquor sadeeqi', Doha News, 3 May 2014.

273 **'It is a way of passing the time':** Tristan Bruslé, 'What Kind of Place Is This? Daily Life, Privacy and the Inmate Metaphor in a Nepalese Workers' Labour Camp (Qatar)', *South Asia Multidisciplinary Academic Journal*, no. 6 (2012), pp. 1–28, p. 13.

273 **Eighteen Australians, along with:** Elaine Yu et al., 'Qatar Expresses "Regrets" but Defends Invasive Exams of Women on 10 Flights', *The New York Times*, 28 October 2020.

274 **The Qatari penal code:** '"Everything I Have to Do Is Tied to a Man"', p. 82, fn. 315.

274 **They can find themselves:** '2021 Trafficking in Persons Report', p. 346.

275 **One prison official:** '"My Sleep Is My Break": Exploitation of Migrant Domestic Workers in Qatar', Amnesty International, 2014, 23 April 2014, p. 49.

275 **'It made us feel sick':** '[MAID ON CALL-PART II] When things fall apart', The Life of Umm, 16 March 2014, https://ummon.wordpress.com/2014/03/16/maid-on-call-part-ii-when-things-fall-apart/.

276 **Women like Wazilfa:** Ana P. Santos, 'Where Pregnancy Is a Prison Sentence', Pulitzer Center, 16 January 2018, https://pulitzercenter.org/stories/where-pregnancy-prison-sentence.

276 **Even if a woman is the victim:** '"My Sleep Is My Break"', pp. 51–3.

276 **Abortion is illegal:** 'Qatar: Gender Justice & The Law', United Nations Development Programme, 2018, https://www.undp.org/content/dam/rbas/doc/Gender%20Justice/English/Full%20reports/Qatar%20Country%20Assessment%20-%20English.pdf, p. 13.

277 **'What danger can a pregnant woman':** Santos, 'Where Pregnancy Is a Prison Sentence'.

277 **'[And] I was walking out':** Ana P. Santos, 'Migrant Life in Qatar', Pulitzer Center, 30 October 2017, https://pulitzercenter.org/stories/migrant-life-qatar.

277 **Pardis Mahdavi, a researcher who:** Pardis Mahdavi, *Crossing the Gulf: Love and Family in Migrant Lives*. Stanford, CA: Stanford University Press, 2016, p. 46.

CHAPTER 14

284 **'Close to half':** Ben Bloom, '"Really scary and daunting: World Championships women's marathon chaos as 28 athletes pull out amid soaring Doha conditions', *Daily Telegraph*, 28 September 2019.

284 **Purdue, who dropped out:** Ben Bloom, 'Charlotte Purdue: Sebastian Coe should apologise for dangerous Doha World Championships marathon', *Daily Telegraph*, 2 November 2019.

284 **Average temperatures have already risen:** Steven Mufson, 'Facing unbearable heat, Qatar has begun to air-condition the outdoors', *Washington Post*, 20 October 2019.

285 **Recent scientific research:** Jeremy S. Pal and Elfatih A.B. Eltahir, 'Future temperature in southwest Asia projected to exceed a threshold for human adaptability', *Nature Climate Change*, 6, no. 2 (February 2016), pp. 197–200.

286 **the new law stated that:** Fakhroo, Decision of the Minister.

286 **According to the academic Mari Luomi:** Mari Luomi, *The Gulf Monarchies and Climate Change: Abu Dhabi and Qatar in an Era of Natural Unsustainability*. New York: Oxford University Press, 2016, p. 174.

286 **If the increase is more:** Owen Mulhern, 'Sea Level Rise Projection Map – Qatar and Bahrain', Earth.Org, 17 September 2020, https://earth.org/data_visualization/sea-level-rise-by-2100-qatar-and-bahrain/.

288 **In 2018, the World Bank labelled:** 'CO2 emissions (metric tons per capita)', World Bank, https://data.worldbank.org/indicator/EN.ATM.CO2E.PC?most_recent_value_desc=true&view=map.

288 **Many in Qatar take umbrage:** See for instance Hisham Aljundi, 'UN report on Qatar per capita carbon emission unfair', *Qatar Tribune*, 21 November 2017.

288 **According to consumption-based calculators:** Based on territorial ($MtCO_2$), data reproduced by the Global Carbon Atlas, http://www.globalcarbonatlas.org/en/CO2-emissions.

288 **Part of the problem is:** Jim Krane, *Energy Kingdoms: Oil and Political Survival in the Persian Gulf*, New York: Columbia University Press, p. 142.

288 **A shocking 70 per cent:** Ibid., p. 69.

288 **(compared to around 15 per cent):** Mufson, 'Facing unbearable heat'.

289 **Top-end shops:** Ibid.

289 **it claims to be organising:** 'The FIFA World Cup Qatar 2022 Sustainability Strategy: Executive Summary', Supreme Committee For Delivery and Legacy, October 2019, https://www.qatar2022.qa/sites/default/files/docs/FWC-2022-Executive-Summary_EN.pdf, p. 11.

289 **and at the 2019 UN Climate Action Summit:** 'HH The Amir Speech in Climate Action Summit', Amiri Diwan, State of Qatar, 23 September 2019, https://www.diwan.gov.qa/briefing-room/speeches-and-remarks/2019/september/23/hh-the-amir-participates-in-climate-action-summit-2019?sc_lang=en.

289 **World Cup stadiums have huge buildings:** Mufson, 'Facing unbearable heat'.

289 **The new inner-city neighbourhood:** 'Solar panels installed at Msheireb project', *Gulf Times*, 31 July 2013.

289 **In its 2015 submission:** 'Intended Nationally Determined Contributions (INDCs) Report', Qatar Ministry of Environment, 19 November 2015, https://www4.unfccc.int/sites/ndcstaging/PublishedDocuments/Qatar%20First/Qatar%20INDCs%20Report%20-English.pdf, p. 2

289 **(it has since submitted):** 'Nationally Determined Contribution (NDC)', State of Qatar Ministry of Municipality and Environment,

August 2021, https://www4.unfccc.int/sites/ndcstaging/Published Documents/Qatar%20First/Qatar%20NDC.pdf, p. 2.

290 **In 2021, the Al-Kharsaah solar plant:** Sebastian Castelier, 'Sunshine-Rich Gulf Slow to Adapt Solar, Clean Energy', Al-Monitor, 27 July 2021.

290 **But in the same year:** Rania El Gamal, 'Qatar Petroleum signs deal for mega-LNG expansion', Reuters, 2 February 2021.

290 **The World Cup's pledge:** 'FIFA World Cup 2022 Greenhouse Gas Accounting Report', FIFA, June 2021, https://www.qatar2022.qa/sites/default/files/documents/greenhouse-gas-accounting-report-en.pdf.

290 **Qatar has been accused:** Kyle McKinnon, 'Qatar touts dismountable stadium for "sustainable" 2022 World Cup', Deutsche Welle, 25 November 2021.

293 **Many studies think:** Sandra Laville, 'Dumped fishing gear is biggest plastic polluter in ocean, finds report', *Guardian*, 6 November 2019.

299 **Bottom-up or citizen-led:** Fromherz, *Qatar*, p. 151.

299 **Organisers of public events:** 'Freedom in the World 2020: Qatar'.

304 **There is an understandable irritation:** Simon Evans, 'Analysis: Which countries are historically responsible for climate change?' Carbon Brief, 5 October 2021, https://www.carbonbrief.org/analysis-which-countries-are-historically-responsible-for-climate-change.

305 **He points to the introduction:** Shabina S. Khatri, 'Qatari men report for first day of mandatory national service', Doha News, 1 April 2014.

305 **Even Qatar's emir:** 'Speech of His Highness Sheik Tamim Bin Hamad Al Thani The Amir of Qatar at the Opening of the 44th Session of the Advisory Council', Qatar Government Communications Office, 3 November 2015. https://www.gco.gov.qa/wp-content/uploads/2017/08/HH-Sheikh-Tamim-bin-Hamad-Al-Thani-the-Emir-of-the-State-of-Qatar-Speech-at-the-Opening-of-the-Advisory-Council-44th-Session-copy.pdf.

CHAPTER 15

312 **Surveys of university students:** cooke, *Tribal Modern*, p. 42.

312 **Young Qataris are some:** Ibid., pp. 126–7, Harkness, *Changing Qatar*, p. 135.

312 **Today in Doha:** Harkness, *Changing Qatar*, p. 124.

313 **Government statistics from 2019:** 'Marriage and Divorce in the State of Qatar, 2019', Planning and Statistics Authority, June 2020, https://www.psa.gov.qa/en/statistics/Statistical%20Releases/Population/MarriagesDivorces/2019/marriage_divorce_qatar_2019_En.pdf, p. 17.

313 **'it is also proof of the purity of Qatari bloodlines':** cooke, *Tribal Modern*, p. 47.

313 **Today, only around 13 per cent:** Harkness, *Changing Qatar*, p. 188.

313 **Tamim was the driving force:** Roberts, *Qatar*, p. 160.

317 **In 2012, a Qatari poet:** Tim Hume and Schams Elwazer, 'Qatari poet accused of insulting emir freed after 4 years, UN says', CNN, 16 March 2016.

317 **Sheikh Tamim is careful to stress:** 'His Highness Speech at the Opening of the Advisory Council 42nd Session', Qatar Government Communications Office, 2013, https://www.gco.gov.qa/en/speeches/his-highness-speech-at-the-opening-of-the-advisory-council-42nd-session/.

317 **'To be frank with you, I'm not a feminist':** Nick Anderson, 'Sheikha Moza: The Woman behind Doha's Education City', *Washington Post*, 6 December 2015.

318 **'State-imposed normality':** Henri Lefebvre, *The Production of Space*, translated by Donald Nicholson-Smith. Oxford: Blackwell Publishing, 1991, p. 23.

318 **But in his brilliant book:** Pascal Ménoret, *Joyriding in Riyadh: Oil, Urbanism, and Road Revolt*. Cambridge: Cambridge University Press, 2014.

319 **'As we walked ...':** Sophia Al-Maria, *The Girl Who Fell to Earth: A Memoir*. London: Harper Perennial, 2012, p. 151.

320 **up to fifteen years in jail:** 'Everything I have to do', p. 82 fn. 315.

320 **Only 61 per cent:** A. A. Arbab et al., 'Prevalence, awareness and determinants of contraceptive use in Qatari women', *Eastern Mediterranean Health Journal*, 17, no. 1 (2011), pp. 11–18, p. 17.

320 **In 2009, a social rehabilitation centre:** 'FAQ', Al-Aween, captured by the Wayback Machine, 22 May 2012, https://web.archive.org/web/20120522104612/http://www.src-qa.org/English/Pages/FAQ.aspx.

320 **There is a great deal:** An example is the boyah subculture, something

akin to a tomboy or butch lesbian. See, cooke, *Tribal Modern*, pp. 145–151, Harkness, *Changing Qatar*, pp. 165–168. Al-Maria, *The Girl*, pp. 134–140.

320 **'We have to do what our family':** Harkness, *Changing Qatar*, 167–8.

321 **Qatar topped a 2015 survey:** 'Qataris Lead Way in Luxury Middle East Spend With $4,000 a Month', Bloomberg, 19 April 2016.

321 **The Qatar Investment Authority:** Claudia Cristoferi and Elisa Anzolin, 'Exclusive: Qatari investor to float 25 percent of Italy's Valentino – Source', Reuters, 20 December 2017, and Lauren Sherman, 'Mayhoola: Inside the Secretive Qatari Luxury Empire', Business of Fashion, 11 February 2018, https://www.businessoffashion.com/articles/luxury/mayhoola-inside-the-secretive-qatari-luxury-empire.

321 **A 2018 government report:** 'Qatar Second National Development Strategy: 2018-2022', Qatar Planning and Statistics Authority, 2018, https://www.psa.gov.qa/en/knowledge/Documents/NDS2Final.pdf, p. 220.

321 **Spending beyond one's means:** Tom Finn, '"Social curse" of huge personal debt raises worries in wealthy Qatar', Reuters, 3 March 2016.

323 **'Future economic success':** 'Qatar National Vision 2030', General Secretariat for Development Planning, July 2008, https://www.psa.gov.qa/en/qnv1/Documents/QNV2030_English_v2.pdf, p. 13.

323 **Central to the plan:** Ibid., p. 24.

324 **'Qatar aims to build':** Ibid., p. 13.

324 **But in 2020, University College London:** Ellie Bothwell, 'UCL to Close Qatar Campus in 2020'. *Times Higher Education*, 2 January 2019.

324 **The remaining universities:** As told to author by a senior administrator at an Education City university.

325 **Qatar has publicly stated:** Regen Doherty, 'Qatar's modern future rubs up against conservative traditions', Reuters, 27 September 2012.

325 **The Qatar Investment Authority:** Julia Kollewe, 'Olympic Village snapped up by Qatari ruling family for £557m', *Guardian*, 12 August 2011, and Eliot Brown, 'Qatar Buys Stake in Empire State Building', *Wall Street Journal*, 24 August 2016.

325 **The *Daily Telegraph* has suggested:** Rhiannon Curry, 'Qataris own more of London than the Queen', *Daily Telegraph*, 17 March 2017.

325 **parts of the German car makers:** Una Galani, 'BREAKINGVIEWS – Qatar's sovereign funds: A guide for the perplexed', Reuters, 2 October 2012.

325 **the British supermarket Sainsbury's:** Sarah Butler, 'Qatari shareholders uneasy over Sainsbury's Home Retail Group bid', *Guardian*, 6 January 2016.

325 **and a string of French companies:** David Hellier, 'Total, Lagardère, Vivendi ... les emplettes du Qatar en France' [Total, Lagardère, Vivendi ... the products of Qatar's shopping in France] *Capital*, 21 March 2012. https://www.capital.fr/entreprises-marches/total-lagardere-vivendi-les-emplettes-du-qatar-en-france-706570.

327 **Prior to the collapse:** 'How Qatar Came to Host the Taliban', BBC News.

327 **It upended the global gas industry:** Yergin, *The Quest*, p. 325.

327 **It managed to see off:** Bobby Ghosh, 'Qatar Exits Gulf Embargo with a Much Stronger Hand', Bloomberg/Yahoo! Finance, 8 January 2021.

328 **At the first partial elections:** Lisa Barrington and Andrew Mills, '"I am not weak": Qatari women unsuccessful in first legislative elections', Reuters, 3 October 2021.

EPILOGUE

333 **It has opened its national day:** Natalie Koch, 'Is Nationalism Just for Nationals? Civic Nationalism for Noncitizens and Celebrating National Day in Qatar and the UAE'. *Political Geography* 54 (September 2016), pp. 43–53.

333 **It speaks in its National Vision:** 'Qatar National Vision 2030', p. 11.

334 **(unless it looks like the stadium):** Sean Ingle, 'Migrant workers and children to pad out crowd for World Athletics Championships', *Guardian*, 23 September 2019.

335 **Low-income male workers:** Finn, '"Bachelor ban"'.

335 **It is illegal to house:** 'MME to strictly implement law on workers' accommodation in family residential areas', *Gulf Times*, 29 September 2019.

336 **'More work needs to be done':** 'Qatar Committed to Improving Worker Welfare, Says World Cup 2022 Organiser', Reuters, 23 June 2021.

Acknowledgements

First comes everyone I met in Qatar. I am grateful to the hundreds of people from all walks of life who, with little to gain (and often a lot to lose), opened up their worlds to me. Thank you to all those who chatted with me over coffee, arranged introductions, offered me lifts, showed me around, disobeyed orders, or took hours out of their day to answer my questions. Bereft of their generosity there would have been no book to write.

There are two institutions whose support was vital in turning the book from a fledgling idea into a viable project: the Wenner-Gren Foundation, whose post-PhD fieldwork grant funded my research, and the Gulf Studies Center at Qatar University, who provided me with an institutional home in Doha. My thanks in particular to Dr Mahjoob Zweiri for his support.

The work of Nick Walters, a thoughtful ally and advocate, was also essential to the book seeing the light of day. I am grateful to him for his astute agent-ing on two books now.

I was lucky enough to have a fantastic editor in the shape of Ellen Conlon. From her enthusiasm at my initial idea through to her perceptive comments over the final draft, she has been a sharp, collaborative and supportive presence. I thank her also for superb marshalling of the many others at Icon Books whose input was essential, in particular Luke Bird for the fantastic cover design, Sara Mulvanny for her excellent illustrations and James Lilford for a meticulous copy-edit which tightened the writing and caught many embarrassing mistakes.

Thanks to everyone at the British Institute at Ankara – my professional home for over six years. My gratitude in particular to Dr Lutgarde Vandeput for her continued support, despite my research interests wandering away from both Turkey and academia.

In Qatar, Craig LaMay has been a well of support. I'm grateful for his friendship, enthusiasm for being interviewed and willingness to provide me with a place to crash and clutter up with cricket equipment. Without Savitri Rajali Chapter 12 would not exist – my thanks for her tireless research, excellent translation and unrelenting good nature. Edward Posnett and Ross Griffin provided helpful feedback on sections of the book. Matthew Cullen did the same, as well as putting me in touch with a host of important people. Mehul Srivastava provided help with nomenclature and translation. Alex McManus lovingly proofread the entire text and, along with Gerry, provided eternal love and support from afar.

It's exciting to be able to thank Maggie, who was a kicking, twirling presence through the final stages of research, a snoring, sleepy one while writing, and a babbling, tottering one while editing and finishing. Thank you for ensuring that I keep my work in perspective.

Finally, and most importantly, to Laura Pitel. For enduring the continual absences and unreasonable editing requests. For stepping in at hairy moments despite her own workload. And for encouraging me on the rather unorthodox path I seem to be taking through life. I could not do what I do without her companionship and love.

Index

Note: a page reference followed by 'fn' refers to a note on that page. 'Al-' is ignored in the filing order, e.g. Al-Jazeera appears under 'J' rather than 'A'.

Extracts from *The Girl Who Fell to Earth*
by Sophia Al-Maria © 2012 reprinted with permission from
the author and from HarperCollins publishers in the USA